C. Graham

The True Philosophy of Mind

C. Graham

The True Philosophy of Mind

ISBN/EAN: 9783337079628

Printed in Europe, USA, Canada, Australia, Japan

Cover: Foto ©Thomas Meinert / pixelio.de

More available books at **www.hansebooks.com**

THE

TRUE PHILOSOPHY OF MIND.

By C. GRAHAM, M.D.,

AUTHOR OF "MAN FROM HIS CRADLE TO HIS GRAVE," AND OF "THE TRUE
SCIENCE OF MEDICINE."

No creed is too absurd for faith; no doctrine too sanguinary and monstrous for human credulity. The lives of former generations and the condition of the present, I give as lessons to posterity.

LOUISVILLE, KY.:
PRINTED BY JOHN P. MORTON AND COMPANY.
1869.

DEDICATION.

Tins work I dedicate to the reader with the following requests : That he will look with an eye of sad regret and see where the Christian world is drifting. That he will have independence enough to know that he has a mind of his own, by which he can judge as well of its own operations as others can judge for him. That he will throw perplexing and unmeaning words aside, as worthless in thought; for brutes, and the deaf and dumb, feel, think, and act promptly and correctly without words. That he will read the history of his race and see that there is, at this time, more than a thousand human victims daily immolated upon the altars of a dark and sanguinary superstition, prescribed by an inhuman and domineering priesthood. That he will seriously meditate upon the fact that more than two thousand years of preaching, and of teaching the nature of mind, its duty to its fellow-man, and its relation to its God, has only served to divide the human family and make the science of mind more laborious and incomprehensible than ever. That he will keep constantly in view the cause of every thought and act of his life, which will soon give him a perfect and practical knowledge of mind, a boon that no closet-book of assumed and artistic minds can possibly give him. That he will be watchful of the artifice of authors and teachers in quibbling out of the influence of motives in the production of will and action by affirming as Haven, the great text-book writer, does, that motives, though the *reason* and *occasion* of will and action, are not the *cause*. With your mind thus fortified, read on, and you will find all the laws of mind fully developed, illustrated, and demonstrated.

TABLE OF CONTENTS.

PREFACE.

My object in the following essays will be to show that we are creatures of education, and consequently should be charitable to each other, no two on earth having the same organization or being impressed with the same circumstances or objects, which make up, through life, our honest and unavoidable convictions. For the want of this knowledge, man has ever been the greatest enemy of man. Yes, from the intolerance and inhumanity of man to man countless millions have bled and died. Look back through mouldering ages at the hills of slain and the rivers of blood caused by men's difference of opinion, and we must grant a wrong, a sad and grievous wrong, in the hearts of men. All history of our race will testify that not only the crusades, but that the persecutions, as well as the wars of nation against nation, have arisen from a false view of religion. Yes, fanaticism, bigotry, and human idolatry have been at the bottom of it all.

From the time Cain slew his brother Abel, from a difference of opinion (*conscience*), whose offering was most acceptable to the Lord, has this malicious and cruel *conscience*, doubtless planted by Satan himself, been busy in all the wars and persecutions of the world, each one feeling that his inward divinity justifies the murder of his brother and of his inward divinity. The slaughter of seventy-four thousand Protestants, men, women, and children, all between the hours of midnight and the rising of the sun, on the occasion of St. Bartholomew's feast in France, in the name of a sacred *conscience* and of God, with the two hundred broiled at the stake, and thousands otherwise put to death during one short reign in England alone, are but as one grain of sand on the seashore, compared with the terrific and fiendish march of this divine *conscience*, which swept with desolating might all over the Christian world. The fearful intensity of this wild fanaticism, urged on by the clergy of whatever denomination got the upperhand, was such that sadness, sorrow, and

2

mourning was in every true Christian heart—the black banner of
death was unfurled and spread upon the family altar, and their pious
prayers to the God of mercy were watched and choked down till
fearful became the name of religion itself. Were all the shocking
atrocities committed by this (so-called) unerring *conscience* brought
up in panoramic review before a feeling man, he would shudder at
the sight, and doubt the infallibility of his own *conscience*. Yes, were
all the gory locks, the mangled and charred bodies, to rise from their
graves, the world would stand aghast.

And now, marvel not at this, my reader, when you have seen before
your own eyes, only a few years back, the bloody struggles and
devastation in your own land, all undeniably from the same divine
and unerring *conscience*, which tells all mankind what is right and
what is wrong, according to the false teachings of our present schools.
The northern people being taught a *conscience* that the domestic
institutions of the South were a sin, and the southern people being
conscious that their rights were invaded, their divine and unerring
consciences brought them into deadly conflict. Feeling assured that
all these sad and melancholy tragedies have sprung from the influences of the pulpit and the teachings of our schools in false theology
and mental philosophy, my aim will be to show the fact, and, as far as
possible, correct the error; for just so long as we are taught that we
have a sacred monitor or dictator within us which condemns the
same in all others will we feel it our religious duty to punish each
other.

In preparing the mind of the reader for the better understanding
of the subject under consideration, I shall have to crowd my preface
with many original, vital, and leading principles by which all things
are governed. God, in his wise and preconceived plans of creation,
has left nothing to chance, but stamped everything with his undeviating laws, called certainty, force, or fate. There is nothing in his
universe which can create itself, move itself, or, when moved, stop
itself but by other forces, but all are *dualistic* and *dynamic* dependencies, no one atom acting upon itself, but acting upon every other
atom. The heavenly bodies are kept in motion by *dualism*, or, in
other words, by centripetal and centrifugal power; while the universal vegetable and animal kingdom has its laws of vitality,
attraction, and repulsion, which makes everything what it is and
nothing else. Though every pore of nature is thrift with organic
life, there is nothing self-created; but all is forced into existence by
their antecedent archetypes, and pressed or forced forward by the

fixed (fatal) laws of organic life. The acorn brings an oak and the apple seed an apple tree, yet neither of them would be developed to a tree but by the force of circumstances. The egg doubtless comes to the world with a germ in it, yet no chicken would ever be quickened into life but by the forced laws of incubation. All beings are forced into existence and held in their alloted spheres by fixed laws that govern them—nothing self-created; nothing left to chance. Man, like all other things, has a forced existence. He comes into the world without his own knowledge or consent, is forced through life by laws irresistible, and, in like manner, is forced out of existence. To know the fact of his forced destiny is but to know that he would as quickly perish without support as fire would die out without fuel. The elements of food and the vitalizing powers, the *modus operandi* of which he has no knowledge and over which his will has no control, forces him forward. All the functions within are forced conditions by the laws of Conservative Wisdom. The stomach can not act or live upon itself, but acts upon the food which comes from without itself. The liver has no power over itself, but is destined to secrete bile from the blood, which is forced by the heart upon it and through it, while the heart is forced to dilation and contraction by the stimulus of the blood, whose stimulating and vitalizing powers it receives from the oxygen of the lungs, which oxygen the lungs receive from the external atmosphere. Nothing self-existent; nothing self-sustaining. All is cause and effect—*dualistic* and mutual dependencies upon the First Great Cause. The blood, like the fertilizing waters of earth, which flow through their bidden channels to the great ocean, and are again taken up on the wings of the wind and wafted to the extremes of earth, is forced in one eternal round, to and from the heart in ceaseless currents, giving life and growth to every portion of the myriad functions of the moving miracle—man. Force motion, all perpetual motion, is the order of nature. If the air or waters become stagnant, they are sickly, and were motion to cease, universal death and destruction would be the result. Yet nothing is self-moved, but moved by an antecedent force, which alternately becomes cause and effect, *ad infinitum*.

In addition to the *dualistic* order of nature, it seems that all things are antagonistic—as God and Devil, heaven and hell, pain and pleasure, light and darkness, heat and cold, attraction and repulsion, good and evil, up and down, big and little, long and short, and so on throughout the whole range of nature—all wisely ordered to act in harmony, like our antagonistic muscles, as flexors and extensors without which we could have no locomotion.

Thus it will be seen that were we to search throughout the whole arcana of nature, there would be no exception found to the divine law of *dualistic* antagonism, nor can it be supposed that man, either in mind or body, constitutes any exception. If mind be not an inseparable part of the body in their sojourn in this world, I ask when and where did it come from? It is born with the body and developed and matured with the body, and all the investigations of the laws of life and of sound philosophy forbid the idea of God creating minds separately from the body, by myriads, and ingrafting them into the body at some unknown place and time, when the bodies are ready made for them. This now, as ridiculous as it may seem, is actually the doctrine of our modern schools, and it is, by the by, the professed faith of Brigham Young, who enjoins it upon the latter-day saints to bring forward as many bodies as possible as tenements for those lone and naked souls who are floating about in search of a home, and that have been heard to shriek in the wintry blast. History tells us that this question was settled by the learned prelates of the world, who decided that souls were made separate from the body, and also the time they entered the body. In solemn conclave at Sarbonne, in France, met these ecclesiastics, sapients, bishops, cardinals of divine authority, and determined that the soul entered the body at four and a half months after conception (the period of quickening), and as soon as possible thereafter should the mother be injected, per *vagina*, with holy water, as a baptism by the Holy Ghost, for should the child die after that period when the soul had taken up its residence in the body, born or not born, it would, without baptism, certainly go to hell for Adam's sin, and not from any sin these little creatures had committed of their own. How unphilosophic and unjust; for if souls are not propagated from Adam, in common with the body, why punish them for Adam's sin, when they are in no way akin to him, but made by God himself. And now, though more modern authors might eschew this celebrated edict, so-called by history, they teach, in reality, the same doctrine of a mind independent of the body, with innate ideas and a divine CONSCIENCE that tells us what is right and what is wrong. And now I make the following quotation as a fair specimen of the mental text-books in our schools:

"There is born with us an original sin, and there is also in human nature a primitive faith, which precedes and transcends reason, and is in reality the self-development of Deity in our thoughts and discernment of truth: a spark of Deity himself, independent and apart from the body." Every mother, without the aid of metaphysics, will contradict this mystic philosophy, for she knows her child is born a child, has childish ideas and childish ways, that every year adds to its ideas and ways, and that it knows nothing but what it gains by self observation or is instructed by others—nor does that divinity within tell the infant what is true or false, right or wrong. The universal verdict of mankind is against this doctrine, and our courts of justice forbid the testimony of infants, distrustful of their intuitive divinity. If asked the reason why men of otherwise enlarged minds and of world-wide fame should teach such folly, I would answer that they are mostly divines, like Bishop Berkley and Swedenborg, who feel that they are advancing their spiritual cause by excluding all influences of matter, and even matter itself (as Berkley did) from this world, and claiming God's constant presence and personal influence in every thought, word and deed, instead of working by wise and efficient laws, as I shall aim to show he does. If we came into the world with innate and unerring ideas, we should certainly recollect them, as our first impressions are the most lasting; and surely that divine and protecting spirit would not let us run into the fire and commit so many errors as we do in infancy.

"Great wit and madness, sure, are close allied,
And thin partitions do their bounds divide."

Those soaring divines scorn nature, and under a spiritual hallucination fall into transcendental and elysian reveries, losing sight of earth and all earthly things. These facts found in the history of mental philosophy, I bring forward to induce the reader to think for himself and look within himself in order to know himself.

My object in leading the reader through the kingdoms of earth and on to the celestial spheres, has been to show him that there is nothing in God's universe self-created or self-moved, but that all is *dualistic* and *dynamic*, and dependent upon the first great and moving cause for their harmonious and eternal rounds; and thence to render it improbable that the human mind should have been left a vagrant to its own whims, subject to no law or divine rule of action. And, further, that as we have seen there is nothing in the universe which can act upon itself, is it probable that the mind can act upon itself and give itself its own thoughts, words and actions; for if so, the infant would be intelligent, the blind man could see, the deaf man hear and know all about the external world and the relation of things around him, simply by creating ideas and intelligence within itself.

I shall aim at no artistic taste or manner of divisions, subdivisions, technical bewilderings and mystic refinings, but shall push my argument straight forward in a plain and familiar style that every reader may understand; and to rest the mind from a close and constant stress of thought, I will digress in examples, illustrations and consequences, and again and again return to the argument. As the subject before us is a difficult and perplexing one, I shall often use the same terms, and as often duplicate and recapitulate, in order to more fully elucidate the subject and fix it upon the mind. In condemning false writers and teachers, and particularly the leaders of religious parties, who I know have done infinite and grievous mischief to mankind, I hope not to be disrespectful, as no one can have a higher regard for religion and the teachers of a true and rational religion than myself, and my following essays are intended to teach them to throw aside all mystic mummery, and study well the natural laws of their Maker in their own minds, that all the isms, cisms, dogmatisms, church persecutions and wars may cease, and brotherly love and friendship may be restored to man on earth.

My mode of instruction will be entirely new, while the great principles by which I hope to sustain my position are original and exclusively my own, no author, so far as I know, having ever discovered or made known the universal law and order of *dualism* by which all things are made, moved and sustained, nothing having the power of creating itself, moving itself, or sustaining itself. Detached parts may have been observed in regard to this fated law of all organic being, but it has never been applied in the investigation of science; and just so with all other principles and discoverings that have been previously known but in part. Every old woman who had boiled a tea-kettle knew the force or power of steam, by seeing it lift the lid, but no one till the days of Fulton applied the principle to boats and navigation: everybody had seen lightning, and many suspected, yes, knew the analogy between it and electricity, but no one proved their identity till the days of Franklin; nor did any one ever apply or harness this wonderful principle and set it to carrying the mail but Morse. This *dualistic* law I shall apply to mind, and demonstrate that it has no more power to create itself or the ideas forced upon it, than a stone has to create and to move itself. I shall also show that the mind is an indivisible unit, without *faculties* (such as are ridiculously given it), and without power, except such as is given it by the force of objectivity and the unavoidable organism and condition of body—just such power as water has to run down, when made to run down. The mind has the same power (a word without proper meaning) to receive ideas that the paper has to receive the sentiments written upon it, or the wax to be stamped with its endless ideas, fatally corresponding with the objects that impress those ideas; nor can the mind any more than the wax alter or annihilate these ideas.

I shall strive to drive innate ideas, as witches have been done, from the world, and to show that this thing called divine *conscience* is a parasite—an effect—is not a principle—has no separate existence from the prejudice and education of the mind; and though destructive to the lives and liberties of others, is the best excuse we can have for own conduct; so that the vicious acts of one intending a crime, to him it would be a crime, while to another the same act would be a virtue, if done with a virtuous intention. Saint Paul says, speaking of faith: "I know and am persuaded of the Lord Jesus that there is nothing unclean of itself, but to him that esteemeth any thing to be unclean, to him it is unclean." That is, it is wrong for any man to violate his own sense of duty, it matters not how much it may differ from that of others.

I have made but few quotations, and they from memory and a few scrap notes, having not a single book of any kind before me in my solitary retirement, my library being consumed by fire years ago, and never renewed; and I will here say to the mechanical and artistic critic that he must excuse my loose and incoherent style and literary defects, as I have not spent my time in the art of composition and the driveling conventionalties of man, but in the pursuit of nature and the laws by which we "live, move and have our being." My life has been one of great hardships and hazards, as I wandered through the wide world. Besides, I write hurriedly, just as my ideas are brought by association. Nor have I copied or revised a single line of my first original draft, aiming not at show, but to make myself understood in the great principles I advocate and the position I aim to sustain. In closing my preface, I say to the reader that if he doubts the perfect originality of my views and illustrative mode of instruction throughout, all he has to do is to look over the index of any and all authors on mental science, and he will find as much space taken up by classifications, divisions, subdivisions, apartments, departments, active and passive powers, with *faculties* innumerable, as is here taken up with the whole science of mind, which I could, aside from explanations and illustrations, have condensed into a single short chapter—as the whole phenomena of mind is this—*God has endowed us with sensibility, from which arise pleasure and pain, and consequently a desire or will to do or not to do!* Thus is solved in a short sentence, the mighty question, the great enigma of psychology, soul, mind or intellect, all meaning the same thing. To excuse the repetitions and sameness of views which may be found under different heads, I will here say, it is the same subject by different names, the sameness in description is unavoidable; besides, I have not striven to avoid it, knowing that recapitulation fixes an abstract and perplexing study more fully on the mind. It must be recollected that I treat of mind as a unit, and though I may speak of its different modes of action by different names, it is all one and the same thing—like giving the character of an individual man under different names and titles. To make a big book on mind, it must be divided into many parts and each part treated of in artistic style, as separate faculties and powers, independent of each other and of the mind itself.

THE TRUE PHILOSOPHY OF MIND.

WILL.

MUCH has been said and written for past ages in regard to the human will. The question has been, whether the will acts under the influence of motives, or, in other words, the promptings of an object presented to the mind for its choice; or whether it has a self-creating and controlling power to act upon an object without any causal influence of that object. Various definitions have been given to the word volition, but no agreement has been settled upon by authors. My position is, that it is simply the choice of one thing rather than another, for we can not choose a thing contrary to our will, nor will a thing contrary to our choice. In this I am backed by the authority of Locke, who sustains the same view here laid down. I will say to the reader, in the beginning, that he must have constantly in view the simple fact that will is nothing more nor less than the indivisible mind making a choice, and that no choice can be made without an object of choice, which object leads the mind to its choice; and farther, that nothing can not produce something, and as the will is something it must have been produced by something, which something is not the mind that can not act upon itself, nor upon nothing, but is an object acting upon the mind, just as medicine acts upon the body, producing its result, which result being the offspring of the motive and the mind, can not have been the author of its own existence. Yes, and moreover, the proof of the will's being an effect is a proof of its not being a cause, or of its having the power of origination within itself or the product of nothing. To quote authority for and against this subject would make a large and profitless book of abstract refinings and technical nonsense, and I will therefore introduce a few sentences only from the pen of Sir William Hamilton, the greatest and best of modern and Christian philosophers.

"Will, they hold to be a free cause, a cause which is not an effect; in other words, they attribute it to a power of absolute origination. But here their own principle of causality is too strong for them. They say that it is unconditionally promulgated, as an express and positive law of intelligence, that every origination is an apparent only, not a real, commencement. How to exempt certain phenomena from this universal law, on the ground of our moral consciousness, can not validly be done. For in the first place, this would be an admission that the mind is a complement of contradictory revelations. If mendacity be admitted of some of our mental dictates, we can not vindicate veracity to any. If one be delusive, so may all. '*Falsus in uno, falsus in omnibus.*' Absolute skepticism is here the legitimate conclusion. But, in the second place, waving this conclusion, what right have we, on this doctrine, to subordinate the positive affirmation of causality to our consciousness of moral liberty—what right have we, for the interest of the latter, to derogate from the former? We have none. If both be equally positive, we are not entitled to sacrifice the alternative, which our wishes prompt us to abandon." (Page 586.) "How the will can possibly be free, must remain to us, under the present limitation of our faculties, wholly incomprehensible. We are unable to conceive an absolute commencement; we can not therefore conceive a free volition. A determination by motives can not, to our understanding, escape from necessitation. Nay, were we even to admit as true what we can not think as possible, still the doctrine of a motiveless volition would be only casualism; and the free acts of an indifferent are, morally and rationally, as worthless as the pre-ordered passions by a determined will. How, therefore, I repeat, moral liberty is possible in man or God, we are utterly unable speculatively to understand."

Thus we see, in accordance with my position, that in the above language "it is impossible to conceive of a free volition," and again, "how the will can possibly be free, is, to our faculties, wholly incomprehensible, and the reason he gives is truly philosophical, "that we can not conceive of absolute commencement," that is, the beginning of the series of causes that unavoidably brings about the result. The remote cause may have been our organization, education, health, and a thousand other events, as passions, wants, etc.

Upham, in his "Mental Philosophy," page 265, when speaking of mental emotions, writes as follows: "We are at first pleased or displeased, or have some other emotion in view of the thing, whatever it is, which has come under the cognizance of the intellect. And emotions, in the ordinary process of mental action, are followed by desires. As we can not be pleased or displeased without some antecedent perception or knowledge of the thing which we are pleased or displeased with, so we can not desire to possess or avoid anything, without having laid the foundation of such desire in the existence of some antecedent emotion. And this is not only the matter of fact which, as the mind is actually constituted, is presented to our choice, but we can not well conceive how it could be otherwise. To desire a thing which utterly fails to excite within us the least emotion of pleasure, seems to be a sort of solecism or absurdity in nature: in other words, it seems to be impossible, from the nature of things, under any conceivable circumstances. At any rate, it is not possible, as the mind is actually constituted, whatever might have been the fact, if the mind had been constituted differently."

Thus did this author, in one of his lucid moments, argue the case justly. But soon did he, like Hamilton, craven to the cry of fatalism, and abandoning sacred reason, fall back into the interminable vortex of superstitious mysticism—a divine conscience.

It is to avoid the Gorgon phantom—this scare-crow word fatalism, that authors have traitorously abandoned the sacred laws of God, grounded in our constitutions and in the kindred and causal relations of all things, and thus reduced mental science to that contempt which, in its present dark and vacillating condition, it justly deserves.

But to proceed:—Every rational being acts with a view to some end, and his desire for this end is just as certainly the exciting cause, of will and action, as the moving of a body is the result of something that moves it, and the contraction of the heart the effect of the stimulus of the blood within it. I can no more conceive of a will begetting itself than of a child begetting itself. Both require parents, and those other parents on and on through the series of ages to the first man, Adam, from God's own hand.

We may as well look for new, spontaneous and self-created animals, in violation of Jehovah's harmonious order and causal dependencies of all things, as to grant the accidents of self-creations of the human will. I also maintain that nothing can act before it is—that is, when it is not and where it is not; and it is equally absurd to admit that the will can create itself or move itself without an antecedent or something that causes it and brings it forward. To say that the will is very different from other things, and that in its own self-creating power it can bring forth without a parent, can act without a motive, choose without a choice, and prefer without a preference, is to talk nonsense, and say nothing in support of such miracles. All things are different from each other,—no two in the wide world alike; and yet they have their laws stamped upon them from creation, that under certain conditions each shall bring forth of its own kind. Everything in God's boundless universe is "*sui generis*," or in other words, it is what it is and nothing else. And the myriad of ideas that are impressed upon us are linked results of those objects. It is from the necessary existence of these laws that the mind can regularly step from effect to cause, on and on, to the existence of a God. And it is this, and this alone, that enables us to infer the future from the past, and to know that we are identically what we are, and not by whim of casualty another, from day to day. The many objects presented to the mind from hour to hour force us to know, and to think, and to be led this way, that or the other—to walk, to talk, to cry, to laugh, or to be quiet and meditate. Suppose yourself in the midst of pleasurable scenes that produce merriment and mirth, and you are informed of the sudden death of one of your family; how quickly would all your feelings be unavoidably changed, and a will created to move you homewards, which incident alone should be sufficient to show us how the mind is impressed and governed by assailing objects through life.

The muscles are free to act, yet forced to act in obedience to the will, and the will itself is free, and yet forced to act by its motive impulse—its antecedent and prompting power. The billiard ball, in like manner, is free to act when struck with sufficient force by another, and this may strike and freely move a third, and so on. But

when we look back, we will find that the motive put the
first will in motion, and that the mace or cue put the first
ball in motion. As well might we attempt to think without an object of thought, as to act without a motive to
act. There is a fixed and uniform relation between
motive and action, imperious and indissoluble as the connection of cause and effect. It is a law of mentality that
the desire is always prompted by the object of desire, and
the deed will always follow the desire. When asserted
by a free-willer that we can do as we will, see proper, are
disposed, choose, prefer, desire, have an inclination, or
mind to do, he is right; and why? Simply because we
witness the invariable result; the deed, in accordance
with a mental law, as before stated, following the desire.

Let us now, by familiar example and by the observation
of common sense, test the thing and see how it will work
out. The free-willer says exultingly to a necessarian:
It is folly, sir, to spend your breath in the advocation of
a cause so repulsive to my intuitive convictions. Why,
sir, I am now sitting and desire to rise and walk; do n't
you see I can do it; and look here, I will to extend my
arm, and now to flex it, and it is done. Truly it is, and
all according to the will or desire so to do, and here rests
my strong position against the freedom of the will, as
understood and taught by free-will writers. Will or
desire being nothing more than the bent of the mind in
the choice of an object or end to be obtained. Think for a
moment what it was that claimed the attention of your
mind and caused it to desire to rise and walk; then will
you understand aright the subject under discussion. As
an honest thinker, you are compelled to admit that my
doctrine and doubt of your doctrine excited your ambition, and caused you to desire to rise and walk, as you
did. In this question is the whole principle of volition
involved, and an honest answer at once explodes the

dogma of free-wills without an object or antecedent
cause of will. And now, though your admission has
settled the question, I ask you once more to think how
impossible it is to desire or will for nothing, and consequently, without an object and end of desire and will, and
you can no longer doubt. Suppose yourself, for instance,
in great want and a sum of money within your grasp,
and you were to take it, would it not be the money which
claimed the bent of your mind and caused the will to
take it? Again, were you to refuse to take it, would not
the fear of detection or a sense of moral turpitude be the
cause of that refusal? Yes; and when you will farther
think and know there is no alternative but to choose or
refuse, you must see that the stronger motive seals the
fate of will and action. Thus, when we find ample cause
for every act of volition, why foolishly assert volition
without a cause?

If we could voluntarily act contrary to our desire or
will, and without a causal object of desire or will, then,
indeed, would we be free, but so long as we are forced to
act in accordance with the promptings of the will or
desire, are we under the law of necessity, or in other
words, our unavoidable nature; for there is not a being
on earth, brute or human, but what is endowed with a
susceptibility of pleasure and pain, from which necessarily arises desire and aversion, and consequently a will to
do or not to do, according to circumstances. Thus it
must now appear to every reader that there is no rational
possibility of a denial, but that we can do as we will,
desire, or see proper, and, moreover, that such is the fixed
and immutable relation or tie between desire and action,
that no man can voluntarily act contrary to his will or
wish so to do. This indissoluble link, then, between the
desire and the deed, being established, it only remains to
show how this will, the cause of all human action, is got

up, and whether it be a self-created, self-controlling and independent entity in violation of all the laws and causal dependencies throughout God's universe, or a fated link in the immutable and eternal chain of causality. Will is not a real, substantial and lasting entity, any more than a shadow, which has no existence separate and apart from its substance; or fever, or any other condition of system that depends upon its cause. Love, though powerful even to death, cannot exist separate from the object of love that begets it, and may be transformed by the force of circumstances to hatred, and so with all our other passions and emotions, which rise and sink forever like the ripples upon a troubled stream, one hour placid and the next perplexed. These ripples can not beget themselves, but are produced by external causes; and just so it is with all our desires, passions, and emotions of soul, which succeed each other like waves of the ocean, rising and subsiding by the renewed force of circumstances. We hunger and desire food; we thirst and desire water; we are kindly treated and love the object; cruelly treated, and hate it. If cold, we approach the fire, because pleasurable; but if we get into it we seek to escape, because it is painful; and just so it is with the myriad feelings and consequent actions throughout life, each and every object producing its specific effect upon our sensibilities, just as plainly as vinegar tastes sour and sugar sweet, or that calomel purges and tartar pukes, simply because God has so ordered it. This is the doctrine of fatality or necessity, over which man has no control, and from which there is no escape, but by subverting the mandates of Heaven and the eternal fitness of things.

A man to know that he acts from the strongest motive at the moment he does the act, has but to feel his own regrets at past acts of his life, and farther to see his friends even commit suicide to avoid a long life of hopeless degradation and misery, from irrevocable deeds which he would not for the world now commit. Every passion and emotion of soul, from the fondest love to the fellest hate, and from the purest feelings of philanthropy to the sordid grasp of venality, has its motive object that as certainly begets the will as that the parent begets the child, and the cause its unavoidable effect. Thus it will be seen that the motive begets the will, and the will begets the deed, and further, that as the motive is prior to and independent of the will, the will can no more create the motive or author of its being than a child can beget its parent, or an effect create its cause. This, then, being a settled point, we will now illustrate how it is that there can be no will without a choice, and no choice without an object of choice, and as this object of choice prompts the will to choose, such will can not in the nature of things be free. For example, we come to a precipice of a thousand feet, to the ocean, or to a great river; these objects create a desire or will to avoid them. We find a treasure in the road, and at once there is a will to pick it up; or we are cold or belated, and see a fire, there is a will that moves us to it. We are in bed and wearied with one position, there is the will to turn this way and that way, or stretch ourselves out at length, as ennui may prompt the will to do. We sit down to eat, and this dish, that dish, or other may become the motive to action, and thus many wills be created, and the many muscles of cutting, eating, and swallowing put into motion. In dictating, in writing, the hand obeys the will, and executes its myriad desires to the letter, but the subject of all this writing and the object to be obtained was the author or parent of every thought and action, for it must be seen that we can not think without an object of thought, nor write without something to write about. It has been said that inasmuch as all men do not act identically alike from identically the same given motives, that the will must have some liberty aside from its motive, but a slight observation of the facts will show that this objection to the doctrine of necessity is a shallow shift, unprotected even by the shadow of science. We might, with equal propriety, say that digestion has a liberty, and is not governed by necessary laws, because the same food does not equally agree with, or act alike upon all men. Medicine that claims no powers of volition, sees proper, like the will, to act very differently upon different persons. A given quantity of spirits will intoxicate one man, and not be felt by another, and more than this, it will make some men furious and others friendly, showing plainly that it is just as free as the will to act by its own whims. Even beggars have discovered the philosophic fact of the gastric and dietic influences upon man, and that a full stomach makes a generous soul, so that they never call for alms upon an empty stomach.

These things I mention to illustrate how wonderfully the mind is wrought upon from without as well as from within, and a volume of such secret and unobserved agencies from our physical organism and internal stimuli might be given to show that those operations of the mind not depending upon external objects, and consequently called by authors intuitive thoughts, divine monitors, angel whispers, and such like mystic powers. But I will give only one more prolific source of mental development. The annals of medical science show that the most intrepid heroes and generous souls have been produced by the seminal stimuli, and that quickly such souls may be reduced to cowardice, roguery, and insignificance, simply by emasculation; and history shows that Abelard, the most eloquent orator, profound philosopher, and divine in the world was instantly reduced to dementation and puerility in this way. We may run through history from the days of Solomon and David, Cæsar and Mark Antony, to Napoleon, Jackson, Clay, and Webster, as well as all others of great note, for the confirmation of this fact. We may also by analogy refer to the stallion, the bull, the boar, and rooster for the powerful influence of internal and corporeal stimulants.

The history of eunuchs proves the fact that the mind deprived of this stimulus becomes cowardly and universally false and roguish. The cause of original thought is not inherent in the mind, but, like love and hatred, in the objects beloved and hated. Why, for instance, does a man not fall in love with man, and marry him instead of a woman? Simply because the will-making cause or motive power is not in the mind, nor in the man, but in the woman, that no authority short of God can alter. This is a fatality of God's own appointment, and no quibbling writer can write God out of his rights. But the question may be asked, Why did such a man fancy such a woman? and the simple answer is that he had a will so to do, and could not do otherwise—the motive will or cause being in that particular woman. Yes; but she is not to me an object of love, but is disgusting. True; but a dog will leave a bed of roses for a rotten carcass simply because it is in his nature so to do: the cause of choice or motive power being in the object chosen. But could he not have married another woman, if he had chosen so to do? Certainly he could, and could not have done otherwise, and yet it was impossible for him to do so under the circumstances; because he had no will at the time so to act. A man could as easily make a good bargain as a bad one, if he had the will to do so, and save himself many sore regrets; but I ask the honest thinker to say whether the present circumstances of the moment did not beget the will of a bad bargain. To farther show the controlling influence of motive power over the will, and demonstrate that the will does not beget itself, I will give an additional case. Suppose two boxes, exactly alike in appearance, be presented to the mind for choice, but one is known to be filled with rich jewelry, and the other empty. Now the mind will be in equipoise suspense, and no choice for the moment can by any freedom of the will be made; but let it be seen or said, in this box are the precious diamonds, and how quickly does that box beget the will to take it. These are simple and undeniable facts, showing demonstratively that in every case there must be some motive or impulse which excites the will. Vanity, ambition, love, hatred, gain, and ten thousand other causes of human will and action are found to have their governing influences over the human mind. When I say to a man, he cannot raise his arm, and he in triumph and defiance does so, my voice and the ambition excited that will, which otherwise would not have existed.

Suppose a jet-black object be presented to the eye, could a man, if he had a mind so to do, will or believe it white? Most certainly he could, if he had a mind to do so; but here, as in all other cases, it would be impossible for him to have such a mind or will without the ability to change the object itself that begets the will. And now this single case should decide the whole question about free will; for if the mind can not change black to white, nor sugar to vinegar, the convictions or determinations of the mind are governed by the nature of things; and as the will is the mind, it cannot in the nature of things be free. Suppose, again, that a Catholic should say to a Protestant, If you have a will, you can believe that the holy faith of the Pope is the only true religion on earth, and if you do not, you shall be put to death; would this, I ask, change his honest convictions, or would it give him a will to hate his cruel and unjust oppressor? These facts should, surely, give us a more brotherly toler- ance and kind forgiveness for each other's opinions, which

I teach to be as variant and unavoidable as our physical and mental appetencies.

I have thus somewhat digressed, in order to occupy the whole of the ground, and in some instances have thought it well to pass over it more than once, in order to fix the ground-rights more fully upon the mind of the reader.

There is no subject that can engage the thought or fix the conviction of mankind so firmly and so universally as the consciousness of being able to do as we will or please, and the fault of necessarians heretofore has been to oppose this self-evident fact; for certainly we can do as we please, as I often assert, and cannot, to save our lives, voluntarily do otherwise; and yet this granted fact does not derogate in the least from the laws of necessity; but, on the contrary, shows the fixed and indissoluble relation between motive, will, and action—the motive having control over the will, and the will over the muscles. The deception here is that we only feel the two last links in the moving chain, which are certainly free to move, or they would not move; but we never look back to the fixed and antecedent links that necessarily move the last series in that chain. If it be said that the will is not material, and therefore exempt from the laws of dependence or necessity, I answer that an agent as potent and productive as the will must have an existence, and whatever has an existence must have come into existence, and as it can not have created itself before itself was or had an existence, it must of positive necessity have an immediate antecedent or cause that excited it for the occasion, and shaped it to suit the occasion, or it is uncreated and self-existent from all eternity, as many authors teach, and that our thoughts are emanations from the eternal Godhead. If the will's self-existence from all eternity be assumed, it must be a definite character; that is, it must be what it was in the beginning, and nothing else; and if of this identical character, it can no more alter itself, or shape itself to the emergencies of life than it can create itself. Then how, I ask, will this gratuitous assumption of free will apply to the uses of life? From day to day, hour to hour, from minute to minute, are our actions called for, according to the necessities of our nature, and this unchangeable statue of an eternal will cannot supply or serve our wants. It is easy for the common reader to see, that if God were created, that as certainly as the mechanic is superior to his work, would God's creator be superior to God himself, who, we affirm, has no superior. It is equally axiomatic that God cannot have created himself, as to do so would be to suppose a thing designing and creating itself before it had itself an existence, which is the same as to say that a thing can be and can not be at the same time, or that it can act when it is not and where it is not. Many divines have gone so far, and most truthfully so, as to say that God has not given to the mind to conceive how he could himself create something from nothing, and hence, that it is most rational to suppose that matter, or the materials of which he has formed all things, was self-existent, co-eternal, and co-extensive with himself. Then, having taken from God a self-creating power, shall we impiously assign to the human mind—a created being, a power superior to Jehovah, a self-creating power, in defiance of the nature and fitness of things, and against all motives for good or evil.

This is the naked and ridiculous position of a free-willer, for, if not governed by existing causes and wants that hourly assail our sensibilities from without and from within, it must, independently of all these potencies, create its own causes. Thus must an effect create its cause contrary to every principle and law that sustains the harmonious universe, and leads us, step by step, through the unerring paths of causality up to the throne of God—the first and only cause of all created existence. If the will could create, annihilate or alter the nature of things we will or desire to obtain, then, indeed, could the will be free, not only to create its objects or causes, but to create and annihilate itself at pleasure. But suppose a will to annihilate itself, where is the next will, out of the thousands which daily arise, to come from? If we could suppose them to create themselves before themselves had an existence, still it would be a puzzle how they could come fitted exactly to the object we desire to obtain without any causal dependence upon that object. If we desire bread, and earth be presented, we have no will to eat it, nor can the will convert it into bread, and consequently, is forced to act upon the inherent nature of things. Suppose, again, that putrid flesh be given you to eat, the senses would at once revolt against it, and there would be no will to take it, nor could your will, with all its creative power (so falsely given it,) convert it into savory flesh; and yet you might have a will given you to eat it. Ten thousand dollars in gold laid down might beget a will that could not beget itself or act contrary to the nature of things desired. The gold now becomes the object of desire and the prompting cause of the will to take it.

That our minds are inclined by something that inclines them, cannot be denied, and to suppose a volition counter to the prevailing inclination, is contrary to all experience, so that our volitions cannot be free and independent of motives. It is by the laws of necessity alone that we can know the certainty of anything physical or mental. If the mind be left to chance, the study of it, and the inferring a man's future conduct from his past character, is all in vain. And why lecture, preach, or teach, if these impressions are not to influence the mind? The law of necessity is nothing more than the law of God, established

to make all things sure. It is nothing more nor less than
that indissoluble relation between cause and effect, and
but for the full conviction of all mankind in the fact, and
his reliance upon it, all transactions of life would cease.
Why eat and drink, or cultivate the soil, hoping to be
sustained thereby, but from our confidence in the doctrine
of necessity; and why offer rewards or punishments, or set
examples to good and evil, if there be no necessary connection between these things and the convictions of the
mind. We can as certainly anticipate the operations of
the will, when temptations are set to excite it, as we can
the products of our crop, or the explosion of powder by
the touch of the spark. It may not always succeed from
unseen and counteracting causes, nor may the powder
always explode, being wet or otherwise imperfect. The
chemist, though acting upon the necessary laws of science,
is as often disappointed in his results from the endless and
unseen counteracting influences, as the man well acquainted with human nature is of the anticipations of his
results. The physician, in like manner, is constantly
perplexed and disappointed in the sequences of his pre-
scriptions; for though calomel be a purgative, and tartar
will puke, calomel may vomit, and tartar purge, from
some necessary existing, yet unseen, condition of system.
Constitution, temperament, and disease that blunt or
sharpen the sensibilities, and a thousand other causes
from without and within, may intervene to disappoint our
anticipations, and yet the laws of mentality are just as
certain as those of matter, wherein we are also as often
disappointed. If a rock be cast into the air, the law of
gravitation will certainly bring it to the earth, yet it may
lodge upon some intervening object, and not fall; so in the
like manner if you offer a miser two dollars for one, the
law of motive will certainly control his will to take them,

but should a suspicion intervene that there is a trick in it, he will not do so.

These are no exceptions to the uniform laws, both of mind and matter, but the very proof of it, each counteracting law producing its legitimate effect. A feather may start in a direct line in the air and yet be driven in a thousand whirls and zig-zag directions; but in every motion it has a definite cause. So it is with mind: it may be carried here, there and elsewhere, just as motives may be presented of this, that, or the other strength. A man may start to a designated spot and yet be driven from that spot in various directions by the cry of fire, of murder, and other deterring or attractive sounds or sights. Here were no self-creations of will which were produced by ample causes over which he had no control; and this will be found to be the case in every action throughout life. The will or desire is invariably excited either by external or internal causes, and the action will as infallibly and unavoidably follow the will or desire to act, as the will itself follows the motive. Why then talk of a free will without motives in such case any more than the freedom of the billiard ball to move without a cause, when struck with sufficient force to move it. If the ball, when struck, had the feeling that we have, it would at once declare its freedom to move, as we do when we feel the stroke or liberty given us by the will or desire to move. This might seem to a careless reader a surrender of the point. But not so, for I have previously granted that the action or motion (for there is no action without motion) is not only at liberty to follow or proceed from the will, but is forced to do so, and is just as much under the law of necessity as is the ball under the law of the impinging power.

It is a common and silly remark that we do many things which we do not want to do, which must be seen

4

to be a glaring inconsistency. I will give a few striking
examples to show the fallacy of this position. When a
man goes to the stake voluntarily for his religious
opinions, it may be said that he dies unwillingly and
without a motive. But this, when investigated, will be
found to be false; he, having a motive stronger even than
the miser, who exchanges one dollar for two, for he
exchanges temporary torments for eternal happiness.
Again, we set ourselves up to be shot at in a duel, or walk
to the gallows voluntarily to be hanged, which, when
understood, constitute no exceptions to the necessity of
will.

It may here be taunted then, that we must prefer death
to life. But not so; we are forced to the gallows by the
unavoidable laws of necessity, from which the poor will,
this non-caused and self-created being, has no escape.
We walk to the gallows like a man, rather than be
dragged there and hung like a dog; and we prop ourselves up to be shot at in a duel in order to escape a
greater evil—the blighting clamor of cowardice and disgrace. We submit willingly to the loss of a limb rather
than the loss of life, but unwillingly if we could will it
otherwise. The man who commits suicide weighs his
motives, and prefers instant death to a long and lingering
life of hopeless misery. I introduce these graphic cases
to show that the mind is the subject of circumstances or
motives that surround us and force themselves upon us
from day to day, and that it has no power to create, annihilate, or alter these motives that beget the will and force
it to action. To test the sovereign power of this non-
caused cause, this deceptive sound, this wonderful thingless thing, called will, let us exercise it awhile and see
what it can of itself do. Can it create a desire or will?
No; because it is itself a desire or will, and not a cause,
but a result; not a principle, but an agent; the mere

creature or menial of a motive. Can it create a thought?
No; nor get rid of one. Can it soothe a pain? No; nor
cure a fever. Can it put us to sleep when restless and
worn out upon our beds? No. Can it make a blind man
see, or a deaf one hear? No. Can it create a single
idea? No; no more than it can create a world. Then,
what can it do more than move as a fated link in the adamantine chain of mental causality—the first link of
which is held by the hand of Almighty Power? In test-
ing this creative power or inventive will a little farther,
we will see that it can not call up a single idea that has
not already been impressed upon the mind, through our
senses by the external world. Nor can the mind by any
power of will even call up those ideas at pleasure that
have once been before the mind. We are apt thought-
lessly to say that we can think of anything or any idea
we may will to think of. I think of London or of Paris,
for instance. Yes; but London and Paris were in my
mind, and the objects of thought; or, in other words,
they were thought of before I could name them as objects
of thought. Think, and you will find it to be impossible
to think without a thought, or the existence of a causal
and prompting object of thought. I know we can think
as we think, live as we live, and die as we die, and can
not, to save our lives, help it. I say to you: now think
of Adam, and you can not help but do so; and now cease
to think, and the more you try to cast off thought the
more you think. But now I say call up the Hebrew
language and read a single sentence, and you can not, by
any power of will, do so; and the reason is, as I often
repeat it, we have no innate ideas; nor have we a will that
can create or get rid of an idea; and, consequently, the
mind has no knowledge but what is forced upon it.

One may say: I can see any object you may name
within the sphere of my vision, which is true; and more

than this, such person, with open eyes, could not, to save his life, avoid seeing. Now, open your eyes to mid-day, but do n't see light or any anything around you; and you must reply, in the language of fate, I can not help seeing light and all things around me. I might say to a man : "Now, think of Heaven;" and he can not only do so, but can not help doing so. My voice having put Heaven into his head—a name or thought that otherwise could not have been there, and consequently could not have been thought of without being there. A person may affirm that they can think of what they please, or name any person they may see proper; for instance, that they will name and think of Washington. But here, as in the other case, Washington was thought of before they could name him as the object of thought. Now, all this is as simply and plainly true as it is possible for any proposi-tion to be.

But reflect upon these facts for a moment, and you will see how impossible and how ludicrous the position of being able to think as we please, without that very object of thought being present and prompting us to think, is. Now, I ask, in the name of common honesty, can we call up a thing by its proper name without knowing the name of that thing, or think of an object that is not an object, or, in other words, has no existence, or which is the same thing, is not already in the mind, and the immediate ob-ject of thought. I might say, now, think of what I am thinking of; when your proper answer would be: "I can not do so, but I can think of what I am thinking of myself." Thus, if the reader will go on slowly and care-fully, he will see that it is as impossible to call for a thing without knowing what to call for, as to speak a language that is not in his mind, and of which he has no knowledge. Nor can he think of a thing without having that very thought already in his mind. I have here repeated the view, and turned the picture about to show the careless observer how obvious the fact is, that we can not create or originate anything, and that all our actions proceed from will or desire, and that will or desire is begot by motives that we did not create, and over which we have no more control than the eye has over light, or the ear over sound, when sensitive and assailed. The blind man can not, by any exertion of will, see; no, nor think of light; yet open his eyes with visual impressibility and he can not avoid light. He then becomes the subject of this self-evident doctrine of necessity. He can not open his eyes to mid day and think it or will it to be midnight; nor can he look around him and not have the objects that there exist, as has been shown, fatally forced upon him.

This is necessity—the immutable and eternal law of God's own mechanism; and why eschew or impiously oppose it?

As the words will and desire are of the same import, and the term desire being expressive and less ambiguous, I shall frequently use it in the course of this essay. We have all our lives been in the habit of giving to the word will complicated and wonderful powers, but which, when. analyzed, we find to be nothing more than a simple result, the product of motive; and yet it is like all other inveterate habits—hard to be broken of their faults and mischievous associations. It is this false association that has produced so much bewildering, ludicrous and disgraceful contentions amongst divines in their heated discussions upon the subject of will. As for example: between Rev. Jonathan Edwards and Dr. Whitby, with a score of Armenian pigmies, who have pounced upon him with their vulgar prejudices and vociferous unmeanings of free-will.

Presuming that the testimony furnished the reader has proven to his satisfaction that God has so constituted us

in mind and body, that will or desire shall be the immediate precursor of all human action, from the tongue that
speaks to the feet that walk, and the hands that execute,
we will ascend one step higher in the ladder of truth.
Feeling, then, that all our acts are the result of will, and
seeing that will can not, from any possible contingent or
law under God's universe, have created itself, we shall
next search more fully for its cause. I here call the
attention of the reader to the great and universal doctrine
of *dualism*, which I have laid down as of my own discovery and application to mind as well as matter—namely,
that there is nothing in God's universe which can create
itself or act upon itself—showing the law of mutual dependencies throughout all nature. Thus informed, we
see that mind can not act upon itself, as it is itself, nor
can it desire a nothing; and hence is positively dependent
upon its existent and natural objects of desire for all its
wants, wishes, wills, and acts. Why is there a universal
will to secure diamonds instead of pebbles, and gold in
preference to lead, but for the qualities in those objects,
the nature of which the mind can not alter; and any man
who will affirm we are not fatally bound by the nature of
things as things are is either ignorant or dishonest.

Excuse me in giving a short explanation of the nature
of *dualism*. In conversation with a learned divine, pres-
ident of the first college in the West, and a lecturer of
science for twenty years, he admitted the general application of my doctrine; but, pausing for a moment, asked,
rather tauntingly, But where is your *dualism* when a man
cuts his own throat; does he not operate upon himself?
Nominally, sir, he does; but in reality does not. Man is
a generic term, and a universe within himself, and, like
the vast universe, made up of many parts. The stomach,
though belonging to the same system, is not the liver, nor
is the liver the lungs or heart; which fact answers the

question negatively and confirms my position. The mind
determines the deed, and the muscles, through the nerves,
execute it—the mind acting upon the nerves, the nerves
upon the muscles, the muscles upon the knife, and the
knife upon the throat. But now take notice: the mind—
the author of the act—is not the body, nor the throat, but
a part of that chain of causal events that cut the throat;
which throat did not, nor could not, cut itself. A motive
forced the mind, and the mind's menials grasped the
knife, which knife did the cutting; so we see the throat
did not cut itself. I know I am a part of the universe, as
the throat is a part of the human system; but I also
know that I am not the universe, nor the author of all
that takes place in the universe; but a subject to be acted
upon by the fatal laws that have forced me into existence and will eventually force me out of existence.
Now, though all the wheels of a time-piece, like the parts
of the human system, are in active play, no one wheel
acts upon itself, but is acted upon by others, and the
whole is dependent upon the main-spring that gives the
law of motion; which main-spring was not self-created,
but dependent upon an antecedent agency, and that again
upon the material created and the law designed by the
First Great Cause of all existence and all motion. The
seed put in the ground did not create itself, nor can it
sprout or grow but by the fatal laws of its unavoidable
nature and the vitalizing elements that force it forward,
and by its limited time force it out of existence. Just so
with the human system—mind and body—nothing self-
created, nothing self-sustaining, or self-moved; but all
are forced conditions—*dualistic* and *dynamic*. The aggregated universe, of which man is but a part, is governed
in like manner. The celestial orbs, that roll their hidden
and eternal rounds through trackless space, are ruled by
the law of *dualism*. Nor is the human mind, which can

not think without an object of thought, nor act without a motive to act, any exception to the fatal law of *duality*— not being able to do anything of itself—all our ideas being begotten by the action of objects upon the subjective mind, just as the child is begotten by the union of the father and mother. An alkali can not act upon itself, nor can an acid; but bring the two in contact, and an action takes place, and a new being, like an idea, comes into existence.

We can not voluntarily act without a desire or choice so to act, and desire as unavoidably implies an object of desire that begets it as the word "son" implies a father who begot him. Trace back the death and the reproduction of man through mouldering ages to the first man, Adam, or glance forward through ceaseless duration to the last man who may hang upon the verge of time, and there will not be found a single gap or broken link in this eternal chain of causality. Pause but for a moment and think of these things, and how impossible the doctrine of casualism must be; for if God had created things contingently, and allowed beings to come into existence without a designated and fixed cause, the world would be filled with new nondescript and motley spontaneities without an archetype, and without the pale of God's government, so that we are preserved only by the uniform laws of Providence; in other words, divine fatality. These are the fixed and immutable laws of Supreme Wisdom, and is as applicable to mind as to matter. Every motive or object of desire begets its appropriate desire, or will; and all our movements, improperly called free volitions, are as much forced as the rifle ball is forced by the powder behind it. The ball has no liberty but to obey the impulse, and human action has no liberty but to obey the will, and the will itself no liberty but to obey the cause, the motive, or impinging power behind it. I will to raise my arm, and it is done; I will to walk, and the limbs are put in motion. Now, the motive here, whether from a banter or from the ten thousand other incitements, caused the will, and the will caused the muscular motion. The powder explodes, and the ball is driven before it. In like manner, the steam is let upon the engine, and the vessel is put in motion. But in neither case is there a self-creating and independent power. But for the spark that causes the explosion, and gives it its quickening power, the powder would remain forever unexploded and powerless. In like manner would the mighty engine, the will of the vessel that sends or makes it walk with magic power through the waters, remain a lifeless tool, as it is, but for the steam that is let upon it. In this case, everybody looks at the astounding might of the working engine as it wields the ponderous mass, without thinking of the power behind it; and just so it is with the workings of the will upon the human body. Every one sees and feels the energies of the engine will, without looking at or feeling the silent motive-power behind it, that begets it and forces it to act just as it does act. We differ greatly in regard to the potency of this will or engine, and the regularity of its action for good or evil, owing to our mechanism, constitution, temperament, prejudice of education, and to the interminable aptitudes to the impulses of passion, and of the impressions that are momentarily made upon our sensitive being through life. Precisely so with a vessel of less complicacy; yet, from defect in construction, or from the machinery becoming deranged, it may go astray like the madman, and even be reversed in its motion; but it is still moved by the same engine without violation of principle—not being able to alter its own condition. The deranged man is under the same necessity, yet he is governed by the same principle as a sane man, who has not a jar or a crack, or a screw

loose in his system. He is governed in all his various
and apparently inconsistent movements by his firm and
honest convictions, or that same will forced upon him by
external circumstances, or excited within by the feverish
or otherwise disordered condition of his system. Nor is
there any escape from the workings of this engine will,
as long as the steam is let upon it. If the steam wears
down or becomes exhausted, the will of the vessel no
longer works, and the vessel sleeps. Identically so it is
with the mind—when the sensorial power or steam becomes exhausted by over-working, the engine will cease
and the body sleeps; but the stomach, like the furnace of
the vessel, being constantly supplied by food or fuel, the
steam is again and again renewed.

We can not have a sensation of any kind, whether of
pleasure or pain, but that there is a desire or will got up
to do or not to do—in other words, to embrace or avoid.
Even when asleep, and the doors of knowledge are closed
to the external world, the laws of the animal economy
are such that we are stirred by functional influences to
pleasure or pain, and often to act, as though we were
awake. When the bowels are disturbed, we dream of
stooling; the bladder, of urinating; when hungry, of
eating; when thirsty, of water and drinking; and there
are many other normal and abnormal phenomena, all
arising from a definite organism, and the uniform and
fixed relation between mind and body, and which is as
indissoluble as the tie between cause and effect. Both in
the cases of somnambulism and somniloquism the unconscious will, stirred by internal forces, puts our machinery
in motion. The sensible observer may daily see that
when his dog is asleep and dreaming of the chase he will
bark, while his legs are in motion, as though convulsed
by galvanic influence. If we then, when our senses are
locked up and we are unconscious of all around, are thus

forcibly operated upon without a choice or a self-created will to bring about these results, is it not proof positive that we are governed by the irresistible laws of our nature, in which we have no hand, any more than in the creation of ourselves, or the pulsations of our heart? The internal workings of our vital functions, of which we are not conscious, are truly wonderful; and here lies the secret of the various mystic systems, that refers all human actions not produced by external agencies through our senses to an internal and self-moving power of the mind, called by different names, as inherent or intuitive conceptions, sacred monitors, angel whispers, and such like. Digestion, absorption, circulation, nutrition, and assimilation, with all the sustaining and renewing both of our mental and physical energies, is carried on as well when asleep as when awake, and the conservative vigilance of these vital powers is the marvelous work of Divine Wisdom, and indicates a mind of body as well as of brain. Yes; marvelous it is indeed that we may take into the stomach a homogeneous substance, as milk, which is itself a secretion, and it will soon be converted into muscles, bones, cartilages, tendons, nerves, and many other solids, and a thousand secretions; all differing greatly, both in their visible appearance and their chemical properties. The wear and tear of mind and body by day is restored by night; and the insidious and stealthy encroachments of morbid influences are watched at every pore. Organic breaches that disturb the vital functions, as a cog out, or a broken wheel, are quickly repaired; a wound is watched and healed, and a bursting blood vessel or a broken bone is soon mended. Prick the hand or flesh even when asleep, and there is an instantaneous recoil; let us stumble or lose our balance, and quicker than thought does this law of nature right us up. Indeed, we have no time to think, nor has this exotic will time to create itself and come to our aid. A thousand facts of equal wonder and sure design are seen in our physiological researches into the animal economy, too numerous to doubt the existence of an all-wise and ever-present Designer, who numbers the hairs upon our head, and suffers not a sparrow to fall to the ground without his notice. If these mere material and tangible operations of body are carried on without our consciousness or knowledge of their *modus operandi*, and without a self-created will that creates these results, how is it to be supposed that in the more inscrutable and subtle mind we can scan those ultimate causes that belong to God alone? To cover this ignorance, a thingless name and powerless phantom has been got up in the dark ages, called will. The physician, when ignorant of those occult workings upon his patient, and pressed hard for explanations, treats the case with deep gravity and most learned technicality; such as morbid irritation, normal and abnormal condition of system, loss of sensorial power, accumulated excitability, revulsion, translation, concatenation, and, above all, "*vis medicatrix natura*" is dragged in as the universal panacea of medical ignorance. In like manner does the superficial metaphysician, when unable to go back through the labyrinth and lengthened series of causation to the more remote and true causes of human action, most sacrilegiously call into existence a non-created and self-willed being, that can with impunity violate all the laws of God, sever the connection of cause and effect, render void his potent and harmonious dependencies, and—what is of all most wonderful in this wonderful, uncaused, and efficient no-cause without the pale of God's government—make something out of nothing, and create and annihilate itself at pleasure—a power that no philosopher or divine on earth ever supposed God himself possessed of. Hence

it is that he is held to be uncreated and from all eternity.
This paramount god of all gods—will—however, is said
to have no antecedent or cause of being; but to rise spon-
taneously from nothing, and from moment to moment
through our existence shape with exact design—but
without a designer to suit the million of emergencies—
the emotions, thoughts, and actions of man as he runs the
gauntlet of life, and is assailed by warring elements on
every side. The God of the universe can not be and not
be at the same time; nor can he act inconsistently with
himself, and yet be a consistent God. But this god,
will, can rise from nothing, can be or not be, as it may
will, without a parent will; can make incompatibility
compatible, inconsistency consistent; can move by con-
trarieties; can make virtue vice, and *vice versa;* can act
without a motive; prefer without a preference, and choose
without a choice. These things, ludicrous and impossible
as they may appear to the reader, are actually the legitimate results of the doctrine taught by the free-willers.

Dr. Whitby, the great Armenian champion of free-
will, seeing that desire is in some way always connected
with our volitions, is recreant and traitorous enough to
truth and sacred reason to boldly affirm that we do not
choose a thing because we desire it, but desire it because
we have chosen it without a desire—making the will
thus free to choose without a choice or desire so to do—
the exact converse of our mental process and order of
exercise in willing; for this would be to will contrary to
our will, or choose a thing contrary to our choice, or
desire, in order to obtain that desire. He farther speaks
of an indifference of choice, or an equipoise condition of
mind, leaving it free to act without a choice; which is
again impossible in any case: for in such case there
could be no choice, change, or act of mind—quietude and
action, or rest and motion, being antagonal and incom-

patible. That a man can do what it pleases him to do, I grant; but to say that he wills to do what does not please him is absurd. We might wish circumstances were different, could the will so make it.

The only obvious and satisfactory way of meeting these abstract and subtle plausibilities is to direct the reader to the exercises of his own mind, and ask him, if a fine orange be presented and he accept, whether it was not the orange that induced him to accept it; and his answer, if honest, will decide the whole controversy about will; for it can not be that without the orange such effects would ever have taken place. A free-willer might answer, as Haven and Dr. Whitby would: True; but it was the mind, and not the orange, that accepted and acted as it pleased; and who could wish to be freer than to do just as he pleases. This every body knows; but ought also to know that the orange caused the mind to be pleased, and made it do just as it pleased. Apply a red-hot iron to your surface, and the mind will instantaneously flinch; in which case it was not the iron that flinched, but the mind; which did just as it pleased. And now, here, as in the case of the orange, and all other cases of will and action, it was the red-hot iron that made the mind do just as it pleased. Was not the mind, however, at liberty not to flinch. No; under the motive power, pain, it was not; and if it had been, it would not have done as it pleased, for that would have been to be pleased with pain, instead of pleasure—a thing impossible in the nature of mind—and by which fact you now see the whole secret of will and action. From the nature of the delicious orange, your mind was pleased to accept it. But now, hark to the fatal fact of how the mind changes with the change of circumstances and causal power—of objects or motives, of pleasure and pain, of loss and gain. Now, if, after the pleasure of

accepting the orange, you saw poison in it, that pleasure
would instantly change to pain, and the mind as fatally
certain as turns the needle to the magnet, would turn
from the orange and refuse to eat—still doing as it
pleases; or, in other words, just as prompting motives,
under its decreed law of mentality, cause or incline it
to do; thus showing that to do or not to do is the same;
and in reality it is all to do, and to do just as the unerring
law of causality makes us do. Reflect upon this, and then
notice every act of your life, and, in so doing, ask yourself, Why I did thus and so, and not otherwise. To say
that the mind, and not the motive, is the proximate cause
of all muscular acts, is obviously true, yet positively false
when applied as it is by Haven and all free-willers; for
the question is not what the mind does, but what it is
that makes the mind do what it does. The man who
shoots another might, with equal philosophic propriety,
say: I did not kill the man, nor did I touch him; it was
the lead, or a ball, that killed him. And this, though
certainly true, would not excuse him, nor one who kills
another by poison, from criminality before a court of
justice. The ball, like the poison, was the proximate
cause, and only cause seen, of death; but if we will trace
back upon the lengthened chain of causality, we will find
the barrel which conveyed the fatal ball, the powder that
sent it, the cap which exploded the powder, the cock or
hammer which struck the cap, the main-spring that forced
the cock, the trigger that set the main-spring loose, the
finger which pulled the trigger, and so on to the remote
and true cause of all these events. Just so with motive
and its events—the will being the proximate cause of all
willing acts; and, as in the case of the ball, we see
nothing and are conscious of nothing but the will or
desire to act, and yet it is just as certain, as in the above
case, that there is an antecedent or remote cause that sent

or excited the mind (take notice) and induced the mind to choose and act—there being no effects without cause in either case. The mind, like a leaning tree, is always just as nature inclines it to be; and when the tree falls, it will fall just as it is inclined or made to fall—does not grow itself or fall itself—the laws of the vegetable kingdom forcing it up as we see it, and gravitation, winds, or other causes forcing it to fall just as it seems inclined and does fall; having no intrinsic power to make itself, grow itself, or to stand or fall of itself. In like manner, the mind did not make itself, nor can it prolong itself beyond its destined end; can not act upon itself, create ideas and volitions within itself, nor even renew itself when exhausted; but is as dependent upon its decreed laws as are all other things under God's government. And now, as the mind can not act without a choice, and can not choose without an object of choice, we at once see its dependence upon those objects which it did not create and can not alter.

In every act of life we instinctively look for a cause, and it is in every body's mouth, Why did he do it? What could have been the motive? And, to answer with free-willers, There was no cause, no motive, no object or end in view, good or bad, would not be satisfactory.

And now, the whole controversy in regard to the human will practically resolves itself into this : — A man bad by nature or education, or both, will certainly will and act badly, in accordance with his nature and the circumstances attending it; while a good man, in like manner, will will and act differently; for the same reason that a Mahometan will act like a Mahometan, a Catholic like a Catholic, a Protestant like a Protestant; and that a Frenchman will speak French, and an Englishman will speak English. These are self-evident facts, which I have demonstrated elsewhere, and I will now proceed.

In returning again to our analogies and illustrations, it may be recollected that I gave the will the place of the engine, which, in reality, is a nullity, a perfect nonentity in regard to an intrinsic, or self-existent power. Like the powder that would remain powerless without the spark that explodes it, the engine would lie for ever dead but for the vitalizing steam, which gives it its executive office. Explosion is a new creation, and is neither powder nor the spark, but a powerful and efficient effect or offspring of both, and which becomes in the fated chain itself a cause. And so in regard to steam, it is a new creation, brought into existence not of itself, but by water and fire. Of this creative power, through the influence of objective and subjective unity, so little understood or applied in our investigations of science, we have many examples in chemistry ; as the union of an acid and a base, forming a saline substance or agent, new and efficient in all its appliances, and yet wholly different from either of its originals. All our thoughts, ideas, and wills are in like manner new creations, not from nothing or from individual influence, but the result of objective action upon the subjective, or, in other words, the influence of the external world acting upon our sensibilities, or the soul within, through our senses. It was from the revivescent and plastic hand of nature, in the death and reproduction of organic matter in its various forms, and of the new and strange productions in the mineral kingdom, that doubtless gave to Zoroastre the idea of the transmigration of souls— the Pythagorean doctrine and religion of Persia. True, the reader may say ; but now for its application to the subject of will, to which I answer that it is by giving a familiar knowledge of the result of those occult and wholly inscrutable laws that bring into existence such results that we can conceive of the workings of appropriate agencies in the human mind in the production of their results, and it will be found that there are more things in this analogy than the giving of a religion to millions of our fellow-beings. And to prevent the barking of cur-critics, who may strike upon a false trail, and cry materialism, I here say, that though chemistry and machinery, used in my analogies, are not identical with mind and will, such analogous principles are common to all things. Were I to say, a good man and a good dog, it would not necessarily mean that man was a dog. And again, were I to say man was an animal, and a goose was an animal, it would not prove man to be a goose, and yet little critics, fonder of controversy than of truth and honesty, might find excuse for a tirade of Puritanical invectives upon this point, for I have read books against Locke's Metaphysics, and the Rev. William Paley's Moral Philosophy, not a whit better founded, which only proves the fact that " dogs may bark at dead lions."

But to return from illustrations to the argument. You say that you can do as you please. I say so too. You reply : this, then, is surrendering the question. Yet not so, for it incontestably confirms my position. I grant that you can do as you please, but I affirm that you can not, to save your life, avoid doing what you please, which is a plain proof of necessity—the very thing I want. You may be determined to a vicious act, but turn it to a virtuous one, or alter your will in ten thousand ways, and yet every act must be in obedience to the motivity of will. You may determine upon an intrigue or fraud, and have that will changed by fear, either of God or man, in each of which cases we plainly see the motive. You will to raise your arm, and it is done. I say now, put it down ; but you reply triumphantly, I won't do it, and so hold it up in defiance of my will, but in full

accordance with your own will, which will and act was
in defiance of my command—the evident motive cause of
such will and act. A link of connection in the machinery
of man may be severed, as in palsy; a screw may be
loosed, a bone broken; and in that case, though the engine
will may work intensely, the legs remain still and the
body unmoved. Just so it is with the vessel—the wheels
will not walk, nor the body of the boat move, if the
connection between the wheels and engine be cut off.
This fated necessity of connection as of cause and effect,
or will and action being established, we will look farther
into the origin of will, the moving engine of the human
system. I have elsewhere said that every rational being
acted with a view to some end, and that that end or
object to be obtained was the motive or cause of will, and
that this exciting object of will bears precisely the same
necessary relation to the will of man that the steam does
to the engine or will of the boat. The steam, though a
new creation, and got up to suit the occasion, is not a self-
created being, but is a separate entity, the offspring of
water and heat. The generators of the will of man are
also actual objects, and work just as simply and plainly
to be seen as the action of one billiard ball upon another
in the production of motion. For example, a child is
hungry and sees an apple, and now the will to obtain
that desired object is certainly created by the apple,
and the efforts that follow are the necessary results
of the newly created desire or will to fulfill its destined
end. The apple created the pleasure and caused the
child to do as it pleased; or in other words, it certainly
led the mind to its choice. Now, in this case the apple
as certainly created the will and the will as certainly
stretched out the arm, as that any one thing in science is
the cause of another. It must farther be seen, that without this apple such will would never have existed; and

again, that there is no such thing as steady, or living and lasting will beyond its immediate motive or causal object. Ten thousand wills are created daily, and as quickly do they pass off, for ever succeeding each other like waves of the ocean. The movement of children who are never still will show the nature of volition, and how every new object or turn of their toys, produce motive, will and action. Put tobacco in a child's mouth, and its effect, aside from sickness, is obnoxious, while sugar has a very different influence. And so with all objects that assail any one of our five senses, aside from what I call the sixth, or functional sense, as hunger, thirst, dreams, pains, and sickness, with our endless neuralgic sensations. We need not study artificial text-books, or go beyond the nursery to learn human nature. The child may be seen to follow the sugar bowl, or stick of candy, as certainly as a horse will follow a bundle of fodder, or an ear of corn. Scatter dimes or candy, and just such a scramble will ensue as we daily see taking place in the selfish acts of the trafficking world around us, that only gains more cunning and fraud by age. Will is not an entity, but simply a conditional or correlative term, like hunger, thirst, love, hatred, and other sensations that constitute neither matter nor spirit, and like motion, that inheres only in the moving object. Music, for instance, has no real, lasting, or separate existence apart from the instrument that produces it. It is a mere momentary sensation, or one of the many evanescent modes of mind. Will, like effect, has no separate existence from its cause. Every word we speak, step we take, and movement of the body in the execution of our hourly vocations, require a new will generated by the object of desire to do what we do. I am cold, and approach the fire; here the fire creates the will or desire, and the will carries the body. The mind did not produce the fire nor the will to go ot it; but God created the fire, and the fire created the will to go to it, and from this fatality in God's own hand there is no escape. But could we not as easily have staid away from the fire? Yes, indeed, and have suffered or frozen to death, if a stronger motive had caused a counter-will, but no such motive having interfered with the bent of the mind, it was impossible for us, under existing circumstances, to do otherwise than what we did. The difficulty in understanding this subject has ever been, that we feel the desire or will to act and see the result, but never look back of the will to see how it is produced. We may see a puppet dancing, and except we look behind the curtain to see the hand of design that holds the law of motion, we might suppose it to have vitality and intrinsic power. To free the subject as far as possible from vague abstractions and bewildering technicalities, I have striven thus to illustrate, by familiar examples of every-day life, and original, but, I hope, acceptable mode of instruction. And again we may exercise our thoughts in tracing the succession of events. We see a man dead from a shot and accuse the will ball (the only thing seen,) of the deed. It pleads necessity, as being sent by a power called explosion; the explosion accuses the powder; the powder being innocent in itself, refers to the spark or cap that ignited it; the cap to the cock or hammer that struck it, and the hammer to the main-spring; that to the trigger; the trigger to the finger; the finger to the tendon; the tendon to the muscle; the muscle to the nerve, and the nerve to the will, which will is gone forever; but could it be called up, it would refer you to some powerful impulse, passion, or emotion, that begot the will. Such will might refer you to the mind, the mind which did not create itself could refer you back to its nature, or birth, its education, and the circumstances that excited it at the moments of its willing. But

could not a counteracting or paramount will have pre-
vented that fatal will, is the natural question of every
man; which question brings the subject in all its force,
fully and fairly, right up before us. I answer promptly to
this question, that a stronger will would as certainly have
counteracted this fatal will, as that the whole is greater
than a part; but it is equally certain that as the prompting passions and emotions of soul, or in other words,
as the motives then before the mind did not excite such
will, it was impossible under existing circumstances for
him to have such a will, which surely left him as free
to follow the stronger will as a feather is to float with the
currents of the prevailing winds. It would have been
just as easy for water to run upwards, sparks to descend,
and rocks to float, instead of being ruled by the fatal law
of gravitation, as they now are, if God had so willed
it; but as God, in his plans of creation, from the motives
then before him, had no such counter will, he ordered
things as they now are, which renders it impossible for
them to be otherwise than as they now are. Again, if
God had willed us to live for ever, we could not die; but
ah! how, in the absence of that easy will, do we feel
the powerful influence of our fated death? It would
be just as easy for to-morrow to be clear as to be cloudy;
but if cloudy, it will not be without a necessary and
sufficient cause in the unseen and unending series of
ever-moving events. If those who have gone to the
stake had had a mind they could have thought otherwise
than they did, and thus have saved their lives; but
without being able to change the circumstances that fixed
upon them the death-deserving opinion; it was impossible for them to have such a mind. I think, however,
aside from these examples, that the reader must see from
the very nature and fixed relation of things themselves,
that no change of will can occur without a change in the

principle, or laws that govern will. The will is so universally governed by the nature, or property of objects, that every body's will is to prefer a pound of gold to a pound of iron ; yes, and diamonds to dirt, the mind neither being able to create nor alter the nature of things. It ever has been and ever will be impelled to act in accordance with the nature of the motive objects. And again, we are known to will and act in accordance with our own nature. For instance, if a man of quick temper has his face spit in, he will be prompted to strike, before he has time to think, while another, cowardly, or of blunt feeling and slow temper, having time to weigh the consequences, may withhold the blow ; but in each case the parties were governed by the necessity of their nature. And again, suppose a man starts to attend a card party, or a drinking club, but while on the way a thought of evil consequences comes over his mind, and he turns back, was he not in each case governed by a sufficient motive to move him? so that a first will being counteracted by a second will is no proof of a self-created or non-caused will. A virtuous will, then, that counteracts a vicious will is no less a motive, or caused will ; and as whatever is moved is moved by something, and whatever is caused is caused by something, the will must have a motive for action, and be that motive good or bad, real or imaginary, (for ghosts move the mind with great power,) it does not leave the will free to act without a motive.

It is granted by all sound minds in science that the same causes will always produce the same effects under the same circumstances, which renders it impossible that any man could have done otherwise than he did, influenced by circumstances as he then was. It is a common, but thoughtless and false remark in the mouth of every one : well, I am sorry I did so, for I might have done otherwise. One moment's thought will convince us of this most palpable and unhappy of all errors : as the pursuit of every man throughout life, from his cradle to his grave, is that of happiness, and this arises from the first law of our constitution which God has implanted in us for self-preservation. He has given us acute sensibilities of pleasure and of pain, which gives us a desire or will to escape from the one and seek the other, and simple and comprehensible as it may be, constitutes the main-spring to human action, and is the key to the phenominal series of life. How, then, under this granted and governing law, can any rational being voluntarily seek pain in preference to pleasure, and, if not so, he certainly acts at the time he acts with the best light that he at the time had, and were it possible for him to go back with identically the same impressions or opinions, it most assuredly must appear that the same results would occur. From the same principles of our nature it is evident that we should not suffer under bitter and deep self-reproach and anguish for past acts, if the light now shining in upon our souls had co-existed with those regretted acts.

Why, then, so foolishly say we could have done otherwise than we did, or that the will has power to act contrary to the convictions of the soul. And now the result of the examples beautifully illustrate the utilitarian principles upon which this essay is founded; to wit, that, by enlightening the human family and giving them a clear knowledge of the laws of God or nature, and our own constitutions, and how these laws or elements operate upon our sentient and percipient being, that we are to obtain that quiet satisfaction and happiness of mind, for which the world incessantly strives. Having in other parts of this essay fully pointed out to man his only hopes for happiness, it will not be necessary here to dwell upon this point. It may be said, why educate, instruct, or admonish, if all is fate and fixed by laws that can not be altered at will. But I answer that these very laws of fatality are what makes us free to escape destruction or less consequences as the case may be; and farther, these laws being fatal (certain) afford the only rational plea for instruction. For instance, being instructed that water will drown, and fire burn, we keep out of them, and thereby avoid the consequences; the friendly law of fatality making us free to escape the more fatal law of destruction. If, on the contrary, God had left things to chance or contingency, instruction and knowledge would all be in vain. Founded upon these shifting sands, bread that nourishes us one day might prove a deadly poison the next; and a deed of virtue one hour, a vicious one the following; so that it will be seen in a single sentence that the doctrine of free-will and casualism would destroy all knowledge, and leave us a physical and moral wreck.

If a man be viciously taught, his passions and wills will be fatally vicious; and if raised ignorantly, the poor fellow will be fatally ignorant. If Eve had believed in the doctrine of fatality (certainty) she would not, when told what would be her fate, have committed the acts she did. But being persuaded by the free-will, Devil, that there was a casualty in the command that left room for escape, she, in consequence, hazarded the happiness of all mankind.

The physical universe depends wholly upon fatality for its glorious harmony and eternal preservation, and but for the reliable constitution of man in his susceptibility of pleasure and pain, and his steady relation to his Creator, good and evil would be neutralized and lost in the destructive vortex, casualism. Grant the existence of a God, and his steady rule and government over all things, then, indeed, will instruction in his laws, for which he has given us full capacity, prove valuable to ourselves and acceptable to him.

Fatality instructs us that we have no will to speak an unknown language, yet this very fatality gives us the will to learn it; and though we have no will to cure the fever, a knowledge of the fact gives us a will to avoid the malarious region that would cause the fever.

Fatality farther instructs us in morals, that we have no will to save ourselves from condemnation for sin; but a knowledge of this fact gives us a will to avoid sin : knowing that no will we can create of our own can save us from the gallows, gives us a will to abstain from crime; and thus it must appear to the most common reader, that the doctrine of fatality is the only immutable basis upon which to found a rational education; and farther, if events could be brought about without a fixed and known law of God by the self-created will of man, all knowledge of the future, both by God and man, would be destroyed. Arrogant and impious then must be the man who aims by a self-created power to resist the laws of his own constitution, and subvert the mandates of Heaven. The prescience or foreknowledge of God would be impossible, if there were other gods or men who could by their own wills change the result or destiny of things. The future with God is the same as the past with men, and as what is past is certain and unalterable, that which is to come is just as certain and unalterable with God. Now, it will be easily seen, that had God left it to the whims of men's wills to do or not do, independent of fixed and fatal laws of his own, by which he can judge that his future knowledge must be uncertain, for how could he be certain of an event that is uncertain, or to know a thing to be that may or may not be.

Observing, then, as we must, that God's perfect foreknowledge of events and free-wills, whims, or accidents are incompatible, and that the doctrine of necessity is thereby established, some have denied to God his power of prescience. This power, however, can not thus be got rid of, particularly by Christians, for it is recorded in his book of revelation that he did predict the action of men, and they came to pass to the letter. In short, all the prophecies were founded upon God's foreknowledge, from which it must appear obvious to every man, that, if the events and persons spoken of, had had a will of their own, independent of God's will, or known knowledge, and could act from moment to moment even against all temptations, causes, or motives, God could not, by any possibility, have known their deeds, where they might have seen proper to act differently. Stand here for a time unsandaled, for you are upon holy ground, and think seriously of what you read. We can, with our limited knowledge, anticipate the conduct of men, and did we know them perfectly, we could present a motive or lay a bait for every act of life. For instance, we know that a miser will prefer two dollars to one, and that a man who has a strong propensity for drink will take it when the temptation is set before him, provided there be no intervening temptations to draw his mind in a different direction. All other events of life are equally certain, when understood, and why, then, say that we are not actuated by motives and by laws, just as obvious and sure, as the material bodies. I will farther show that will is an effect, as has been often asserted, and how it is created or produced. One man calls another a liar, it creates a will to strike, but a fear of consequences or a regard for moral duty may be the stronger motive, and create a will not to strike. A large sum of money, without fear of detection, may create a will to steal, but if a high sense of honor or moral terpitude, from an early and well grounded instruction in religion, comes in as his stronger motive, the theft will not be committed. Liquor creates a will in a savage to fight, and a kind word and certain benefit to

that savage gets up a counter will. The inhalation of the
exhilarating gas may engender various wills, and reveal
to view the peculiar idiosyncrasy of the individual: one
will dance, and another dash at the audience for a fight, a
third will debate most furiously, while a fourth will sit
silently and weep: showing beautifully and clearly that
will or desire is nothing more than an impression made
upon our sensitive being. This subject is to me so simple
and so clear, that additional illustrations seem really to be
a loss of time.

This doctrine of necessity must show to every reader
the necessity of an early and deeply grounded instruction
in religious and moral principles, it being as fatally certain
that a man of early vicious habits and strong passions
will yield to temptations, as one whose passions have
been early subdued, and mind elevated to more noble
aspirations, will have a strong enough will to resist them.
Some authors, seeing the power of motives over the will,
have granted that the strongest motive or temptation
offered to the mind will move it, as certainly as that the
strongest body in motion will overcome the weaker, or
that the whole is greater than a part. This every honest
man of clear mind, like Hamilton, is forced to allow ; but
some, like Sir William, fearing that bugbear cry of fatalism and infidelity, shift off under the cover of conscience—
a lying witness. Fashions in education are like fashions
in dress, as well as in all other things. A new cut may
at first be uncomely, and even forbidding and ridiculous ;
but soon, from its association with greatness and refinement, becomes beautiful and irresistible over the will, and
the reader who can not see from this single example the
sovereign power of circumstances over the production of
thought and action in the human family, must be blind,
indeed, to the influences of his own mind.

Conscience or opinion (which in reality are the same

thing) are like will—not an original faculty or power, as is falsely taught in all the books on these subjects; but they are effects or results, and formed and changed about by the circumstances that create them. For instance, how are the consciences of judges and juries formed in giving their decision in cases involving life, liberty, and property? They have no legal or just opinion, and consequently no will to act till the case is heard. If the testimony be plain and positive, the conscience is clear, and the will quick and strong in its decision. Here is a simple case that will apply to every opinion and act of human life, and shows, beyond contradiction, that we are governed by opinion, and that that opinion—the father of the will to act—is itself dependent upon circumstances; and farthermore, that those circumstances are themselves dependent upon their antecedents or appropriate causes, and so on *ad infinitum;* and hence, as Hamilton says, it is impossible to find a beginning—one event succeeding another, and the causes of will being as interminable as the sweep of time itself. It is remarkable that Hamilton and other intellectual writers, men of great minds in little things, should not know that the beginning is in God, whose creative wisdom has called all things into existence, and who gave life, laws, and motion to the aggregated universe, and that all was constituted to act in harmony and with undeviating fate.

In speaking of the causes of volition, Dr. Edwards says: "If the mind causes its own volitions, it can only do it by a causal act, and that causative act is itself a volition, and requires another causative act to produce it, and so on *ad infinitum*, thus involving us in the infinite series." Hamilton recognizes this as a legitimate argument, and hence, he affirms, that, as we can see no beginning of self-caused or free volitions, they are inconceivable—yes, impossible. But aside from all great names, with their abstract and equivocal doctrines, I here give my own views as plain and undeniable facts: First, that all events and all productions are alternately cause and effect—as the reproduction of man from Adam down, nothing standing as an independent and universal cause, save God alone; secondly, that every effect must have its cause; thirdly, that every cause must act to produce its effect; fourthly, that there is nothing self-created or self-made, but everything is moved by other forces, otherwise we could have the perpetual motion, by a self-moving power, a thing I have elsewhere demonstrated to be impossible, the fatal and inflexible law of *dualism* forbidding it.

And now, from these great and universal principles, decreed by the Maker of all things, we must infer that the mind can not create itself, or act upon itself to create ideas and volitions within itself, but is dependent upon other objects that operate upon it—the causal power of *dualism*. Haven calls the doctrine of Edwards and Hamilton the *dictum necessitatis*, which subjects the mind to the causal law of all other things, and tauntingly says, "The mind thinks, and has it to think before it thinks any more than to have a motive to act before it acts?" Now, this, though plausible in words, is obviously false in principle and in the nature of things; for, though the mind does not have to think before it can think, it can not think without having an object of thought, any more than it can choose without an object of choice, or will without a motive to will. As I constantly repeat, the great error of this author, like all free-will writers, is in dividing the mind, an indivisible thing, into many parts, powers and *faculties*, and making them so independent that Dr. Alexander says, in his book on Moral Science, that the soul is not responsible for the acts of the will, nor can vicious qualities of the soul vitiate its essence; as

though the soul was not like everything else—made what
it is by its parts and properties. This constantly deceives
and misleads the reader, and indeed, both writers and
teachers of metaphysics; so much so that Haven says
the mind, by aid of its *faculty*, will, can create its own
wills, motives, thoughts, and acts, as though the will was
not the mind and the mind the will, which is the same as
to say, that the will can create its will, or the mind can
create its mind. Will, like faculty, is a word of false
sound; for what is it, I ask again and again, but the
simple bent or inclination of the mind itself, and what is
the bent or inclination of the mind itself but the turning
of the mind itself to the objects of its desire or aversion?
The mind that laughs one minute and crys the next is
identically the same mind, governed, not by extra wills
and faculties, but simply by the objects presented to the
mind, over which none of these creative wills or faculties
have any control. The needle turns to the magnet, its
causative object, just as the mind turns to its creative or
causative objects, and one has just as many faculties and
wills as the other. There is nothing in the whole science
of the mind but sensations of pleasure and pain, and
consequently, desire or aversion to do or not do, just as
such pleasures and pains may incline this feeling thing
we call mind. If suffering pain from thirst and we see a
cooling spring, the mind, without the aid of faculties, at
once carries the body to it. Charming music, through
the ear, leads us to enjoy it, while, on the other hand, if
we see or hear something frightful and dangerous, we at
once, without the advice of faculties, escape it. Thus is
solved the mighty enigma of mind and the great science
of psychology. I have no objection to the mighty array of
faculties, wills, volitions, and powers necessary for making
up big and mystic books, and livings for thousands of
teachers; if such book-makers and teachers should tell

the student they are mere high sounding nothings
introduced to fill up and give the appearance of much
learning. And now, I ask the reader to see Haven, the
great text-book maker, where, under the head of a contrary choice, he creates a faculty, sticks it into the mind,
and makes it so paramount to the mind with all the other
faculties, as to choose, will, and act, contrary to the
choice, desire, and determination of the mind itself. I
say, see Haven, and read and think for yourself. He
repeatedly says, We can voluntarily do what we do not
want to do, and moreover, that we can feel differently
from what we do feel, as well as think and believe
differently from what we are inclined to do. Such a
faculty I should like very much to have, as it could make
pleasure out of pain, mitigate all sorrows and afflictions,
and feel that we are rich when we are poor. Yes, I now
ask such writers whether this thing they call will, has
any actual existence separate and apart from the causal
object, and if so, when and how did it come into existence?
The idea of its designing itself and bringing itself into
existence before it had an existence, is too absurd and
impossible to entertain, so that it must have a cause aside
from itself, which I hold to be the causal object such will
desires to obtain. Should the alternative be assumed, that
the will is no separate or independent thing, but is in reality
nothing but the mind itself, which creates its own wills, we
are thrown right back into the absurdity we aim to escape,
of self-creation, as it would be just as easy for the will to
create itself and its objects of will, as for the mind to create
itself and its objects of choice. The mind, with all the faculties and powers we falsely give it, can of itself create nothing, any more than the mother alone can create her offspring
or product. I say, and say again, will is an effect, a product
of the subject mind and the motive object, neither alone
being able to create themselves, but are results, the pro-

duct of God's decreed law of *dualism*. But to be done with this view of the subject, (for I am weary with proving a self-evident proposition,) I will once more ask the reader, if invited to a party which he attended, whether the will created the party, or the party and his invitation to it created the will which took him to the party? But now vary the question, as free-willers would do, and affirm, you did as you pleased? I again ask, was it not the party that gave you the pleasure to do as you pleased? so, vary the question as you may, it terminates in the self-evident fact, that motives are inevitably and invariably the cause of will.

My natural turn of mind led me, in early life, to moralize upon all events, and caused a pleasure (no self-creation, take notice) in me to do just as I pleased, which was to read everything I could find upon the subject of the mind. With this foundation I commenced my practical study of mind, and having for more than fifty years mixed with all nations and languages of the human family, from the native Indian up, or rather, down, to the snobs, parvenus, and paragons—the fashionable folly of our race—have sought to find where happiness dwells.

Whether Diogenes, Alexander, Cæsar, or Napoleon lived and died the rational and happy life, is a question of doubt.

It is at once seen that the will or conviction of mind to decide any case is not a self-created, fortuitous, or contingent nature, but is dependent upon the testifying facts that make the case what it is, or upon impulses arising from love or hatred to persons or objects, which loves or hatreds also had their foundation in the nature of things. It appears to me to require but little expansion of mind to see this relation of causal dependencies, or the immutable and indissoluble connection of cause and effect, and that the investigation of which must as necessarily lead

us upwards and onwards to the First Great Cause, as the
rounds of a ladder lead us upwards, or the tracing back
the causality of man from son to father will, through the
series of generations, lead us back to Adam, the first man,
from the hand of God himself. Nothing stands alone, or
has a self and independent existence, but all things bear
a kindred and causal relation, in time, space, and nature,
and is doomed to incessant and eternal succession. There
is no first beginning, no last end, but in God.

The mirror has no power to create pictures, but can
reflect the impression made upon it, nor has the daguerre-
otype-plate power to alter or obliterate, except by time, as
the fading of memory from the tablets of the mind. The
wax, in like manner, is susceptible of ten thousand stamps
or impressions, but has no will to resist or change them.
And so it is, likewise, with a blank paper, like the child's
mind at birth—without a scratch or character of any kind
upon it—but languages and whole books of science may
by-and-by be written upon it; nor has it any more power
than the mirror to speak a language that has not been
taught it, or change the nature of things that are impressed upon it. The materials in the mind received
through our senses may, like the materials in the kaleidoscope, be turned about, exhibiting endless forms—as
in case of imagination, and dreams by internal and
functional excitations or emotions, and we may even
become furious madmen by disease; but in all these
cases the will can do no more than the mirror. The
will, I have said, is nothing more than the result—the
reflection of our sensations and thoughts—and the madman's will is just as much the result of his unavoidable
feelings and thoughts as the man better balanced. And,
if there be an unerring conscience and will independent
of circumstances, why ever act amiss, as we often do,
greatly to our own disadvantage—as in our contracts

and other acts of life. As before stated, if cold, we approach a fire, because the sensation in this case is pleasurable; but if it burns us, we have an instantaneous and strong will to withdraw from it, because the sensation is painful. These are plain and simple facts, and apply to every act of life. If we could perform an act without a motive or cause, then we should have events or effects without causes; and if this be so, which is impossible, then man can not be free. Every act of life proceeds from desire, and desire indicates an object desired; which object the will did not create, and consequently is not free.

We hunger, and desire food; thirst, and desire water; are in love, and desire the object; hate, and avoid the object; and just so it is with every other act of life, called free-willing. The mind, as previously stated, is a unit, simply with the sensation of pleasure or pain, as external agencies may impress it, so that all resolves itself into desires and gratifications. God himself is under the necessity of acting according to the nature of things, as acknowledged by Clark, Chalmers, Dewey, Scott, Dick, Butler, and other able divines. For instance, God's will is not self-created, nor inconsistent with the nature of things eternal, but is the result of immutable wisdom and infinite goodness, and comprehension of what is right and best; and truth, honor, and justice being uncreated, underived, immutable, and eternal, God can not act contrary to the nature of these independent entities and paramount motives; for that would be acting ignorantly, untruthfully, dishonorably, and unjustly, which would make him neutralize his own attributes and sink beneath the dignity and honor of a God. So that in accordance with his own nature and the laws he has stamped upon all things, he is under the moral necessity of acting with an undeviating rectitude of purpose.

These are august realities and sacred principles, grounded in the constitution and nature of things, that can not be denied by Christian nor by Deist. Haven says upon this subject, in treating of taste: "The beautiful, the true, the good exist as simple, absolute, eternal principles. They are in the Divine mind; they are in his works. In a sense, they are independent of Deity. He does not create them. He can not reverse them, or change their nature. He works according to them. They are not created by, but only manifested in what God does."

God's laws, then, are not right simply because of his authority, or his having willed them, for he willed them not from any arbitrary feeling, but because they were in themselves independently and eternally right. We do not, then, derive morality from the mere dictates or commands of the law; but from a higher and anterior source, from which all law, if just, both human and divine, must be derived.

After having shown, then, that God himself had a foundation and reason for all he did, shall we assign to man a power to originate things from nothing, and to possess a will that is governed by no law or rule of action?—a broken link in the great chain of causality, and without the pale of God's government; a thingless thing, and an efficient nothing and effectual no-cause, that can act without a motive, choose without a choice, and decide without a difference; and, above all, that can create and annihilate itself at pleasure. If will be the result of our judgment, it is not free; and if determined by reason, or the dictates of conscience, it is equally a result, and not an efficient and independent entity. We have farther seen, as in the decision of judges, juries, and in all other cases, that our reasonings, judgments, and convictions of right and wrong are dependent upon the facts of the case, or in the nature of things, so that it must be seen that neither the will nor the foundations of will are free—all dependent upon antecedent circumstances, and consequently under the laws of causality, or, in other words, necessity. Even after all the testimony has been heard and a judgment formed, a speech will change that judgment, and, consequently, the conscientious decision of a jury. Where, then, is this innate and immutable, immaculate and divine conscience thus warped and driven before the breath of eloquence as a feather before the storm? In short, if we had that infallible monitor, maintained by model copyists, we could as well decide without law and testimony as with them. I at this moment think of a case which of itself is sufficient to decide the question whether we have a will that can, under any circumstances, come to our aid, or decide anything without the causes or objects that create that will. Suppose, for instance, we come to the forks of a road of equal size (as I have often done), and no finger-board to decide or beget this wonderful will, so independent of all causes. We have no will with us, nor can we summon it to our aid, but let a man come along and say this is the right road, and then does this paradeful and no-caused will rise up and claim the honors of an infallible guide.

If we will disregard the abstract and inexplicable refinings to be found in the innumerable and perplexing books upon metaphysics, and apply the mind itself to the practical purposes of life, we shall find no difficulty in understanding all the laws of mentality; which are so few and simple that a child, as before said, may master them in a short time, and that, too, by the most pleasing exercise of its own mind. But the schools now destroy the mind by stupifying it with memorizing abstract and technical nonsense, instead of enlarging, elevating, and enlightening it by familiar conversations and lectures on

science, and upon those laws of our nature by which we
are to be made healthful, prosperous, and happy. Our
youths are not now taught to get rid of local, petty,
and personal prejudices, and to believe in one God, one
church, and one brotherhood; but are early stultified
and blinded to truth and justice by idolatrous isms,
schisms, and dogmatisms, that sear the heart and vitiate
the soul, thus engendering fiendish and implacable parties, who in religion drag each other to the stake, and,
in violation of the laws of both God and man, assume
the authority of God's partial favoritism and approbation, get up bloody wars, and subvert governments, thus
making man the greatest enemy of man.

But to return from those reflections upon the results
of education to the argument. It is admitted by many
free-will writers, that where the mind is under a prepon-
derating influence, that it has no power itself to change
itself and make a choice contrary to its own choice—
which in reality is as impossible as to be and not to be
at the same time: but, say those authors, throwing off
part of their absurdities, there are conditions of mind,
as in a state of perfect equilibrium, where things are
equal, and there is no choice, then can this will come
forward and make a choice. In proof of this, they offer
a case that has figured through their numerous and
bewildering volumes for centuries past. It is simply
the old stone balancing the grain, and they have not
yet seen how to do without it. This celebrated and most
notorious case is the offering of the choice of two guineas
to a beggar or miser, wherein it is contended there can
be no difference in the thing chosen to create a choice.
Now, the choice being made, as they think, without a
difference, they thus exultingly affirm it to have been
done without a motive or preference in the thing itself:
therefore, the will is free to act or choose without a choice

or distinction in the thing chosen; which is an absurd
mistake, for it must be seen by the most common reader
that indifference and .choice are wholly incompatible;
and, moreover, that the question, when properly understood, and as acted upon is simply this: a guinea or no
guinea? for the beggar or miser sees at once that, *if he
makes no choice, he gets no guinea,* and as there is no difference, it makes no difference which. This case, well
known to every man who has studied psychology, actually proves the reverse of what it is intended to do,
to-wit—that will acts upon the motive for action, or, in
other words, according to the motivity of things, and the
immutable laws inherent therein. This proposition of
a balanced or equipoised will of the two equal guineas
reminds me of the Greek's jack that starved to death
between two hay-stacks, because his mind was thus
equal and he could go to neither. Such propositions
have a seeming something in them that might perplex
the pupil or common reader; but it is like the question,
whether, if one stove saves half the fuel, two, by the
rule of three, may not save all? These are abstruse
and ingenious subtilities, it is true, but profitable only
to mechanical teachers, and stupid book-makers. Bring
such mystic and misguided teachers to the light of nature,
and they are as blind and dumb as owls and bats. I have
seen unthinking persons perplexed to account for what
becomes of all the old moons when the new ones appear;
a problem of equal weight with the guinea question, and
many others that support the schools, and make *big*
books so vague, tangled, and mystic as to be as indeterminable as the tenets of witchcraft itself—but a short
time since so gravely and grievously maintained by law.

It is a very common remark by free-willers: Well, I
would not suffer such and such thoughts to come into my
mind, I would cast them off; when as easily would it

be for the leopard to change his spots as we to cast off
our nature and its thoughts. Why not cast off all
disease and mental affliction, and these wandering
thoughts that keep us tossing all night upon our sleep-
less beds? Say to the mother: cast off all affection
and distress for your dying babe, and she will say in her
heart, you are an unfeeling fool; and so may we say
to all superficial thinkers, and false teachers, who are
wholly ignorant of nature and of their own constitutions.
I do sincerely pity the youths of our country who have
to undergo the drudging and dwarfing influences of
our present schools. It is memory, memory of arbitrary
nothings, till the mind is actually incapacitated for
those enlarged and ennobling thoughts of God and of
his mighty works, which alone can make us wise and
good. If we had schools freed from the galling yoke
of the dark ages, and teachers that would lead their
pupils out into the groves, and before the unfolded
book of nature, their bodies would be strengthened, and
their minds stored with wisdom from the God of reason.
If the books studied in the schools be worth anything,
they are founded upon nature and the eternal fitness
of things, and as the mind, which we carry with us by
day and by night, is the substratum of all knowledge,
why not apply it to nature itself, and instead of a copy of
ten thousand copies that may have been corrupted by
ignorance or design. To show the natural propensity
of the mind for new and novel things, I make the following quotation :

> " In the pleased infant see its power spread,
> When first the coral fills his little hand ;
> Throned in his mother's lap, it dries each tear,
> As her sweet legend falls upon his ear ;
> Next it assails him in his top's strange hum,
> Breathes in his whistle, echoes in his drum ;
> Each gilded toy that doting love bestows,
> He longs to break, and every spring expose."

Lead the little child out into the flowery meadows and along the purling streams, and his desire for nature will induce him to throw aside his artificial toys, and oh! with what delight will he paddle in the water, and play with the pebbles. As the larks skim the air before him, and light with their soft, shrill notes upon the tops of the waving weeds, he with extended arms struggles after them, and by his joy-lit countenance and ecstatic manner, speaks in the language of nature : " Oh ! see, see!" Soon a child becomes an ardent florist, and while yet young, might become scientific without ever looking into a book, and without the aid of the degrading lash and stupefying drudgery of our commonplace and routine schools. A lisping child may be led onwards and upwards in the laws of its Creator with as much delight as it is known to take in exciting narratives. ghost stories, and things new to the mind. And should it be, that by casting off the stale and mechanical details of dead languages and other dwarfing studies, we too early learn all that is to be learned in this world, (as such teachers say), we can direct the mind of the pupil from the dazzling streams and verdant fields of earth to the gorgeous and glorious universe where clustering worlds in heavenly harmony roll their hidden and eternal rounds. Here may science exhaust her every rule, and imagination roam in these untrodden fields of endless space and ceaseless time. But I would say to these nut-shell teachers, who grovelingly, yet gravely, maintain that the human cranium, contracted as it is, may, by the innumerable apartments and departments they have so liberally assigned to it, have ample room for all the arbitrary and unmeaning trash they have doggedly drilled and crammed into the brain, and yet have room for everything that is to be learned in this world. That this assertion will stand as a glaring and grievous error,

7

till we shall have learned the laws of life and enough
of our own constitutions to rid them of all disease and
bodily afflictions, and leave old age as the only outlet of
life, and till the statesman and divine shall have learned
enough of their own minds to live at peace with themselves, and to unite the human family in one harmonious
brotherhood, that wars may cease and murders and
misdemeanors be unknown.

To relieve the reader's mind from a constant stress
upon abstract thoughts, I will as briefly as possible
contrast the book of nature with the petty driveling
staid and stale arts of man, found in the paper books of
our drudging schools.

Thus the reader will have seen what he has yet to
learn, and that we are at this moment living in gross
ignorance of the wonders of the world and of the
unnumbered and undiscovered elements and laws around
us, equal to astronomy, railroads, and telegraphs, which
has taken us thousands of years to discover. And why
is this so, other than that our lives are taken up with
languages, logic, rhetoric, and other such pedantic
trifles that have never discovered or invented anything,
not even a plow or a harrow, and in the nature of things,
never can. Think, I beg you, why it is that men living
two thousand years ago were more original, profound
and eloquent in thought than any of the present age?
the answer to which is that their thoughts through life
were devoted to the laws of science and the voice of
nature. No orator has ever equaled Demosthenes.
Euclid, who lived near three hundred years before Christ,
still stands far ahead of all the mathematicians who have
ever lived. Æsop, though a slave, has never been
equaled. Socrates, Plato and Aristotle are still the
masters of philosophy, while Homer is justly adored as
the divine father of poetry; and though Milton has
gained an immortality in his " War of God with Satan "

by stealing from Homer's " War of the Gods," he is but
a feeble imitator. Shakespeare, the only modern child of
nature, and the glory of England, is entitled to a rank
with the sages of antiquity. Those truly great men
retreated from the petty scenes of society and sought
wisdom in caverns, forests, and in the sacred fanes of
nature; and I must say that my thoughts have been
greatly more enlarged and elevated amidst the voiceless
wilds and slumberous solitudes of gray old forests, than in
the busy marts of men; and who is it, when standing
as I have done, upon the watch-towers of creation, and
viewing the ramparts of eternal ages just as they were
reared by the hand of Almighty Power, will not have
sublime ideas and solemn thoughts? Here, and not in
the man-made church, will you meditate with awe and
admiration, and feel that you are in the presence of the
great Jehovah himself. Amidst old decay and ruin wide
you see marine organic beings sleeping in their rocky
tombs of unknown ages, yet tell you of a former and
ruined world, which leads you back through the dark
and lengthened vista of time into past eternity! But
we must cut short these thoughts, solemn and sublime
thoughts, created by the objects of nature, and return
to the argument, my only object being to contrast the
study of nature and the works of God with the puerile
works and machinations of little man and their disgusting vanity. And now, though this might seem
to the reader to be a digression, I could use no argument
to more fully convince him of the power of circumstances
over the mind, and to show how the mind, as I have been
throughout striving to do, may be stultified and degraded
by petty and puerile studies, or ennobled, expanded and
elevated by the meditation of nature—God's own immutable and eternal laws of science.

The illustrated book of nature speaking in the un-

mistakable language of God, is ever open before us, and
the interminable chain that binds the physical, intellectual and moral world is to be examined, link by link,
while but few rounds of the ladder of truth that reaches
from earth to heaven have as yet been ascended. The
whole phenomena of nature are presented to our view
and her classification is simple, her nomenclature perfect.
As the light of heaven is adapted with kindness to every
eye, so is the language of nature to every tongue and
capacity on earth. The outer eye requires no arbitrary
learning, nor does the inner eye of the mind; it is but to
open either and see for ourselves. The great enigma of
the universe is yet to be solved, and we have, if untram-
melled, the capacity ample for the task. From the grand
and colossal exhibitions of nature, we infer boundless
power and infinite wisdom, and from the exquisite designs and adaptation of means to ends, we infer a
Designer. Through immensity, we launch into eternity,
and in endless variety we find an eternal unity. Transcendent beauty, order and harmony fill all the departments of God's vast domains, while vitality and thrift
spring from every pore of nature. Search from old
ocean's oozy bed to the concave heavens that span the
whirling globe, and from the hidden caverns of earth to
the star-lit skies, and all is filled with life and activity.
The glowing heavens are replete with light, and the laws
that rule the celestial orbs, while the waters beneath,
team with organic being. Plenitude and power are seen
everywhere, and the unmistaken presence of the great
Jehovah is made manifest to the most common observer.
God's own hand-writing is seen upon the face of nature,
leaving no room for subtle follies or verbal quibblings.
No *hic, hæc, hocs*, or further struggle between the rule of
truth and the errors of education. Those glittering
diadems that stud the mighty dome of heaven, and the

green earth, with its rolling rivers, its waving forests and
blooming lawns, are all sweet expositors of their Maker's
greatness and goodness. "The heavens declare the glory
of God, and the firmament showeth forth his handiwork;
day unto day uttereth speech, and night unto night
showeth knowledge." The heart is no longer chilled by
the stern and wrinkled brow of the technical pedagogue,
but bounds with exulting rapture, while the emancipated
soul bathing in the pure and sparkling fountains of nature,
rises with renewed strength, like the noble eagle from his
dirty cage, and soars high in heaven's unfathomable blue.
No odious selfishness or fraudulent creeds can be found in
God's natural revelation. No theological chimeras or
sordid mummeries of a knavish priesthood are there to
be found. No confused relations of vague and complicated abstractions, conventionalities or factitious entities,
no cheerless mystery or desponding gloom, but all is held
out in bold and bright relief to the glowing light of day.
There are

"—— tongues in trees, books in the running brooks,
Sermons in stones, and good in everything."

I have thus briefly striven to show the reader what we
have yet to learn, and to restore the book of nature to the
church of God, which book, in the dark ages, being pronounced heterodox with the artistic canons of theological
philosophy, was thrown out, and an absurd and suicidal
system of mystic philosophy ordained in its place. Of all
the delusions this was the most unfortunate. It dethroned
God, degraded the human mind, and dishonored religion,
and after the vast expenditure of mind and money, during
a lapse of eighteen hundred and sixty-eight years, the
religious world is left in doubt and distraction.

There are but few who can account for their own
actions; yet strange, yes, truly strange, that any man
of sound mind, seeing that his own actions are always

directed to some end, should not know that that end was
the cause of such action instead of referring it to casualties that have neither motives nor ends for action. The
whole deception of this long perplexed question is in
feeling the undeniable fact that we do as we are inclined,
desire, or please, but search no farther to see why we do
as we desire or please, or what it is that begets that desire.
As we desire to exist and feel that we do exist, were it not
from palpable contradictions we should certainly imagine
that our desire begot our existence, simply because we
desire to exist and do exist, just as we desire to act and do
act. It is this delusive feeling that begot and sustained
the doctrine of witchcraft, and the power of spells. Desir-
ing an event and finding it follow, will naturally beget
a belief that the desire was the cause of such event. The
daughter of the Governor of Massachusetts, as recorded in
history, wished that the arm of a certain young lady
might be shriveled, and that her tongue might be palsied,
and such coming true, she confessed before the court, and
had her own tongue bored, the least punishment then
inflicted for witchcraft. Hundreds have confessed their
guilt before the courts of England and suffered the
dreadful ordeals of fire and water, showing how necessary
it is to guard against our false and imaginative feelings.
Amongst the last prominent cases brought before the
Court of England was one of a poor old woman, who was
formally arraigned before Lord Mansfield, and though the
facts were plainly proven by the most respectable witnesses, that she had been seen riding through the air upon
a broomstick, he humanely let her off, by granting that
the respectability of the witnesses proved the fact beyond
contradiction, yet that there was no law to prevent any
one who might see proper, to ride through the air upon a
broomstick. This case may be found among many others

of similar character, amongst the records of the courts of Great Britain.

Martin Luther, though a man of strong mind, was so ruled by superstition as to say to the churches, I would have no compassion upon these witches, but would burn them all; and history tells us that thousands were annually burned throughout Europe for witchcraft.

As I again and again repeat it, motive begets will, and will begets action, and this, in reality, simple and short as it is, is the sum total of a question, upon which thousands of books have been written. The reader must here take a particular notice of these connections, and by practicing his own mind, will discover the fact that such is the established relation between desire and deed, or will and action, that the moment we desire to act, the nerve of connection with the part conveys the power to the muscle. If a sensitive and high-toned man be called a liar and a coward, the will to strike is at once excited, the spark is put to the powder, and as quick as a flash it passes from the pan to the rifle barrel to send the ball; does the nervous fluid fly from the brain to the arm? We will or desire to walk, and the legs are put in motion, one moving alternately before the other—the mind now commands the legs to stop, and more certainly than a master commands a servant, do they obey and stop.

To witness with what marvelous skill the great Designer has established will and action, exercise your mind upon the various muscles of your body. Will to flex or extend any one finger fixed upon, and it is instantly done, showing incontestably a mental control over our locomotive and procuratory muscles. God, however, has wisely severed the action of the heart, and all our vital organs from any tamperings of the will, and endowed them with separate and more inherent energies. Here is actually a universe of dynamic and normal forces, with vitalizing

and renewing powers of which we are wholly unconscious, and through whose dominions our intellectual and
telegraphic messengers pass from our *censorium communi*,
or head office, to their destined points of execution without interruption. From this short excursion after collat-
eral and amusing facts, we will return to the argument.

We have seen that motives have a full control over our
desires or will, and that will has a like control over our
voluntary or motive muscles, and analytically or synthet-
ically, there is nothing more to be found in this mighty
question about the nature of volition. Let us try the
power of motives a little farther, and test whether our
assertions be correct. Suppose yourself sitting in a house,
and it takes fire, and the flames envelope you, would it
not prove an ample motive or a sufficient power to put
your legs in motion to escape. I hardly think you will
deny it, and if not, the question is at an end. You may
answer, yes, it certainly was a sufficient cause, but I was
at liberty to stay and perish in the flames, for many a
martyr has gone to the stake voluntarily and been burnt.
True, but these are cases full in hand to prove the power
of motive and the doctrine of necessity. You could have
been consumed, had you seen proper, but it is certain you
did not see proper, and now we turn the key that shows
the mighty secret. It is, why did you not stay and be
consumed? and as an honest man you answer, because
there was no motive to do so. No motive—true—true—
yes, true as that there is a God in heaven, and that he
has established his laws, mentally and physically, upon
fixed and immutable principles, that cannot be subverted
by casualties or the whims of man. It was as impossible
for you to stay without a motive, as to fly without wings,
the stronger motive as certainly controlling your will, as
the heavier body will turn the scale. The weight in your
case was in the scale of self-preservation, and it turned

you out of the house and saved your life. But you say, many a martyr has gone voluntarily to the stake to be burned, which is true, and many a man has walked voluntarily to the gallows to be hanged, not that he preferred death to life, but there being no escape, the stronger motive, to die like a hero rather than be dragged up and hung like a dog, prevailed. The man who goes to the stake might escape, but he goes there selfishly, and under the same motive that induces a miser to exchange one dollar for two. The martyr simply exchanges temporal torment for eternal happiness, and instead of getting two for one, as in the case of the miser, he expects a hundred-fold. Perjury to a false faith might release him to a life of disrespect and self-reproach, and at last sink him down to the undying torments of hell; all of which calculations come in as motives to sustain him in his trying but momentary struggles. I could not select a stronger case to show the power of motives, and how the stronger motive will always prevail even unto death. Thousands upon thousands of the superstitious have starved and maimed themselves to death under the powerful motive of rapturous and eternal joys. The man who commits suicide, has an overwhelming motive to get rid of some agonizing distress and hopeless despair. The poor drunkard, whose gastric and nervous influences are aggravated to an insufferable extent, might seem to act upon reverse principles in seeking temporary relief to the hazard of permanent disgrace, want, and squalid misery; and yet, his motive acts are perfectly legitimate. He bears with the urging wants and with his sinking spirits, till his feelings are overwhelmed by a depressing melancholy that obscures the future. Besides, a pride and self-vanity, which blinds us from seeing ourselves as others see us, and then that blessed hope, delusive as it may be, that buoys us up through life, comes in and sustains him with

8

a belief that he will not go like others, and by relieving his agonies for a moment, he will not lose the resolution that is ultimately to reform him. Under a clear sky, however, he sees himself mirrored as he is, when he shudders and shrinks with horror from the sight, and then it is that he takes Bible-oaths and temperance pledges; but soon again, dark clouds overhang his ill-fated star, inward storms arise, and our poor, frail, and afflicted brother, feeling what we can not—the irrepressible monster gnawing at his heart's strings—yields his every earthly prospect and becomes a raving maniac, or a mournful melancholy seizes upon him and depresses him down to hopeless despair. He, under these circumstances, takes palliating draughts, just as one suffering under an excruciating and incurable malady is prone to do. Here is a case that shows the necessity of an early and well-grounded education in sober and steady habits, and in a knowledge of our constitution of mind and body, and the laws of nature under which we "live, move and have our being." If, instead of spending our lives in the study of dead languages and clogging our brains with a chaotic mass of other such trifles, we were put to early training in the active and efficient laws of nature that hourly act upon our sensibilities for weal or for woe, education, instead of being pedantic and degrading to humanity, would become elevating and ennobling. And thus, instead of making an arrogant and supercilious display of a vacillating and artistic nonsense, we should be well grounded and wise in the immutable and eternal laws of our Creator. Were this the case, and nine-tenths of our canting demagogues (who are more corrupt and wily than the devil himself in sowing the seeds of jacobinical corruption and dissipation) made inmates of our penitentiaries, there would yet be some hope of reform from the threatened destiny of man, and the pending dissolution of this happy government.

In recurring to the more powerful passions and emotions of soul that absorb every other feeling, and that often lead us as blind captives to disgrace and misery, I will mention a clergyman of my acquaintance, who, having no resolution to restrain his amative propensities, and believing that even concupiscence was a sin, his motive for honor, virtue and religion was so powerful as to induce him to take the knife and emasculate himself. Poor, silly man! who might as well have considered hunger a crime and cut out his stomach, cursing God for giving us those vulgar passions and brutal propensities, with which he might have made some woman as happy as was Sarah, the wife of Abraham and mother of Isaac, in compliance with the decreed laws of procreation, planted in our very constitutions by God himself. St. Paul was thus much troubled with a member of his body, which he called a thorn in his flesh; but did not aim to destroy that nature which God gave him for the best of purposes. Under an all-absorbing passion for revenge, men often take life, and then, under a change of feeling equally uncontrollable, they destroy themselves; a horrid act which no one would commit had he power to feel or do otherwise, for he could not desire death but as a dreadful alternative from greater evils.

A very common argument in favor of free-will is this—if persons can not control their will, why should everybody think so, and blame them for their acts. The only answer to this seeming something is, that the error lies in our own selfish sensations; so much so, that we hate everything which gives us pain, or that is even unpleasant to our sight, and hence it is that we kill snakes, that are not accountable for their nature, and hate and punish many a poor creature because uncomely to our sight, or run counter to our feelings and interest.

Anything that obstructs our view to happiness, or

excites painful sensation, is at once hated, and hence the
unreasonable prejudice against the innocent vessel out of
which we have taken medicine when sick, and the unavoidable disgust at serving of soup in a night-vessel,
though equally as clean and as pure as a china tureen.
We will by-and-by hate the approach and looks of the
friend who tells us of our faults or brings us bad news,
while we love flattery and pleasing intelligence. We can
not avoid hating the looks of a man scabbed all over with
small-pox, or leprosy, or any deformity, though such
unfortunate person can not help it; and so with every
object of life — our fancies, our loves and hatreds not
necessarily being founded, in justice but in our own
feelings that arise from our individual and varied organ-
izations, sensations and aptitudes to impressions made
by the objects of sense, or arising from our emotions
within. Were love and hatred bestowed upon merit, we
should have more happy matches, and men of moral
worth would fill the offices of government, instead of
canting demagogues, who cater to the lowest and grossest
prejudices of the masses, who are led astray by those very
feelings that I am combating. Hasty and inconsiderate
persons will take up and break an innocent stone against
which they have stumped their toe, and the poor and
undefending brute is unmercifully beaten because unable
to bear the burden imposed upon him; but this prejudice
of ours is no proof of a just foundation in the nature of
things. One who flatters us or contributes to our pros-
perity is loved; but let him become a competitor and
adversary, and he is at once hated, though honorable
and beloved by others. It is a common expression, I
hate such a person (or an object)—not from any merit or
demerit, or willful act, but simply because such are our
feelings and hatreds to all who do not act in accordance
with our wishes. Let any man try whether he can keep

his own temper in riding a blind or stumbling horse, where it is obvious the animal can not help it, and he will find that his flash of passion and the application of his lash to an unavoidable act was actually simultaneous with the inoffensive offense, and before he had time to think or reason upon the injustice of his own conduct—showing that•unavoidable things, as well as avoidable, when they inflict pain upon us, get up at once a feeling of resistance; and, on the contrary, when they give us pleasure, we desire to embrace them. So that we will see from the ever-varying counter-currents and emotions of our own minds, that we should be cautious how we inflict cruelty upon our fellows; for it is impossible, in the nature of things they should feel and think with ourselves, or act to please us. The impartial observance of such facts, then, as I have related, must clearly convince us that, though God has endowed us with watchful feelings of self-preservation, and a hatred of everything that runs counter to our interests, it requires close guarding not to become the instruments of great injustice, and the destroyers of others' rights. He has also given us fire and water as blessings, when properly used; yet, if not strictly guarded, they may become elements of destruction. It must appear, then, to the observing reader, that we are governed by circumstances, and, farther, that we are made to differ as much in mind as we do in body, in constitution, in temperament, in health, and in the various vicissitudes of fortune and afflictions of life—all which tend, unavoidably, to form the character of man. Our feelings, thoughts, and emotions of soul are as diversified as the objects that surround us: every new scene in nature, and all the changing events of life, develop in the human mind their appropriate feelings and affections. The fondest love and the fellest hate may, alternately, possess the same soul; while the most malignant revenge may be quickly followed by remorse, humility, repentance, and forgiveness.

How, then, in the face of all these facts, can any author maintain that we are not fatally influenced by circumstances, but that we have a divine, instinctive, and unerring conscience as a guide, and a will to execute, that is above circumstances, and which can bring the thoughts and movements of all men under one undeviating rule and standard of action? We hear such men constantly saying, Well, I would not let such and such feelings trouble me. The mother is told to dry up her tears, and to consider the loss of her child a blessing. The lover is a fool for entertaining such frivolous and childish passions; and the man who has lost his all on earth is weak to permit a regret to enter his mind. Such advisers are doubtless honest enough in their soothing injunctions, but they certainly fly directly in the face of both God and man, in attempting to subvert the established and undeviating laws of mentality, that can no more be severed from the circumstances that beget them than effects can from the causes which produce them. Just as rational would it be to say to a man whose hand is in the fire, Why, my dear sir, I would not allow the idea of pain to enter my head, but sum up resolution, and consider the feeling pleasurable; or to admonish a hungry man not to allow so vulgar a thing as the stomach to control his feelings.

But, to the point; you will still affirm that you can do as you please, and so I say; and, farther, that you can not, to save your life, do otherwise than as you please; for then, indeed, could you will to be free to act contrary to your will, or, in other words, to all the motives and feelings that beget will. To say that you can do as you please, is exactly the same as to say you can be pleased with what you are pleased, will as you will, and do as you do. This is certainly talking nonsense, and saying nothing in favor of free-will, or will got up without a cause or motive to act contrary to what we please. Pause and think this over and over, till, by-and-by, you will see clear enough, that there is no voluntary act of life without a desire to act; and, farther, that desire can not exist without an antecedent, or object of desire; and again, that the mind can no more alter the nature of that motive or object of desire, or avoid its impression, than it can alter the nature of a red-hot iron applied to the surface, or avoid the pain resulting therefrom. But we constantly feel that we can do as we desire, upon the application of the object of desire, just as we can feel as we do feel upon the application of the red-hot iron ; they both being results, and as unavoidable as the impression of light when it flashes upon the open eye.

How the will can be both the determiner and determined, I can not conceive. Again, for the will to change itself from itself, and make itself what by nature itself is not, is equally difficult. And again, for the will to rise without an object and fit itself to an object without any necessary connection or causal dependence upon that object, is, if possible, still more absurd. The will to change itself from itself, must make a change in itself, and consequently leave itself not itself. So we see, that, by the mutation of self-wills, would the identity of mind soon be destroyed; as, for a thing to change from what it was, is to be no longer the same that it was. How a will can will a will into existence for a particular purpose, without a purpose or motive to will, is again wholly incomprehensible. If the will be determined to a certain purpose, it must be by something that determines it to that purpose. which determiner is assuredly the motive to action, and nothing else. There can be no voluntary action without a will to act. and no will to act without a

choice or object of action. So that it must be found that
the object is the foundation both of will and action. There
being a preference in every active mind, that preference
is the cause of action; otherwise we must prefer nothing
to nothing, and as such preference exists in the quality
and nature of things themselves, the will has no independent or self-creating powers; that which fixed and determined the mind, being just as independent of the mind
as the medicine which acts upon the body is independent
of the body. When tartar assails the stomach, the stomach could say, I can puke just as I please, or do puke, and
the bowels could say the same under the motive influence
of calomel. To say that a man can will as he wills, or
choose as he chooses, or that he can follow his own inclinations, is the same as to say that a man can grow as he
grows, die as he dies, or that water can run the way that
it does run or is inclined to run. And to say that a man
can act contrary to his prevailing inclinations, is to say that
we can choose contrary to our choice, or prefer contrary
to our choice, or prefer contrary to our preference, or that
a thing can be different from what by nature it is. The
mind has no more power to cause itself to prefer contrary
to its preference, or to prefer and not to prefer at the
same time, than it has to cure a fever, or mend a broken
leg, or to be and not to be at the same time. He simply
has power to do as he wills, but has no power over his
will to do what he does not wish or will to do. According
to the free-will doctrine, the good will, in order to get rid
of the ill-chosen will, determines without a motive or
choice to get up a will without a choice, or to annihilate
itself till it can consult with itself upon the best choice.
They talk about one will suspending another will, but
this again must be found grossly absurd. Suspension
and action being as incompatible as motion and rest, for
in that suspension there can be no change of will, and

change and action being the same, there can be no action, good or bad, attending a suspension of will. Now, as it has been shown that all wills spring from motive or design, these motives or objects of design exist without and independent of the will, or the will before it can will must will to give itself a motive to will—which power must be a creative power—no such motive or object having existed previous to such will. And thus it is seen that these free wills are free gods, without God's government and beyond the sphere of his causal dependencies—that they are governed by no fixed law or rule of action, and, what is more startling still, that they give the lie to God's revealed word, that he is the Author of all things, and the Lawgiver and Ruler over all things by fixed and undeviating principles. Thus we find that the doctrine of freewill is encumbered with a thousand vague and self-contradictory assumptions, quibbles, and shallow shifts, at war with nature, while that of necessity, being founded upon the immutable and eternal laws of causality, is as truthful, simple, and comprehensible as nature itself, being nothing more in reality than a conformity to the universal aptitude, fitness, and causal dependencies of all things as founded and fixed by the hand of Almighty God himself.

A few illustrations will show how simple it is to have our wills excited by the things we will to do. Suppose yourself lost in the wild woods, as I have been, and when shivering, hungry, and half frozen, you see your camp-fire, friends, and food at hand, O, what delight at once fills the mind and gives it a pleasure and power to go to it, or rather, it causes or pleases the mind to do just as it pleases. Here, now, (as I often repeat it in different forms) is a case which will fit every other act of life, and as an honest man, I ask you what it was but the fire and the pleasures attending it which took you to the fire? Haven would answer, it was not the fire nor the motive of pleasure,

but the mind which took you to it—a petty quibble un-
worthy the name of philosophy, and which only returns
the question to us in a different form—what was it that
caused the mind to be pleased to take you to it? The
mind of itself, with all its powerful wills and faculties
falsely given it, could give itself no such comfort as the
camp-fire did; but now mark it, the light flashed upon it
and made it pleased to do as it pleased.

Suppose a desire or will comes up in the mind, from
some prevailing cause, to go and see a neighbor, how
quickly will the legs be put in motion to do so; but if
told by the way that the friend is not at home, which fact
the will has nothing to do with, yet this fact at once
creates a will for a counter-movement; and just so with
all the acting, counter-acting, and checkered movements
of life; the nature, or quality, or inducement of the thing
presented for choice being the cause of will or motive of
choice, having neither room nor apology for self-created
wills, independent of, and holding no necessary connection with, the properties and nature of the things themselves. This is all natural and easy, while the idea of the
will creating the quality sought by the will, and then
creating another will to obtain that quality, as free-willers
would say, is complicated and unnatural.

In farther illustration of how wills are gotten up, I say
to a man: Sir, you are not free to get up and walk; this at
once creates an ambition, will, or desire to walk, and he
does so, falsely feeling that the will was gotten up by himself, when, in reality, that will was the necessary result of
my banter; for no such will would ever have existed, or
such movement have taken place but for that banter. The
very expression of a man, that he is free and can do as he
pleases, at once betrays the fact that he is already possessed with a feeling, inclination and ambition to do so,
which feeling, inclination, and ambition are not inherent

qualities, or veritable things in the mind, but mere conditions or modes of mind, produced by the inherent
quality or nature of things that operate upon the mind.
The mind of a man may be in a perfectly pacific mode or
condition, and he is called a liar and thief, and the mind
is at once agitated and belligerent in its feeling, not from
anything internal or from nothing (take notice) but from
the words spoken. Here were no self-creations of words
or thoughts; but you will say, now is the time to show
that a man can do as he pleases, strike or not strike in
revenge, and I will agree with you that he can, as he may
please, strike or not strike; but his being pleased to act
or not act, is to be the result of agencies, over which he
has no more control than he had over the words which
excited him. If by constitution he be apathetic and
cowardly, or if by education he is in principle opposed to
vulgar conflicts, he will not resist; but if on the contrary,
he, by his unavoidable nature, has an irritable temper-
ment, and has by his education a different view of what
constitutes honor, and obtaining chivalrous cast in society,
he will certainly, if not a coward, strike. All the temptations, passions, and emotions of soul, are alike governed
by their exciting causes. The best tobacco in the world
offers no temptation to me; where, then, is the virtue in
me for avoiding both it and spirits, for which I have as
little desire. These are, however, irresistible temptations
to others, when no counteracting inclination prevails. I
can not help, from my nature, but dislike both whisky
and tobacco, while others can not, from their nature,
avoid liking both.

It will be seen that the mind is governed in the
exercise of faith by abstract things, just as our desires
are by concrete things; and it also must appear, upon
investigation, that there is neither merit nor demerit
in faith ; for where is the merit in believing that which

we can not help but believe? and where the demerit in
disbelieving that which it is impossible to believe? For
instance, that two and two make four, carries a conviction to the mind that can not be resisted, while the
assertion that two and two make six, conveys as
irresistible a disbelief; and these simple facts and illustrations show the principles upon which all faith is
founded. There is every degree of natural organization
and temperament; every degree of education and of
maturity and experience in life; every degree of circumstances that hourly impress us; and there are endless
vicissitudes of fortune and affliction moulding us to
the necessity of the case. Sore afflictions beget sadness,
sorrow and sighing, while the flush of fortune and
buoyancy of health produce mirth and laughter, and
these vacillations of soul are the necessary results or
effects of their appropriate causes. The Protestant and
the Catholic who go to the stake, and the Hindoo who
is crushed under the wheels of Juggernaut, are governed
alike by their unavoidable faith, and each are entitled to
equal merit, if merit attaches to that which it is not
in our power to resist; so that the man who believes
either in religion or in the common affairs of life, is upon
a footing with him who unavoidably disbelieves. Now,
though a man can not help his belief, we hate him for
it, and even put him to death, because his unavoidable
faith runs counter to our unavoidable faith, and lessens
our interests and prospects of happiness, here and
hereafter. We hate a disagreeable sound, and things
that are unpleasant to sight, smell, taste and touch; and
even hate a man because he is homely, or loathsomely
ugly, while we love those that are beautiful and
charming, though we know they cannot help their
nature, and that they have neither merit nor demerit
in them. These illustrations I introduce to explain

the constant question asked—why are people punished? and everybody think they ought to be punished if they could help the belief, or faith, for which they are punished. Though it is impossible that God, without violating his attributes of love and mercy, can punish us for an honest belief, yet it is necessary that man should punish man with a view of reform in himself or example to society, or confine him to avoid evil to others; just as we will kill a snake, shoot a mad dog, or confine a madman, though all of them act under their unavoidable nature, and the injurious power of circumstances. Punishments and examples have their necessary influences upon us to do good as well as evil, and hence the consistency of punishment under the law of necessity. The most honorable and best regulated nation in the world is in South America, they having but four laws—no murderers, no thieves, no liars, and no idlers; all put to death, thus begetting such a terror to evil doers that evil is almost unknown; and no taxation to support a vast army of judges, lawyers, and other parasites who live upon our substance. A man who knows he will be punished for certain acts will be necessarily impressed with the fact and the fear which counteracts the temptation to indulge. Knowing, for instance, the fatal fact that fire will burn and water drown, will deter us from running into them; so that it will be seen, as before exemplified, in the early part of this article, it is the doctrine of an early and well-grounded education in whatever direction we wish the youth to be guided; for be assured that education has as powerful a government over the youthful mind as the rein has over the guidance of the horse. The Hindoo widow mounts the funeral pile, and is consumed with the dead body of her husband, while the Christian widow holds to life and looks out for another husband; showing the wonder-

ful power of education, and circumstances in giving us
faith (a conscience) as well as a will to execute. But
to the text:—

A man, I repeat it, can certainly do as he pleases,
and he can not do otherwise ; but in every pleasure to
act, there is a sufficient, and, consequently, necessary
cause of pleasure, which cause is not the subjective mind,
that can not act upon itself any more than a stone can act
upon itself, but is without the mind, and an object of
desire by the mind; which two, when brought into
contact, create a new condition of mind (this pleasure we
so much harp on) to act. This is simple, and in full
harmony with the universal laws of causality, while
for a thing to act upon itself and bring forth a new
creation within itself, without materials on which to
work, is complicated and incomprehensible—yes, impossible. How one thing can operate upon another, everybody can understand; as an acid upon an alkali or
salifiable base, where the product is a new creation by
the union and combined agency of them both ; nor is
there a conception, action, or product of any kind, mental
or physical, short of God himself, but what must proceed
from the fixed and unalterable laws of *dualism.* It is just
as reasonable to suppose that the mind has made itself,
that it can resist the tragical scenes and unnumbered
fluctuations and afflictions, yes and even death itself,
as to say it can create or originate ideas within itself.
If the reader will reflect a moment, he will see that this
would be to make something out of nothing, a thing,
I have said, and say again, impossible. If a man's
thoughts and desires have an existence, they either
came from something or from nothing ; and as they
invariably come fitted to some object, end, or desire, such
object, end, or desire must have been the cause of that
desire. It is just as simple and reasonable that the mind

should turn to the object, as the needle point should turn to the pole.

I here relate a little incident that illustrates two great leading principles: I had a sprightly and interesting puppy, to which the cook often threw egg-shells, thus teaching it to eat eggs; the result being the breaking up of all my setting hens and loss of chickens. All this, however, my fond attachment induced me to put up with; but another branch of education caused its death. Breachy sheep occasionally entering my yard, I set little Fidel after them, and was often greatly amused to see the little creature in full chase, tight and tight, after a flock of great sheep; when on its return it would frisk around me, and looking up with innocent laughter, seemed to say: "I did what you told me; wasn't it funny?" By and by, however, its training led it to killing sheep; but not, however, till I thus lost ten or twelve by its example in learning others to help it, had I courage to take its life, knowing that the fault was not in the dog, but in myself; nor had I myself a heart, or will, to perpetrate the deed, but hired another to do it. This illustrates two vital principles: 1st. The force of education for good or for evil, even upon the brute; 2d. The necessity of punishing, or taking life, to prevent disastrous consequences, and to save the lives of many. Parents and friends often think it smart to hear their little ones swear or commit innocent depredations, as I did little Fidel, not thinking it might lead to their destruction.

The question under consideration, when properly understood, is not whether we can do as we will to do—for that is granted to be unavoidable—but what it is that causes us to will or desire to do what we do; and whether that will or desire be in the object willed for or desired, or a mere spontaneity of mind, having no antecedent or

necessary cause of existence—an offspring of nothing? and
what more miraculous, that a self-created will should
come fitted to a specific purpose without a purpose. This
proximate feeling and conscious fact, that we can do
as we desire, is like the feeling that we can call up to
mind, by memory, what we desire to do; but in neither
of which cases do we feel or are we conscious of the
remote causes that brought these desires to the mind,
any more than we feel the miasma of fever or the cause
of small-pox; though we acutely feel, and are conscious
of the present action, and see the results; just as we do
those of will, without knowing what caused us thus to
will. Now, it would be just as rational to say that
diseases and excitements of our bodies are self-created
things and without a cause, because unconscious of a
cause, as to say that our mental phenomena is without
a cause.

Persons will assert that they can call up by name
anything they may please, without knowing the fact that
that very thing is already in the mind, for otherwise
they could not name that thing as an object of thought.
For instance, a man says, I will now call up Australia;
but, except he first thought of Australia, how, I ask,
could he call for Australia any more than to call up
an unknown language and speak it? To call for a
thing without knowing what to call for, or name a
thing without already knowing the name of that thing,
is too ridiculous to argue about; and just so in regard to
our strong and conscious present feeling of being able to
do as we desire; so long have we been in the habit of
acting from the immediate promptings of our feelings
(like seeking the cooling water under a burning fever)
that we never search back for the remote cause; and
thus it is that we naturally enough imagine that our own
will, before we have a will, begets a will, aside from all

causes, motives, inducements, or qualities in the things sought for. One may say, I will now repeat the alphabet; but who could ever do so, simple as it is, without first learning and knowing it?

Volitions often arise, not from any immediate, external, or obvious cause, but from internal rumination, or reflective thought—as in acts of revenge long after an injury or insult. The dark and dreadful act of Col. Sharp's assassination, at Frankfort, Ky., was of this kind, which took place years after the alleged offense. Many better opportunities were doubtless offered during this time to commit the bloody deed; but we must account for the delay from the murderer's health or condition of system, which enabled him to resist the temptation. We are often reminded of things past and forgotten by our dreams, and thousands of hidden and functional causes prompt our wills to action that otherwise would never have existed. Many persons live an honest life for many years, and then take to stealing; sober men in later years become dissipated, while sane men may ultimately die in a lunatic asylum. These mutations of mind are not from divine influence, or God's immediate presence, but from physical and functional causes, and can no more be helped than any other morbid condition of system. Mental, as well as bodily, afflictions—as hydrophobia and consumption—may lie dormant for many years, and ultimately kill. Everything, mentally and bodily, as well as all organic being, has its period of incubation and time for development. We gain not our knowledge in a day, nor does the child grow to manhood but by time, and this is the fatality I aim to teach. These obvious facts may be granted, and yet the question asked, whether, when such inclination, desire, or will arises, we may not have resolution to resist it, by a counteracting and stronger will? To which I answer, Certainly we may, if a stronger

will should arise from a stronger motive not to obey the
command than to obey it. Suppose, for instance, a man
is commanded by high authority to do a certain act. He
is, at once, given a will, by the command so to do; but,
as in cases of martyrdom, if a silent command arises
within him, from a belief that God's command is greater
than that of man, a counteracting and paramount will
will certainly control his actions; and now, though the
first command was from without, and the second and
prevailing from ruminating causes within, they were
both the result of actually existing and uncalled-for
causes. Yes; causes that the will did not create. Nor
is the result in such cases any more obscure or difficult
of comprehension than the testimony which forces conviction to the mind; the will to do or not to do being
the invariable result of prompting passions, or of deliberate judgment, founded upon anticipated results; in
neither of which cases are there any self-creations of
wills without causes—the will being as unavoidable a
result as was the cause, both being as firmly linked
together as is the endless and eternal chain that binds
God's vast and harmonious universe. We may not see
or feel but the first, second, or third moving link, but,
could we trace them back, they would unerringly lead us
on and on to the throne of God—the original seat and
foundation of all causality. Here, by infinite wisdom
and boundless power, were all God's laws, both mental
and physical, designed and irreversibly fixed beyond
the power of earthly vanity to subvert.

Thus having established the supremacy of God's unalterable laws, all we have to do, is to understand and obey
them. If we plant and pray to God to cultivate for us,
he will not do it; and should we plunge ourselves into
the ocean, and cry, Lord save? he will not heed us, nor
will he even administer an antidote to a poison, though

ignorantly and innocently taken. Those laws of our vital and normal existence are fatally fixed, and the health and happiness of man depend upon studying them well, a thing least thought of by the present artistic age, when men with their idle hypotheses, religious creeds, and political squabbles distract the human mind. To these debasing influences over the mind may be added the stultifying nature of dead languages and unmeaning technicalities, which engross all the early and more susceptible portion of our lives. Were we to study well those laws to which we are hourly subject through life, the doctor then would practice upon a science, and we should not daily bemourn the loss of our friends, butchered through ignorance; for old age would, as certainly as we now exist, be the only outlet to life; for, as sure as there is a God, there is a law of hygiene ample for every morbid influence that can assail us. The wonderful discoveries which have been made in science, as the telegraph, compass, navigation and railroads, for instance, can leave no longer doubt of the powerful agencies and counteracting agencies that are at play around us and of which we are wholly ignorant. In proof of our medical ignorance, and as a reproof to the vanity of our little technical popinjays, I introduce the following introductory lecture by the great Magendie of France:

"GENTLEMEN: Medicine is a great humbug. I know it is called a science. Science, indeed! it is nothing like science. Doctors are mere empirics, when they are not charlatans. We are as ignorant as men can be. Who knows anything in the world about medicine? Gentlemen, you have done me the honor to come here to attend my lectures, and I must tell you frankly, now, in the beginning, that I know nothing in the world about medicine, and I don't know anybody who does know anything about it. Don't think for a moment that

haven't read the bills advertising the course of lectures
at the medical school. I know that this man teaches
anatomy, that man teaches pathology, another man
physiology, such-a-one therapeutics, such-another *materia
medica. Eh bien! et apres?* What's known about all
that? Why, gentlemen, at the school of Montpelier (God
knows it was famous enough in its day!) they discarded
the study of anatomy, and taught nothing but the dispensary; and the doctors educated there knew just as much
and were quite as successful as any others. I repeat it,
nobody knows anything about medicine. True enough,
we are gathering facts every day. We can produce
typhus fever, for example, by injecting a certain substance into the veins of a dog—that's something; we can
alleviate diabetes ; and, I see distinctly, we are fast
approaching the day when phthisis can be cured as easily
as any disease.

"We are collecting facts in the right spirit, and I dare
say, in a century or so the accumulation of facts may
enable our successors to form a medical science; but, I
repeat it to you, there is no such thing now as a medical
science. Who can tell me how to cure the headache? or
the gout? or disease of the heart? Nobody. Oh! you
tell me doctors cure people. I grant you people are
cured. But how are they cured? Gentlemen, nature does
a great deal. Imagination does a great deal. Doctors
do—devilish little—when they do n't do harm. Let me
tell you, gentlemen, what I did when I was head-physi-
cian at the Hotel Dieu. Some three or four thousand
patients passed through my hands every year. I divided
the patients into two classes; with one I followed the
dispensary, and gave them the usual medicines, without
having the least idea why or wherefore; to the other I
gave bread-pills and colored water, without, of course,
letting them know anything about it; and occasionally,

gentlemen, I would create a third division, to whom I gave nothing whatever. These last would fret a good deal—they would feel they were neglected, (sick people always feel they are neglected, unless they are well drugged—*les imbeciles!*) and they would irritate themselves until they got really sick; but nature invariably came to the rescue, and all the persons in the third class got well. There was a little mortality among those who received but bread-pills and colored water, and the mortality was greatest among those who were carefully drugged according to the dispensary."

Thus spake a man of great learning and world-wide fame as a physician.

And were divines in like manner to become thorough-bred students of nature, instead of burthening their minds with selfish creeds and theological follies, they would neither respect the dogmas of men, nor glory longer in their own folly; no, nor could those detestable demagogues, the veriest varlets of earth, humbug a community thus enlightened by the elevating and ennobling study of God's harmonious and glorious works, that will unerringly lead us to health, to happiness, and to Him. But we will return from consequences and examples more directly to the argument, and show how we are influenced by physical causes that make us happy or miserable in this world.

The influence of disease upon the mind every man in community has both seen and felt. To a sick man the luxuries of life lose their zest—nothing tastes or smells pleasurable, and sights and sounds are disagreeable. All his feelings are as whimsical as his appetites. The brave man becomes timid, and the imperturbable and generous soul becomes irritable and selfish. The patient and affectionate mother grows fretful and captious towards her children. Every vocation and profession in life loses

its interest, and our resolutions for any enterprise become
weak and capricious. The aberrated mind is dark and
vacillating in its religious and moral affections. Even
toothache, gout and sick headache will spoil the temper
and greatly afflict the mind; and O! how often do we
become silently demented or harrowed up to raving
maniacs, while others sink under the crushing weight of
accumulating afflictions down to a settled and hopeless
melancholy. Now, if these afflictions of mind be unavoidable and incurable by the will, the will can not be free to
control itself or the destinies of the mind, but is itself
controlled by the unavoidable destinies of the system.

To show how we are led captive through the dark and
checkered paths of our anxious and toiling existence here,
not by the power of disease, as above named, but under
the guidance of natural and normal influences, I will
give a few additional examples. Our journey of life is at
best but a day, and affords us but little knowledge of the
innumerable and wonderful agencies in nature that play
around us, and in which and through which we uncon-
ciously live and move, being seduced by more sensible
objects to follow our veering fancies. We set out in the
morning of life, unconscious of guilt and fearless of
consequences; the whistle, the drum and hobby-horse,
with the nightly legends of the nursery, filling our cup
of innocent and early joy. Little do we think how "one
generation passeth and another generation cometh," nor
have we yet any knowledge of our own flitting and
transient lives; but on we journey, joyously picking up
by the way the early flowers, and chasing the butterfly
with his gilded wings, which gives us more rational
delight than a monarch can receive from the temporal
bauble of a jeweled crown. Charmed with every changing scene of nature, we are led through flowery lawns, by
purling brooks, and into fragrant and warbling groves

where our enchanted minds are lulled into elysian
reveries, and our thoughts elevated far above the vulgar
realities of life, not dreaming that soon we shall enter
the dark and dreary abodes of sorrow, where we
are to be afflicted by cares and torn by contending
passions. Fresh in youth, buoyant in health, and
animated by the hope of future bliss, we still pursue our
unclouded path, nor think we are so near the troubled
ocean of life and the vale of tears. All has been serenity
and sunshine; but now the noon of our day has come
with a clouded sky, and the troubled elements are
warring around us. The day is far spent in the toys of
life, and the unwelcome fact is forced upon us, that we
have a living to make; and now it is that pride
and ambition enters the unstained and tranquil soul.
The tumults of life now begin; and hope and fear, love
and hatred, and joy and grief, with all the distracting
passions, alternately occupy the soul, and imperiously
direct the will to this, that or the other act.

As the evening of our journey approaches, circumstances again change and throw us upon a smoother
path. The stimulus of ambition is gone, and the heart
grows cold to the world. The lengthened vista is closing
upon our sight, and the memory of the past is fast fading.
Our hearts beat faintly, and we feel that every pulsation
brings us one step nearer to the brink of eternity, when
our journey will be at an end. The pleasures of early
life have fled forever, and we worship the Lord of Nature
no longer in his flowery meads, his flowing streams, and
shady bowers; but seek him in a higher sphere, far, far
beyond the confines of earth, where we hope for a happy
haven of rest when our stormy voyage shall be over.
The heart that once glowed with love, with humanity,
and kind affections, has been left but to sorrow. Every
tender tie on earth has been broken, and our friends have

passed to worlds unknown. The lone and feeble soul has now no consolation but in religion, when it again becomes firm, tranquil, and buoyant in its glorious hopes, which warms it with seraph fire and wings it for its eternal flight.

Now all these vacillations of mind and workings of will to suit the occasion must have been from the progress of age, and the power of circumstances; farther showing, what I think has been already amply proven, that the will is governed by circumstances, and, consequently, under the law of necessity; which is not an accident, or broken link in the chain of causality, but a fixed and unalterable law given by God himself to preserve the unity and harmony of his universal dependencies upon the one Great Will.

AXIOMS.

Now, by way of recapitulation, I set down the following axioms as undeniable:

1. That there is no omnipotence in the universe save God himself; nor is there anything which has a self-creating and self-controlling power, either of mind or of body.

2. That all things, mind and body, are *dualistic* and *dynamic*— no one atom acting upon itself, but acting upon every other atom; no one thing having the power of giving itself motion, but is dependent upon the great and universal law of *dualism*.

3. That there is no such thing as innate ideas, and, as the mind can neither create itself nor ideas within itself, it is dependent upon the objects of sense for all its original ideas. Gold begets the idea of gold, and lead of lead; and so with all other things, each and every one creating a knowledge in the mind of its own inherent nature—the mind having no power of rejecting, altering, or converting one into the other. Hence the mind has none of those powers and faculties given it by authors; but is simply a submissive subject, not with a power (which is a false term) but a capacity of receiving impressions.

4. That neither God nor angels are resident in the mind (as almost all authors teach) for the purpose of giving us our ideas and stirring up thought; but that

all our thoughts recur by association with external
objects, or by functional influences within the system
itself. For instance, I never taste or smell an orange
but what it carries me instantly into the tropics, and
brings to mind all the scenes of a long travel—this
being one amongst millions of external causes of reflective thought.

> " Lulled in the countless chambers of the brain,
> Our thoughts are linked by many a hidden chain.
> Awake but one, and lo, what myriads rise ;
> Each stamps its image as the other flies."

> " How soft the music of those village bells,
>   Falling at intervals upon the ear ;
> With easy force it opens all the cells
>   Where memory slept ; where I have heard
> A kindred melody, the same recurs,
>   And with it all its pleasures and its pains."

A large portion of our recurring thoughts, however, are
from internal causes, exclusive of dreams ; a knowledge of
which fact would have spoiled many a transcendental and
beautiful theory, and have curtailed thousands of volumes
on the subject of mental philosophy. As ludicrous as it
appears to me, and as degrading as it certainly is to God,
all the most celebrated authors of the world, as I have
said, have maintained a direct divine influence over our
inward thoughts: so that when griped or troubled with
unpleasant thoughts, we must infer that Satan had ex-
pelled God and taken up his residence in the bowels; to
this certainly the mystic doctrine would lead us.

5. That neither mind nor body has any more power
over their existence than they had in bringing themselves into existence—being firmly bound by the laws
of their unavoidable nature. Man is sustained from his
birth to his death, not by a wish, or will, or nothing
(take notice) but by his food and his vitalizing powers,
over which he has no more control than has the grain

of wheat or corn over the laws that force them into
existence and make them what they are. All existence
and motion are forced states—nothing creating itself,
nothing sustaining or moving itself; but all are *dualistic*
and *dynamic* dependencies. All the reader has to do to
get rid of such astounding folly as now taught on mind,
is to constantly exercise his own mind, and see where
this thought, that, and the other comes from. Think,
also, how mind is led astray by credulity, and that the
more absurd, monstrous, and cruel the creed, the firmer
the faith—as will be seen by more than one half of our
race being at this moment chained down to such faith;
yes, a faith that leads them by thousands to martyrdom.
I say, and say again and again, read the history of man,
both sacred and profane, from the earliest records, and
see the eternal vacillation, both of governments and
of religion, and you will know more of the real nature
of mind than any and all authors who have ever written
on the mind. Read the history of Greece and Rome
alone, and you will find that wiser heads than ours
worshiped the most wicked and degrading gods and
goddesses that ever polluted earth. Nor did any dare
doubt but the divine Socrates—who was put to death
for his infidelity. Yes; I repeat it, that you will, after
thus gaining a practical knowledge of man, agree with
me, that the time is coming when every book on earth on
psychology will be thrown away like trash, as the books
on heathen mythology have been.

Sir William Hamilton, at the close of his great book,
with just humility, says, that "All of our philosophy is
ignorance—we start from one ignorance and repose in
another. They are goals from which and to which we
tend; and the pursuit of knowledge is but a course
between two ignorances, as human life is itself only a
traveling from grave to grave." And again "All we

know is but to know that all our knowledge is but a
learned ignorance, and that true wisdom is to know
that we know nothing." He is right; for what we
know is nothing to what is unknown, and the proportion of the finite mind to the infinite is as one inch to
unlimited space, and as a moment to eternity. The
highest grade of knowledge, and the greatest mark of
wisdom, therefore, is the knowledge of our ignorance,
and of our helpless condition in this our momentary
existence. And here, for the sake of the conceited
clergy in mystic things, I quote what St. Chrysostom
says: "Nothing is wiser than ignorance in these matters
(mystic theology) where they who proclaim that they
know nothing proclaim their paramount wisdom; while
those who busy themselves therein are the most senseless
of mankind." These things I quote and proclaim to
give to man a crushing knowledge of what he is—a flitting, fated shadow, that hangs upon the dial's point but
for a moment, and is gone forever.

6. That neither God nor man created themselves, or
gave themselves their nature; nor can they alter that
nature—the principles inherent in the eternal Godhead
constituting the law by which he is bound. His promulgated laws, therefore, are necessarily founded upon them,
and hence it is that virtue has an anterior and paramount
rightness, in itself independent of the will of God. It is
acknowledged by Clark, Scott, Chalmers, Dick, Douay,
and all other intelligent divines, that God did not promul-
gate his law from any self-willed or arbitrary view; but
it was called forth by necessity from the prior existence
and inherent nature and fitness of things themselves. It
is also granted that the holy angels are so conformed in
their nature that they can not act contrary to that nature;
showing an unbroken chain, reaching from eternity to
eternity, and from earth to heaven, binding God, angels,

and men to abide their nature. This eternal, irrevocable, and universal law of divine harmony and consistency is what I have been aiming to teach.

7. That the doctrine of self-creating power leads to atheism; for if God be not the creator and governor of all things, then may all things create and govern themselves, as Pantheists affirm.

8. That God fits means to ends, and, comprehending all things from eternity to eternity in one most perfect and unalterable view, his foreknowledge must be as unerring as man's after-knowledge.

9. That there is as indissoluble connection between motive and action as between cause and effect, and that all things in God's vast and harmonious universe are dependencies upon the one first great and moving Cause.

10. That both God and man as certainly exist under a law of necessity as they exist in time and space, neither being able to act rationally without a motive in view and an object to be obtained, which motive in view and object to be obtained must be the ground and reason for such action.

11. That the inherent qualities of objects we desire to obtain being wholly separate and independent of the will, the will is certainly bound by these qualities, and not by nothing, as free-willers have it.

12. That an effect does not create its cause, the child its father, nor the will its motive; but that the cause produces its effect, the father his child, and the motive its will, as certainly as that sugar creates the idea of sweetness, fire of heat, and ice of cold.

13. That to say, because we act from our unavoidable nature and the force of circumstances under which we are placed, that our lovely acts are not to be loved, nor our hateful acts hated, is a false position; when all will acknowledge that God, in his unavoidable nature

is absolutely perfect, pure and holy, and yet we adore him because of those natural perfections. The angels are in their nature so confirmed in holiness that they can have no will to do wrong, and yet we glorify them. Christ fulfilled the will of the Father in his preconceived and determined plans of redemption, but we love him none the less. We love an infant that can not help but be an infant, and we hate a snake that can not help its nature; we kill rats because they are rats by the will of their Maker; and there are hundreds of other examples I could give.

14. That no man can help his honest belief, and consequently there is neither merit nor demerit in faith, for where the merit in believing that two and two make four, or the demerit in disbelieving that two and two make ten?

15. That there is no man on earth who is a wilfull disbeliever in religion; for as the whole pursuit of man, from his cradle to his grave, is that of happiness, he can not knowingly seek misery in a doubt of future bliss, and thus live in hopeless despair and misery, an active and conscious hell being preferable to an unconscious and eternal oblivion.

16. That in every act of volition an object of choice or desire must be presented to the mind; and that, inasmuch as the quality or exciting nature of that object begets the will, such will can not be self-begotten and independent of all motives and ends.

17. That if there could be such a thing as a motiveless will, it would be perfectly worthless, as having no object of good or evil in view, and consequently irresponsible for its acts.

18. That as the mind has no alternative but to choose or refuse, it will as certainly yield to the stronger motive, be it for good or evil, as will the weaker force yield to the stronger, or the heavier weight cast the scale.

19. That to say we will do things we do not desire or wish to do, is an obvious error. For instance, we willingly submit to the surgeon to have a limb taken off, and may say we do not desire or wish to lose that limb, when it will be found that the desire, wish and will all agree to have the limb taken off. A nauseous draught of medicine, and thousands of other examples could be given wherein we are perplexed and deceived in regard to the nature of will—willing often to do what we would not do if we could help it.

20. That there may be ten thousand conflicting emotions and passions of mind, drawing this way, that way and the other; as love and hatred, wright and wrong, loss and gain, obligation, gratitude, and so on; but the volition in the end will be decided by the character of the man; if naturally sordid, gain will be the prompting motive; if high passioned, hatred and revenge will decide; when, if religious and conscientious, love and gratitude, truth and justice, will prevail.

21. That the will does not create the motive, but the motive creates the will, proving the will to be an effect, and not a free cause.

22. That if we put our hand in the fire there is an instantaneous will to take it out, which will did not create the fire, but the fire created the will; and so it must be in every act of life, some pleasure or pain, and consequent desire or aversion to do or not to do.

23. That God as well as man is governed by circumstances; circumstances gave him a will to turn Adam out of Paradise; circumstances again created a motive, and that motive a will to destroy the world by a flood; circumstances determined him to destroy Nineveh, and a change of circumstances determined him to save it; circumstances brought Christ into the world for the redemption of man, and his whole life was a scene of

action from circumstances ; circumstances of thirty pieces
of silver gave a will to Judas to betray his Master, and
a change of circumstances (remorse) gave him a will
to go out and hang himself.

24. That so long as the will can not make pain pleasure
and pleasure pain, it will remain subject to those feelings,
and to the passions and emotions of mind, which passions,
emotions, and feelings are not produced by the mind itself,
but by things that operate upon the mind.

25. That the alternative and imperious law of will to
do or not to do, seals the fate of man.

26. That as we can not like what we do not like, and
the will being dependent upon our likes and dislikes, it is
not a creator or originator, but a submissive result.

27. That if will arise from a sense of honor, gratitude,
obligation, love, hatred, or revenge, it is nothing but a
result; and if, from reason, judgment, or any other cause,
it is not itself a cause but an effect, as I constantly
repeat it.

28. That conscience is simply a conviction or belief—a
creature of education, and not the same in any two
countries or in any two men. Aristotle condemned the
poor African to slavery by a single syllogism, thus:
"Black people were made by God for slaves; the Africans
are black ; therefore intended by God to be slaves." Thus
did the Rev. John Newton, of England, and many others,
get a conscience (as he himself has said) to engage in the
trade ; but by-and-by did another vagabond conscience
(right by chance this time) tell him that his other
conscience was a wicked and evil deceiver, and then
did this truly conscientious and pious man eschew and
give up his vocation.

29. That the whole science of mind is in a single
sentence, thus: God has endowed us with feelings of
pleasure and pain, from which arise desire and aversion ;

and, consequently, a will to do or not to do; and this, as
short and simple as it is, is actually the desideratum and
ultimatum of mind. Yes, it is positively the whole of
psychology worth knowing, upon which thousands of
books have been written.

30. That to say man has a veto power over the will of
God, or that he can in any way disappoint or fret him,
is a sacrilegious vaunt; for if so, God would, as Dr.
Scott says, "have fretted himself to death long since."
God, as I have said, seeing all things in one perfect whole,
from beginning to end, and fitting means to ends with
laws to govern them, it can not be that any unseen power
in heaven, hell, or earth can disappoint him in the final
issue—otherwise God is destitute of wisdom, foreknowledge and power.

31. That the mystic system of psychology and theology
have distracted and corrupted the world, abstracted
science, and rendered no practical advantage to man in
his struggles after truth and a just rule of moral rectitude
and brotherly union. After thousands of years' teaching,
and the expenditure of myriads of money, what is our
condition? No honest man will deny that we live in an
age of impiety and of reckless extravagance and lawless
ambition. To look around and see the sordid grasp of
the trafficking world; how neighbor strives to overreach
neighbor, and brother to cheat brother, and glory in his
shame, I see a wrong, a sad and grievous wrong; yes, a
wrong that my pen can not wrong, and that Satan himself, the father of wrong, can not but detest as a wrong
in the education and training of man. Besides, we read
but little else in our daily news but cruel wars, from
combined powers down to fillibustering and plundering
parties. The bloody dagger and the burglar's hand are
rife in their midnight deeds, while forgeries, defalcations,
and debaucheries, from the sacred precincts of divinity and

the high functionaries of government, down to the street
scavenger, have become common. The vicegerents of
God and holy teachers themselves become the inflamers
of war, and join in the struggles of political mobs and
the embroiling elements of human strife. No repentance
in sack-cloth and ashes, but in fine linen, fine cloth ; while
the brainless devotee of fashion becomes almighty over
the minds of men, and as well might the friend to
humanity attempt the stay of time as the march of
fashion. As arise those delusive lights from the beds of
physical decay, that but involve their followers in bewildering mazes, so from the hot-beds of moral corruption
and depravity may arise in Paris a glare of fashion that
catches the eye of the vain and giddy world. Princes
and peasants bow alike to its mandates, and countless
millions are paid for its formula. The veriest varlet in a
prescribed and artistic garb receives more attention from
the fashionable world than a Howard, a man of the
finest attainments; while the giddy whirls and amorous
wiles of the ball-room hold an unquestionable supremacy
over moral worth and modest mien. Books of science
and moral teaching meet with no encouragement, while
works of fiction, that feed only the degenerate and sensual
passions of the day, are devoured as they issue from the
press. Those who do not fall under the dominion of
fools of fashion are led captive by juggling priests and
knavish demagogues. By sermons in Latin, and tricks of
hocus-pocus, men are brought with their tithes to the feet
of their leaders, while women are led as it were by the
hand of love to the altar of confession! The snickering
demagogue, too, knows well how to bait his hooks and set
his snares. He smiles with compassion upon the people,
tells them of the oppression and wrong of party, till he is
soon found riding on the car of state and enjoying the
gifts of popular favor. No anecdote too low and loath-

some, no falsehood too gross and glaring for the public taste. The prognosis from such a gangrenous state of the body politic must be unfavorable, yes, fatal.

Thus have I shown the true character of the human mind.

32. That if man can see himself aright, he will know that he is but a fated link in the eternal chain of causality; that all things originate and terminate in God, who gave the first impulse to life and motion, and who holds firm and fast the two ends of this vast, unbroken, and eternal chain, that binds his mighty universe in one harmonious whole and ceaseless round.

33. That all things are held in subordination to the accomplishment of the one great end—God's preconceived plans of creation.

34. That the wisdom and power of God forbid the doctrine that he has made anything in vain, and that, consequently, he has not regretted, pined, and fretted at his own work—as we weekly hear proclaimed from the pulpit.

35. That all things bear a primary and kindred relation, and are means and ends in the one eternal and irrevocable design.

36. That God has not given the power of self-creation to any being on earth, nor the ability of counteracting and disappointing his sovereign will in the realization of his first and final object of creation. It is the principles, then, of the all-sufficiency of creative power and wisdom which I aim to teach, and to show that the doctrines that God has done things which he did not purpose to do, and that his laws do not act in harmony and with undeviating fate, are untrue.

37. That the free-willer has never given an argument to sustain his dogma, but assumes it, and proves it by a mendacious witness, thus: We are free, because our

conscience tells us we are free; and therefore we are free. Yes; thus, and thus only, is the freedom of the will established, and the whole of the argument and refutation thrown upon the necessarian, who finds it difficult to disprove anything—no matter how false—firmly grafted upon a superstitious and bigoted conscience. Socrates himself could not disprove the conscious veracity of heathen mythology (though now held as contemptibly false and ridiculous); nor can all the missionaries on earth prove, to the satisfaction of the faithful in Buddhism, that it is a false religion.

38. That if the mind could will and act independent of the objects and ends in view that cause us to will and act, we should not halt, hesitate, and reason before we will and act. Freedom of will must lie within itself, and not depend upon exterior or extraneous motives and temptations to will and act.

39. That motive and will stand in the same relation of predicate and consequent.

40. That the universal law of inertia—which requires a moving force equal to the object to be moved—will forever forbid the mind, or any other created thing, from acting upon or moving itself. *And I will here say that it always has, and ever will, forbid the discovery of a perpetual motion.*

41. That a choice contrary to our choice is no choice, but a contradiction in terms; and as the object of choice must be prior to the choice, there* is no escape from the certainty of such objects, motives, ends, and means being the cause of choice, will, and action. As inevitable, then, as the behest of Deity is the fact that, without an object there is no choice, and, without a choice, no will or act.

42. That as the mind can not desire itself within itself or act upon itself to acquire its wants and desires without itself, those wants and desires most assuredly lead the

mind to its choice, will, and act according to the inherent, essential, and eternal nature and fitness of things.

43. That as the mind (as in part above shown) can not live upon itself, and every necessary of its existence, as well as every object and end to be obtained — whether abstract, concrete, moral, religious, or political — being not the mind, but things desired by the mind, every act of the mind to its desired end is as determined as the irrevocable mandates of Heaven.

44. That the mind can no more act contrary to its laws — in other terms, to its desires, wills, and wants, than a stone can rise up (contrary to the laws of gravitation); and, consequently, that the examples given by free-will writers prove nothing beyond their ignorance or dishonesty. The willingness of Abraham to sacrifice his son, Isaac; Brutus in ordering the execution of his two sons, and Virginius in driving a dagger to the heart of his lovely daughter, is no proof of their acting counter to their ultimate will or wish so to do; and no event could be brought forward in stronger proof of the irresistible nature of motive upon the mind. Abraham's devout motive to obey the Lord created a willingness to sacrifice his child. The patriotism of Brutus begot a motive so powerful as to sacrifice every feeling of his fond heart for the good of his country; while Virginius, with a motive to save his daughter from pollution and disgrace, by patrician power, slew her. So it will be seen that the above cases (brought forward tauntingly to prove that we can act contrary to our wills and desires so to do) are in full and satisfactory confirmation of the exact reverse.

45. That an affirmative answer to the question, whether a strong cup of tea does not often operate upon the mind so as to keep it awake all night? at once solves the whole enigma of mind; for it can not be that the mind operates

upon the tea. And just so it is with everything that
gives the mind its ideas, thoughts, pleasures and pains,
wills and desires—the mind operating upon nothing, as I
often, and again, say; but everything operating upon the
mind, just as medicine operates upon the body.

46. That if one will reflect back how often he has
moved about (changed his location, as well as vocation),
he will find a motive and a reason for it all, and for every
other act of his life; and, also, that as neither houses,
lands, nor other necessaries of life were in the mind (but
out of it, and things desired by the mind,) he will know
more of mind than all the authors who ever wrote on
mind; for they acquire knowledge, not of nature and
the objects of life, but from the closet and superstitious
mysticism. Yes; and let him reflect how often he has
reproached himself for past acts of loss and distress, and
say, Well, I might and ought to have acted differently,
and now I do and ought to suffer; when it is fatally
true that he at the time acted up to the best lights then
afforded him. Nor is it probable that his after acts—
with all his powerful will, divine dictator (conscience),
and the thousand faculties given him—will prove any
more satisfactory.

47. That the horse has a liberty (like man and every
other animal) to do just as he does and desires, or is
pleased to do; that is, he desires and acts just as his
nature, his training, and the motives presented cause
him to desire and act. And now, if the acts of beasts
do not make God the author of wrong, why should those
of man, when they are both equally bound by the same
laws of their unavoidable nature. The brute does wrong,
in our opinion (though acting under the will of their
Maker), and we punish and put him to death (just as
we do man); but whether God will punish either brute
or man for his own defects (as free-willers unwittingly

affirm them to be) we know not; but are fully assured
that he, the Maker, Lawgiver, and Ruler over all, suffered
no sin (mark it) *in his estimation*, to enter the world;
otherwise, having a perfect foreknowledge of the evil
results of his works, willingly permitted the curse of
sin to attend his works, and can not, therefore, punish
his own works. We, moreover, believe (yes, know, and
can not help but know) that it no more makes God the
author of sin to use one man as an instrument to kill
another, or to use more protracted, painful, and distressing means to kill men — as fever, rheumatism, steam-
boats, earthquakes, famine, pestilence, and war — by
which means he kills men, women, and children *en
masse.* Why, then, so foolishly oppose a self-evident
fact in science—an unquestionable law of God—by our
assertions of its making him the author of sin. And
now, if the reader will reflect here upon this suggestion
by free-will teachers, he will find that it charges God
with sin in making man, and everything else that runs
counter to our interests, passions, prejudices, and contracted views of right and wrong. Man can injure man
(as other works of God do), and we call it sinful; but
he, with preconceived wisdom, having made things as
things are, has not been disappointed or grieved at his
own work (as free-willers say); and, consequently, can
not pronounce them sinful, or look with approbation
upon those who do so.

49. That I maintain the wisdom, power and perfection
of Deity, and the certainty of his decrees; no casualties,
no powers on earth, in heaven or in hell, being allowed
to counteract or disappoint him of his will and wishes
in the result of his works; while the free-willer robs
him of his wisdom, foreknowledge, and power to carry
out his first and final designs, and giving to man, a thing
created and designed by God, a power to act independ-

ently above and beyond the will and sanction of his Maker.

50. That free will and casualism leads to atheism; for if God is not the unerring creator and ruler over all things, then may all things create and govern themselves, as Atheists and Pantheists affirm.

> "All are but parts of one great whole,
> Whose body matter is, and God the soul."

That is to say, not meaning a personal God, but that the universal, essential, and eternal laws inherent in matter has formed all things as they are—the nature of matter being the God of matter, and nothing existing in the universe but matter. There is a vital and conservative law of adaptation to circumstances attending all the forms of organism, as witnessed in the renewal of our exhausted minds and bodies, the mending of broken bones and the healing of wounds, the influence of habit over mind and body, etc. The blind fish, found in the Mammoth Cave and other dark streams, is a striking instance that matter has a law of its own which conforms to the necessity of the case. The progenitors of these fish had eyes, but their descendants, having no use for eyes, lost them; but a few generations in sunny waters would restore them, when having use for them. And now it matters not whether this law of organism which makes all things what they are, has been independently inherent in matter from all eternity, or the work of an individual God who stamped these laws upon it, for it is a question that never has, nor never can, in the nature of things, be decided.

51. That free-willers are very inconsistent in constantly asking the question, why should we punish man if he acts unavoidably from his nature, his education, and his circumstances in life, that urge him to action when teachers, preachers, and book-builders all teach that the

brute acts like man from the nature God has given them, and that under the direct sanction and will of their Maker, and yet do these very persons not only punish the brute, but often put them to death, because perchance they depredate and offend us just as man does. Why do we give by law a premium for killing crows and lay a fine for killing vultures, when both act in accordance with the nature God has given them? Simply because one interferes with us and the other does not, and if they ran counter to the will of God he would change their nature.

52. Let any one notice his own movements from hour to hour, and he will find that most of them arise from functional causes that are never at rest. The heart never sleeps, the lungs never sleep, nor does the brain, or any other organ ever sleep. The waters are never still, the air is never still, nor is the earth itself ever still; motion, all motion, *dualism* and *dynamic*, is the order of nature; nor is mind any exception to this universal law decreed by God himself, which stamps everything with fate. Our endless dreams, with the acts of somnambulism and somniloquism, should convince the free-willer that our minds are stirred to action by our organism alone, without the aid of a conscious free-will.

53. That writers opposed to necessity, having abandoned science for a mere proximate feeling, tauntingly affirm that we do as we please; and as greater liberty could not be conceived of, which is a seeming something with thoughtless readers, while a smattering of science will at once see there is nothing in it, the predicate and consequent having no connection. The premise here is undeniable—that we do as we please, while the conclusion that we are therefore free is false. I can prove by the same mode of logic that free-will writers

11

are geese, thus : Free-will writers are animals, and geese are animals ; therefore free-will writers are geese.

True, we are free to do as we are pleased, but that is not the question under discussion. It is this, whether we are free to convert pain into pleasure, or be pleased with what we are not pleased, and what it is that makes us pleased? Is the will free to be pleased with the sensation of pain when our hand is in the fire? No. Is it free to be pleased with the loss of fortune and friends? for if not, the question is at an end. And now I ask the honest reader to say whether it is the mind that gives itself the pleasure to do or not to do, without an object or end in view, or whether it is not objects operating upon the mind, and something desired by the mind, which gives it a pleasure and will to do or not to do? Away, then, with your chidings of free-will and a power to do what we are pleased to do, when pleasure and pain are the result of fatal laws and events beyond our control, and the very things that create a pleasure, desire, or will, to do or not to do, just as those pleasures and pains prompt us. If this hackneyed and false word, as here applied, had been called force, simple and just as it would be, it would have cut short hundreds of volumes and livings for thousands of writers, for the sentence and true science would then read thus: We do as we are forced to do, and therefore are not free; instead of, we do as we are pleased to do, and therefore free. False assumptions, false terms, and the dexterous use of abstractions and refinings have given to psychology a mystic charm and artistic beauty, which, having been hallowed by time, is hard for the untrained in the true principles of science to resist; and preachers and teachers, heading all the institutions of learning in the world, may find it to their interest to keep up the old artistic and technical system of psychology. Many more exposures of such chicanery and quibble might be made, but I must

think the reader has, by this, learned enough to know
why it is that more than two thousand years of preaching
and teaching has only darkened and perplexed the science
of mind, made man the greatest enemy of man, and rendered no benefit whatever to society. Metaphysics has
in past ages been nothing more than a hodge-podge, a
pretentious fabric, made up of words without meaning,
distinctions without a difference, with indefinable and
indeterminable mysticisms, neither understood by the
writer nor the reader.

53. That the mind can not make sugar sour nor vinegar
sweet, and, consequently, has no power or will to operate
upon things and make them what they are not, but bound
to be operated upon by things as things are.

54. That instead of controlling our thoughts, our thoughts
control us; for who can stop his thoughts, change his convictions of mind, or make painful thoughts pleasurable?
Consequently, that pleasure which causes the will to do or
not to do in obedience to our thoughts and convictions, is
beyond our power and control; hence it turns out that the
will does not create the pleasure so much harped on to do
or not to do, but the pleasure creates the will to do or not
to do, which pleasure did not create itself, but was in turn
the result of our unavoidable convictions, and those convictions themselves were the fatal product of testimony
forced upon the mind. Thus all illustrations resolve themselves into one—that the mind creates nothing, can operate
upon nothing; but is operated upon by all things, and fated
to abide things as things are, not being able to think black
white or white black, in violation of the fated connection
between subject and object.

55. That life itself is a life of necessity, not having
created itself, but being forced into existence by a Power
anterior to and beyond itself, and being dependent upon
the necessaries of life to sustain itself, its wants become

urgent and innumerable. If in want of means and a sum
of money be illegally presented, our unavoidable organism
and education will be tested. If by nature our appetites
be strong and urgent and our resistance weak, our choice
will be to take it; when, should our nature be the reverse,
and our moral training be well grounded, our choice will
be to refuse it. Now in this is involved the whole science
of mind, for the reader must at once see that we have no
liberty but to choose or refuse; and from our choosing and
refusing issue all the acts of life. Hence, mark it here,
that to choose or refuse, from which there is no escape, is
one and the same, in regard to liberty—each being our
choice, which choice being grounded in our nature and
wants, is as fated as time, yes, and death itself. Thus I
grant to the free-willer, we do as we please; but that pleasure itself which causes us to will and to act, is an effect,
a result, yes, an inevitable result, emerging from life itself,
and that tendency interwoven into our very existence and
the irrevocable nature of things decreed by Deity from the
beginning of the world. Reflect for a moment, and you
will see we are bound, yes, fated to believe or disbelieve,
be pleased or displeased; from which proceed all our acts,
and where then the liberty of mind any more than the
liberty of body? The stomach digests as it does, the
blood circulates as it does, a rock returns to earth when
thrown up, and water runs down just as it is pleased
(inclined) and made to run down by the fated laws of
gravitation.

In recurring to the oft-asked question, whether a second will got up of ourselves may not counteract a
first will prompted by other causes, I answer, as I before
did, that a second will may, if the stronger, as certainly
counteract the first as the stronger power will overcome
the weaker, or the heavier weight cast the scale; but mark
it, the stronger will is got up by the stronger motive,

which motive the mind did not nor can not create; it
being out of and independent of the mind, and simply an
object and end desired by the mind. For instance, an
owner puts a horse up at auction and a bid comes to his
full price or value, such bid creates in his mind a will to
take it, but a second bid says ten dollars better. O how
quickly is the first will overcome by the second, and so
on and on to the end. But none of those bids or motives
were gotten up by the mind itself, as free-willers would
have it, but came from without, and acting upon the mind,
made the mind do just as it pleased. Again, suppose
a man resolves upon the death of another, through revenge or otherwise, and starts to commit the deed, but
on the way a fear (not from nothing or self-produced)
comes over his mind of detection, and a punishment here
and hereafter. He hesitates and stops, the two wills now
being in equipoised conflict; but by-and-by the second
will prevails, and his legs are at once commanded to take
him back. Where the difference I, in turn, ask, in the two
wills in regard to freedom, the first being created by the
passion of revenge, and the second and prevailing will
by a fear of punishment, and not from nothing, or a self-
created nothing. As before made known, there is nothing
which can create itself, live within itself, or upon itself,
but is dependent upon objects and agencies without itself.
The mighty oak, deeply rooted, does not grow itself, but
is grown by elements without itself: nor is the mind any
exception to this universal law of *dualism*, not being able
to grow itself, create ideas within itself, or make something out of nothing. Every idea must have its repre-
sentative that begets it, every will its object, and every
child its father. This is fate, a fixed and determined law
of organism, and of all things short of God himself, the
only Creator and *Primum Mobile* of the aggregate universe.
And now in closing this essay I beg the reader's atten-

tion to the fact that all mankind are governed by their opinions or convictions, which convictions are not by the will, but from testimony, and that testimony being the result of time, of natural mind, of credulity or incredulity, of location and association, intelligence, acute or dull sensibility, and a thousand hidden causes, consequently not voluntary, but an unavoidable result which gives to each man his separate opinion, no two on earth thinking exactly alike. Had this fact been known in past ages it certainly would have made men more brotherly and saved millions of lives from intolerance and persecution. If Michael Servetus, John Rogers, and thousands of others could have changed convictions of soul by a mere act of will, they might have saved themselves from the dreadful death at the stake. More than one hundred thousand of our fellow-mortals are now annually sacrificing their lives upon the altar of their honest convictions of religious right fatally fixed upon them by the country in which their lot has been cast, and the education there received.

56. That God, being absolutely perfect in his uncreated, underived, immutable, eternal, and unavoidable nature, every motive to action must be for the best, and that there is not, therefore, any evil in God's universe, but that all apparent evils are dispensations of mercy, and end in universal good. He, who maintains an all-wise, all-powerful, and good God, can not but grant this doctrine of optimism, which affirms that all things are wisely ordered, and ordered for the best.

57. That to say that God's prescience is perfect and infallible, and yet, that the connecting links of causality, or laws by which events are to be brought about, are fallible, or, in other words, fortuitous and uncertain, is ridiculously absurd, for God himself can not see the evidence of a thing, which in itself has no evidence or antecedent cause of existence.

58. That it is impossible for God himself to know a contingence; as to do so, would be the same as to know a thing to be certain, which, at the same time, he knows to be uncertain, involving the absurd idea and impossibility of to be and not to be at the same time.

WHAT IS SENSATION?

SENSATION is the soul, the mind, the sentient and percipient being, by which we know all we do know or possibly can know. It is the foundation of all knowledge, and the only intentional, innate, congenital, or original principle belonging to the organism of man, mind or body. It is the arbiter of all our actions. It has priority and superiority over all, for it is all in all. It is born with us, giving us all our knowledge, all our pains and pleasures, and hopes and fears, and dies with us—it is our life. We see by it, hear by it, smell and taste by it; yes, and feel all we do feel, externally and internally, by it. We perceive, conceive, imagine, reason, and judge by it. It is our memory, for we could not remember but by feeling the presence of things remembered. It is our conscience, as we can not be conscious of a thing without feeling it. We are conscious we exist because we feel that we exist. It is the foundation of virtue, of morality, and of religion. We have a sense of honor, of pride and ambition; a sense of duty and a sense of gratitude; a sense of condemnation of guilt and sinfulness; a sense of right and wrong, and of truth and falsehood. It short, it is the life, the mind, and the man; without it we are dead, without it we cease to think, and without it we are nothing. Sensation constitutes the first law of our natures, and is given to us by our Creator for self-preservation; it watches every pore of our system from the stealthy encroachment of disease, and everything that may harm or pain us. It admonishes us to avoid or invite as our sensations may be agreeable or disagreeable. When wearied it invites us to rest, and when irksome in one position it turns us over to another. Beauty, symmetry, and utility give a sense of pleasure; while vice, immorality, and deformity produce pain and disgust. All our kind and benevolent affections arise from a delicate and refined sensibility. Yes, and the highest, the noblest, and the most durable pleasure is in a clear conscience—in doing good; while the most bitter sensation of anguish and remorse is in a guilty conscience. Feeling is the highest attribute of God himself. More than all else, without sensation we could have no feeling of obligation to our Creator, nor love for our Saviour; no, nor could we realize the pleasures of heaven or the pains of hell; so that reward and punishment are based upon it. Yes, and the golden rule, to "do unto others as we would have them do unto us."

How, then, any set of teachers can degrade this divine gift and discard it as "low and sensual," except it is that the brute has it in common with man, when just as rational would it be to close our eyes to the glaring light of day, and tear out our stomachs, because God has seen proper to give to the brute those blessings as well as to man. From the examinations of near one hundred authors, I am well assured that it is this supercilious and sacrilegious vanity of man which has induced him to discard the system of sensationalism and advocate the doctrine of mysticism, which has kept science, morality, and religion back for thousands of years. No argument has ever been used against the true doctrine of the mind,

but an ignorant and vulgar tirade of degrading names,
such as skeptic, materialist and deist, have been threatened against its advocates, just such as were impiously
hurled against God's laws of astronomy, geology, and all
other laws of science when first discovered; and yet have
those very objectors, when no longer able to resist the
truth, unblushingly come forward and, making a merit
of necessity, taught these sciences; and the day is not
far distant when they will be compelled to teach the
truth—the true science of mind.

WHAT IS AN IDEA?

An idea is simply the impression of an object upon the
mind, with which the mind becomes acquainted. For
instance, if an elephant be brought to sight for the first
time, and the name given, we have an idea of an elephant, and, should we see it again, we would pronounce
it an elephant; and so it is with all other objects—each
and every one of which impress their appropriate ideas.
Nor is it necessary that those objects should be presented
to the mind in our after thoughts of them, as they often
recur by association, and are even brought up fresh in
our dreams, by ruminating causes within—not from
spiritual or divine agencies (take notice), but from
physical causes. Every original idea or thought, of
every possible description, must come to the mind
through the senses; after which the mind (like the
mirror) can reflect those images (ideas) to the memory
or imagination. The mechanic's shop empty can do
nothing; but fill it through the doors (outward senses)

with materials from without, and those materials may be made to assume endless shapes, with endless names. The kaleidoscope, in like manner, can exhibit no form or feature without materials; nor can wax or blank paper operate upon themselves—but are subjects to be acted upon by objects without.

It is true, we can think of things that do not exist— as a flying horse, a golden mountain, or a mermaid—but (mark it) we have had the materials in the mind of which they are made up. For instance, we have seen a horse, and we have seen wings; gold and a mountain; fish and women.

Fearing the reader may think I am burlesquing in my representation of the almost universal teachings of mental philosophy, I will make a short quotation from Dr. Reid's Intellectual Powers of Man, in confirmation of all I have said, or may say, in regard to the gross falsehoods and the astounding folly yet taught upon the subject of mind and what ideas are.

In speaking of the doctrines of Plato and Aristotle (which are in reality the same now taught by mystic and idealistic philosophers), he says: " These images or forms (ideas) impressed upon the senses are called sensible species, and are objects only of the sensitive part of the mind, [*I wonder where that part of the mind can be which is not sensitive, or has no sense*]; but by various internal powers they are retained, refined, and spiritualized, so as to become objects of memory and imagination, and at last of pure intellection. When they are objects of memory and imagination, they get the name of phantoms; when, by farther refinement and being stripped of their particularities, they become objects of science, and are called intelligible species; so that every immediate object, whether of sense or of memory, of imagination or of reasoning, must be some phantasm or species in the mind itself."

Thus we have the mystic mode of ideas, and the teaching of mental philosophy, and thus do we also see how far a phrenzied fanaticism may lead great men (fools) greatly astray. David Hume (with good sense) converted those strange things, phantasms and species, into more visible and tangible forms, and called them impressions; and Descartes christened these incomprehensibles, and called them ideas; which name they have ever since borne. Now, though I think my own authority (sustained by sound logic and axiomatic facts) will be ample with the philosophic reader, I will make a few quotations for such as are governed by great names and not by reason. Sir William Herschel says, that "The whole tendency of imperial art is to bury itself in technicalities and place its pride in complicated specialties and in mysteries known only to adults." Again; the Rev. Isaac Watts, in his work on the improvement of the mind, says: "A man who dwells all his days amongst books may have amassed together a vast heap of notions; but he may be a mere scholar, which is a contemptible sort of character in the world." These few remarks speak volumes in favor of coming out from the dark and factitious closet of the mystic and mechanical schools to the glowing light of heaven, and the unerring revelation and guidance of nature. And again, Dr. Scott says: "A teacher of divinity may be a living concordance and a walking index to theological follies, and yet know nothing of religion."

These facts I quote as equally applicable to the teachings of mental philosophy, in which I have attempted to show that no amount of learning or labor in abstract or mystic things can ever improve science or aid in the practical lessons of life. I assure the reader that the systems of mental philosophy now taught in our schools are more vague, complicated, and incomprehensible than those

maintained in the days of Plato and Aristotle, two thousand years ago. This want of improvement in so great a
length of time, is owing to the want of original and independent thought, each book-maker being a mere copyist,
and each teacher being of the same stupid and stereotyped
order. I have forgotten to refer the reader to Sir William
Hamilton, the latest author (and the literary wonder of
the world), in farther proof of my assertion, that "all the
labor of past ages in regard to mind has ended in confusion, and without any satisfactory agreement among
authors," who, I say, have lashed the air with frenzied
fury and left not a visible mark behind them. And yet,
strange to tell, Sir William, after prostrating every author
who stood before him, steps upon the same platform of
their "learned ignorance," as he calls it, sets out with a
paradoxical array of high sounding technicalities, of classifications, divisions, sub-divisions, and mystic refinings, too
vast even for the most mystic recluse or the most patient
of alchemic philosophers.

Having, in a single sentence, given you the idea of how
we receive our ideas, I am at a loss what more to say,
other than to tell you, as before done, that our senses are
the only inlets to knowledge (ideas), the arbiters of truth,
and the valid witnesses of the soul, each sense impressing
its appropriate ideas. The eye can not smell, nor can the
nose see, and yet they aid each other in determining the
nature of a thing presented to one alone. For instance,
the ear may be in doubt about a voice it hears, but let the
eye glance upon the person or object, and it will tell the
ear who it is or what it is; taste sugar for the first time,
and look at it, and the eye alone will afterward tell it is
sugar without the taste. We might hear a man speak
and a cow low a thousand times if blind, and we could not
tell which the voice came from; but open the eye to the
object and the ear alone could not afterward be deceived;

or, if blind, feeling the objects at the same time we hear them would aid the ear ever after.

Touch is the great corrective of relative distance, which the sight alone could never attain. All objects presented to the eye in infancy appear equally distant from it, as pictures upon an even surface do, yet greatly unequal in distance, while paintings, though upon an equal surface, may be made to deceive the sight, as looking very unequal, which deception the touch would quickly correct. Why do the heavenly bodies, though some of them millions of miles beyond others, look equally distant? Simply because we can not get among them and, by locomotion and touch, correct the error. This fact is proven beyond all dispute by persons restored to sight from a congenital cataract, who would as soon put out their hand to reach the moon as to reach a man three feet from them; nor can they tell by sight objects they had often felt and knew by touch. The celebrated surgeon, Cheselden, first proved this fact by restoring to sight a man some thirty years of age, who could not distinguish any difference in the distance of objects, and though he had a cat and a dog, which objects he had often felt and easily distinguished, he could not by sight tell one from the other, till at last in his perplexity he eyed them closely, and put his hand on the cat, saying, "Now, pussy, go; I will know you next time." Children will climb to high places to touch the moon with a rod, and infants will stretch out their hand to reach a candle many feet from them.

I will repeat it, in fine, that sensation is the mind, and being subject to all manner of modes of action or sensations, that a single idea is simply a sensation produced by an object of sense. For instance, the table before me impresses by sight the idea of a table, the book of a book, and the inkstand of what it is. Fire gives the sensation or idea, by touch, of heat; the ear gives us a variety of sensations of different sounds; the taste, of different flavors, and the nose has its sensations of pleasure and pain from the various odoriferous objects presented to it. I will further say, that those objects of sense (as great houses, etc.) do not enter the mind, nor are our ideas of them big or little, round or square, soft or rough, red, black, or white; but each and every object, being different in its nature, produces its specific sensation or idea, to which, by language, we give names. The same sensations from the same objects are the same in all ages and with all persons, but are designated by different names in different languages. If black had originally been called white, and A called B, they would have been just as well understood. The knife which inflicts a wound bears no resemblance either to the wound or the pain it inflicts; the pain is not in the knife, but in the mind. There is no fragrance in the rose which has no sensation, nor do the particles emitted from it bear any resemblance to the rose itself. In fine, an idea, the number of which constitutes all our knowledge and intelligence, is an effect, a perception, or, rather, a conception or reception, of objects and instructions forced upon the mind, which, without such objects and instructions, could never have an idea, or become intelligent. Direct and undeniable proof of which is, that blind persons have no knowledge of objects of sight, nor the deaf of sounds or language.

WHAT IS PERCEPTION?

PERCEPTION is whatever we perceive or gain a knowledge of. It is an idea of something—something presented to the senses. For instance, if a horse be presented to the mind, the mind at once perceives it. The picture of a cow is next stamped upon the mind, giving it an idea, or perception, not only of the cow, but the difference between it and the horse. Thus does the perception, idea, or knowledge we gain of the horse and the cow, simple as it is, fully represent all other perceptions, and every description of knowledge we acquire through life. I see an object and perceive it. I hear a sound and perceive it. Smell, taste, and touch, and my mind perceives the object assailing it, through those senses. Thus, we perceive, have an idea, know, believe, judge it so, and have a conscious knowledge of the fact, requiring no great metaphysical books of bewildering technicalities to render all doubtful. God made the eye, and made it ample for all objects of sight; open it to midday, and, without those parasitic *faculties,* it at once perceives it, nor could any artificial book or instruction by man make it more perfect. The birds and beasts, whose senses are more perfect, and whose perceptions are more acute than ours, must, according to the doctrines of our day, have more *faculties* than we, and teachers who understand them better than ours. I ask the reader to scrutinize closely, and consider words and arbitrary sounds worth nothing, for brutes, children, and deaf persons perceive, think, reason, will and act, as correctly without languages as with it; and if he will, moreover, consider God superior to man, he will no longer be led astray by the vain conceit and learned ignorance of man.

What more to say I know not, as the above few sentences have told all that is known of mind, and of its avenues and resources of knowledge, save this—that all its recurrent thoughts and combination of knowledge, whether awake or asleep, are brought back by perceptive association or functional excitement from within, which I call the *recurrent or sixth sense*, of which we know as little as we do how the chicken is, by incubation, brought from the egg in which we see no chicken, or the man, mind and body, is forced into existence from a seminal secretion—how small-pox and vaccination will remain in the system as a preventive for life—how the rabid poison, as from the bite of a dog, should sleep for months, or even years, before development; or why all diseases have their period of incubation, and why certain morbid conditions of system should assume periodic forms. What little we know, either of mind or of body, we gain not from intuitive *faculties*, but simply from perception, and after reflection. Yea, and so very little do we know from life's experience, that we can treat neither with success. We prate much, and yet the sum total of what we know is to the unknown as an inch is to limitless space, or as a moment is to unending eternity. The child may, and often does, confound the philosopher by three questions. Who made the toy? Man. Who made the tree? God; and, who made God? Indeed, such is our ignorance, beyond artistic taste and technical folly, that we should blush at a single question. What is the life of the humblest insect, or of a blade of grass, no philosopher knows. Isaac Newton, after tracing the laws of gravitation from its gentle hand upon the falling apple, to its mighty grasp upon whirling worlds, when asked, what is gravitation itself? answered, I know no more than the ploughman of

the field. St. Chrysostom said, "If asked what is time, I
know, but if asked to explain, I know not." That calomel
will purge and tartar puke, everybody, from perceptive
experience, knows; but of the *modus operandi* no physician
on earth can more than answer with the child, "because;"
and this ultimate fact, like all others, must be left with
God who so ordered it. I had intended a few remarks
upon the modes of mind called dreaming; but as it is not
worth a separate head, or a sheet of paper, I will only say
that we constantly dream, both by day and by night; but
our senses being true inlets of knowledge, and the valid
witnesses of the soul when awake. they limit and correct
our morbid musings; but when fast asleep, place, time,
and space have no limits or correction. All mesmeric
and psychologic exhibitions, so wonderful and inexplicable
to the beholders, are by first lulling the perceptive organs
that gave the mind all its original knowledge, in the
absence of which the credulous mind believes whatever
is told to and commanded of it; but awake these senses,
and how quickly do those phantoms fly. Somniloquism
and somnambulism also have their ludicrous freaks while
the senses are asleep; nor is there any end to the associated ideas stirred up by functional excitement. For
many years I dreamed of nothing but flying, gliding from
height to height on easy wing; but for the last ten years
my dreams have all been unpleasant, owing to some
abnormal condition of my vital functions. Persons have
been known to predict a spell of sickness and death long
before their occurrence. unconscious of the fact that the
seeds of disease were disturbing their vital functions
during the period of their incubation. Persons intending their departure at a certain hour by stage or cars,
will sleep soundly and awake at that hour, the mind
which never sleeps being watchful of that hour. We

often dream of lost articles that have been laid away and forgotten for years, the sixth or recurrent sense reminding our memory of the past.

WHAT IS METAPHYSICS?

METAPHYSICS, as taught in our modern schools, is but a jargon of technical and abstract nonsense—a play of words upon assumed premises, neither understood by the writer nor the reader. I have never read an author on the subject who did not at once obscure and perplex it by classifications, divisions, sub-divisions, and subtle refinings, and, by interminable mysticisms, make himself wholly incomprehensible, thus bringing the very name of metaphysics into disrepute by sound thinkers. Metaphysics properly means the science of mind, psychology the soul—all the same—which is as simple and demonstrable as any branch of physics, when not rendered unintelligible by ineffectual efforts to reach the infinite, even the essence of God himself, by the finite mind. If the reader will but think for himself, he will see how it is that metaphysical writers and stupid teachers become deranged upon this subject, and have never come to any settled or satisfactory conclusion, or bettered mankind in honesty, in morality or in religion; but in reality have rendered the science of mind (by which, of course, the world is governed) more perplexed and doubtful than it was two thousand years ago, during the days of Plato and Aristotle. And now, to convince the reader of what I say, I ask of him to exercise his own mind, and ascertain whether he can even imagine the limits of space or the end of eternity; that is whether he can conceive of a limited place or point beyond which there is nothing nor no space, or of a time when there will be no more time, and he will at once see that his finite mind can not reach or encompass the infinite, and also why it is that mystic and fanatical philosophers have made the science of mind the subject of perpetual vacillation and doubt. False premises, based upon frenzied and transcendental feelings, have led philosophers and divines most shamefully and mischievously astray from that conservative common sense which God has so kindly bestowed upon us, as ample for all the practical purposes of life. The controversy between Bishop Berkeley and David Hume, in regard to the actual existence of the objective and subjective worlds, and by which Berkeley annihilated one and Hume the other, leaving us without soul or body, is a fair specimen of the ideas of our (so-called) great men and their mystic philosophy. To show the common reader the artistic and perplexing mode of teaching mental science, I will make but two short quotations from celebrated authors, thus : " In order to reason, we must have the subject, or that concerning which something is either asserted or denied, commanded or inquired; the predicate, or that which is asserted, denied, commanded, or inquired, concerning the subject; the copula, by which the two other parts are connected. In these two propositions: Cæsar was brave ; men are fallible. Men and Cæsar now are the subjects; fallible and brave are the predicates: are and was are the copulas." See Upham's Moral Philosophy, page 192. Again, I quote from Morell's History of Modern Philosophy, page 421. In treating of what the great Fichte calls the absolute principles of philosophy, but which I affirm to be the essence of absolute nonsense, he says, " In order, therefore, to obtain a starting point for a system of reasoning and for pure science, we must look steadily

into our own *consciousness*, and find some act of the
mind's own spontaneous production, which can be
regarded in every case as axiomatically true; such
being found (but which never was nor never can be
found), it would give us the absolute and unconditional
principle of all human knowledge. This primitive act
is none other than the principle of identity. A=A, a
principle which is unconditionally certain, both as to
its matter and its form. No one will dispute the proposition A=A, when it is not enunciated as though A
implied any particular existence, but simply hypotheti-
cally; that if A is, then A is equal to A; and yet, in
affirming A=A, I pass a judgment—I think; and in
doing so, I affirm myself, so that the identity of me is
here asserted; and the proposition becomes *ego=ego*.
The second absolute principle is the category of negation,
which may be thus expressed: A is not = A. This
proposition is conditional as to matter, because it depends
upon the previous truth, A=A; but it is unconditional as
to the form, viewed as an absolute act of the mind; the
equation becomes the not me, if not=the me. By the
former proposition, the me affirmed itself; by this
second act, the me affirms the not me: that is, it
places something before it which is opposed to itself.
In other words, in the one case the mind views itself
as the absolute subject, now it views itself as object;
forming thus the opposition which is necessary to every
act of *consciousness*."

Thus may the reader see how it is, and why it is, that
more than two thousand years in the teachings of mental
science, and eighteen hundred and sixty-eight years of
gospel instruction, have ended in idle speculation, and
rendered no benefit to society. Were authors to throw
aside their logical forms, rhetorical flourishes, and artistic
vanity, and pursue the simple laws of nature, as even

children are prone to do in their progress of knowledge, mankind would certainly become wiser and better, by a knowledge of their own nature, and of their destined spheres in this life. Man's duty here is action, and not speculation; it is practical piety. through charity and kindness, and not dogmatic theology, with its bitter intolerance and distracting isms.

Modern divines are like Milton's fallen angels, had "reasoned high of providence, foreknowledge, will, and fate—fixed fate, free-will, foreknowledge absolute and found no end, in wandering mazes lost."

WHAT IS MYSTERY?

MYSTERY is a profound secret. unknown to all but imposters, who, being favorites of Heaven, are given the power of disclosing those secrets which God keeps carefully hid from all others! This god, Mystery, has been held in awe and admiration, and worshiped by millions of the demented and duped masses of mankind from the earliest period of our race to the present time. Yes, this great god, the father of all the idols and little gods throughout the world, the father of three hundred and thirty odd millions of gods in the East alone (according to the best missionary authorities), where he has at this moment more than one-half of the human family chained down to the most cruel, gross, and degrading modes of worship; and such is the firm veneration of the antiquity of these gods that reason is scouted as it falls from the mouths of our missionaries. Tell me not, then, ye mystic teachers of the human mind, that we have an intuitive and unerring (conscience) knowledge of right and wrong, and a sacred guide to religious faith and devotion. But read as follows from the pen of a missionary, Rev. Mr. Word: "Instigated by the demon of superstition, many mothers, in fulfillment of a vow entered into for the purpose of procuring the blessing of children, drown their first-born. When the child is two or three years old the mother takes it to the river, encourages it to enter as though about to bathe it, but suffers it to pass into the midst of the current, when she abandons it, and stands an inactive spectator, beholding the struggles and hearing the screams of her perishing infant! At Sangwi Island mothers were seen casting their living offspring among a number of alligators, and standing to gaze on those monsters quarreling for their prey, beholding the writhing infant in the jaws of the successful animal, and standing motionless while it was breaking the bones and sucking the blood of the poor innocent!" Away, then, with your divine *conscience*, which leads to such awful and appalling scenes of inhumanity as the above, and grant, in honesty and in truth, that the brute has a more divine *conscience* than the human, for they will risk their lives and fight to the death for their tender offspring. If such teachers and preachers as write books on nature were to throw aside their abstract nonsense, pedagogical conceit and ignorant learning, as Sir William Hamilton calls it, and study history (not as the parrot learns languages, but moralize upon the philosophy of history), they would gain a crushing knowledge of the demented condition of their race and of their own exceeding littleness.

Mystery is the father of superstition, and the grandfather of bigotry that figures so conspicuously in our modern churches and boasts of its origin. It affords a

living for millions of its appointees who filch the pockets
of their devotees. Fortune-tellers, soothsayers, augurers,
gypsies, and diviners, of every description, have been
sustained by mystery. No one in classic days doubts
the divine authority and power of the oracular priesthood, and such was the faith (conscience) of wiser heads
than ours, that Alexander the Great, after conquering the
world, penetrated far into the deserts of Africa to consult
the oracle of Jupiter Ammon ; nor can we marvel at this
if we will come nearer home and to a later date and read
the philosophy and hear the preaching of our own time.
We see uninspired men of finite minds profess by learning to reach the infinite designs of Deity and to explain
his revealed will. Now look at this with an eye of devotion to divine truth and you will see that to say God
has revealed a mystery, and has given us a guide beyond
the capacity he has given us to understand, is a solecism
in language and an absurdity in the nature of things ;
yes, and a libel upon the Supreme himself. It is to say
man can make God's law plainer than he himself did
or could do. God is not like the bloody tyrant of Rome
who gave to his subjects a law, and wrote it so fine and
hung it so high as not to be read, that he might punish
them for not understanding it. If God has given to
his children a law beyond their capacity, he can not, in
justice, hold them responsible to that law ; and hence it
is that in defence of our Maker, I say there are no mysteries necessary to salvation in the Bible, and if there are
they were never intended to be understood, for the very
word and nature of a mystery is beyond the ken of
uninspired men. The very name of mystery, I repeat it,
carries with it the impossibility of human explanation ;
and why, then, give such a degrading credence to the
vanity of our earthly leaders, who profess to explain
that which, in its very nature, is incomprehensible. I

know that all who may dare the sacredness of long-
established customs must suffer popular censure; and
I can now see Socrates swallowing the poison because
he could not believe in the man-made gods and corrupt
religion of his day, and Galileo upon his knees before
an ignorant and ungodly priesthood. I can also see the
mighty array of holy orders, and the thunder-bolts of
the vatican hurled at Martin Luther, who was anatha-
matized and pronounced by sacred custom " too base for
dogs to eat with." John Wesley, too, in common with all
others who have labored for the freedom of thought and
the improvement of religion, have in like manner been
rewarded by the malevolence and bitter denunciation of
the church. I feel assured, however, that the time is
coming when the light of science will lift the minds of men
from the petty arts and wily tricks of their erring fellow-
mortals, to see the resplendent glory and eternal majesty
of the one God, when their groveling faith in the mystic
mummery of their little psuedo gods will vanish as
does the ghost of night and the mists of morn before
the rising sun. "The heavens declare the glory of God
and the firmament showeth forth his handiwork." Yes,
then, and not till then, will all eyes, to the uttermost
bounds of the earth, be turned to the one great God,
and to Christ, the simple Child of nature, as the archetype of perfection, and their only Guide and Hope for
happiness here and hereafter.

Thus have I aimed to show what the human mind is,
and to prove, by the history of facts, that those who
err most in religion are guided by this deceptive feeling
called a divine conscience, and, moreover, that the grosser
and more foreboding the error, the stronger their faith, a
faith so inveterate and incurable that death is no terror,
but is invited by self-privations and austere severities
even unto death. O mental philosophy, that thou couldst

take a lesson from living and undeniable facts; and not labor as thou hast done to the slander of God, the disgrace of man, and the blight of science. I had thought to be done, but there are great and leading principles in this history that should not be lightly passed over, and one in particular, to-wit: That faith in religion, even to martyrdom, is no evidence of the truth or superiority of that religion ; for if so, Buddhism is the true religion of the world, having ten thousand of the faithful to one of any other religion, and a hundred thousand martyrs to one that can be found amongst all the other religions of the world put together. This bloody conscience, then, which I war against so much, is no safe guide to truth, to humanity, or to justice, but is simply a proof of sincerity in the person who is governed by it, and the crazy man actuated by the same principle (conscience) is equally honest and sure in his convictions. Abraham's faith was such that he was willing to sacrifice his son Isaac, and the faith of a well-known lady in Louisville (the very first in society) was so overwhelming as to *prompt her will* to sacrifice her three children by throwing them out of a fourth-story window upon the pavement, sending them to the Lord. as she said she had pledged to do, as though God delighted, like a bloody monster, in the sufferings and death of little innocents. Thus is reason to be sacrificed upon the altars of this god, Moloch, who is taught by modern writers and many preachers, to be a divine director, and to be implicitly obeyed! O thou mystic monster (conscience) encouraged by divines to murder reason, the first and highest attribute of God himself!

This mystic philosophy and theology was practically carried out by Emanuel Swedenborg, the founder of the New Jerusalem Church, and is now the mysterious lever and main-spring of the spiritual rappers, a new sect, proselyting faster than any *creed* ever before gotten up by a phrenzied imagination ; demonstrating the fact, that to teach a supernatural power or divine influence of mind, is to obstruct science and distract religion, as it ever has done. Did I believe as many do, that my erratic and transcendental feelings were the prompting of angels or divine spirits, I should like, then, to yield my reason and common sense to their guidance. But I have said, and say again and again, that the mind is governed by fixed and physical laws, without which we can never have any science or knowledge of mind.

*

SUPERSTITION.

SUPERSTITION is an over-credulous faith in mystic things (which I have been combating throughout). It is an unfortunate taint and tendency of the human mind to follow the pretended vicegerents of God and the expounders of his mysteries, as though God had hid his will, and given to his children a law beyond the capacity he gave them to understand. It is a belief without evidence, which tends to false religion and false worship, and has been the clinging and clamorous curse (as before said) both of true religion and of science. We need not go back to the Brahminical sages, nor to Oriental Pantheism, to Egyptian astrology, heathen mythology, nor the endless shades of Paganism, to show that man has been chained to the grossest and most degrading superstition, and led as an ox by the despotic opinion of others. This may seem to be a bold and degrading assertion ; but it is one in which the history of facts will bear me out. To grant the mighty influence which the opinion of one man may have over millions of his fellow-mortals, in succession, we have but to learn that Confucius gave laws and religion to China, Socrates to Persia, and Mahomet to Arabia; and thousands of other cases might be named where mind has held despotic dominion over mind. There are men now (who I might name if not offensive to their followers) who, by their dictum, wield millions of their followers with as much certainty and ease as a a boy whirls his top. Joe Smith, the Mormon impostor, is a lamentable instance of this kind. His craft and wily tricks have already grasped the four quarters of the globe, and creatures of all languages and nations are crossing stormy seas and traversing forests wide and wild to worship at his shrine. Thousands of smaller dictators rise up from time to time to lead captive the unthinking in the various isms and degradations of the day. Juggling demagogues and metaphysical fanatics have also entered the vortex of mental distraction and swelled the scene of unhallowed bickerings and revelings without charity. No brotherhood is found on earth; no bonds of union or ties of friendship to be felt. No one God, one people, one church, is granted—all is left in darkness and in doubt—each little party impiously arrogating to itself the special gifts of Heaven! All have agreed to disagree in all things, save only that reason is to be condemned as the enemy of mystery and the faith in things unseen, and that the bulls and thunderbolts of the church are to be hurled with pious fury against poor nature—in other words, the progress of science. And now, to justify every sentiment I may utter, and to render incontrovertible every statement I may make in regard to superstition and fanaticism, I refer to historical facts. Here the reader will find the trial and condemna-

tion of Galileo—one of the greatest and best of men—for
casting off the superstitious and libelous estimates of the
works of God, and bringing his mighty and marvelous
truth to the light of day. Here it is, reader. Ponder
over it, and weep for the ignorance and fanaticism of
man: "I, Galileo, aged seventy years, and on my knees
before you, most reverened Lords and Cardinals, and
general Inquisition of the Universal Church, of heretical
depravity, having my eyes upon the Holy Gospel, which
I do touch with my lips, do swear that I believe, always
have believed, and always will believe, every article which
the Holy Catholic Apostolic Roman Church holds, and
teaches, and preaches; and as I have written a book in
which I have maintained that the sun is the center—
which false doctrine is repugnant to the Holy Scriptures—I, with sincere heart, do abjure, curse, and detest
the said error and heresy, and generally, every other
error, and heresy, and sect, contrary to said Holy
Scriptures."

Cast your eyes all over the world, and meditate upon
the present degraded and melancholy condition of mankind. Then read back, through mouldering ages, the
history of all nations that have come and gone, and you
will see that superstition has produced the most wicked,
abominable and cruel gods that ever polluted earth ; and
yet, none too monstrous and detestable for human faith
and conscious worship.

O, superstition! long hast thou been the slanderer of
God and of his glorious works, and millions of good men
hast thou persecuted and put to death (amongst whom
were John Rogers and Michael Servetus). Thou art a
professor of religion; yet hast ever been pleased to do
Satan's bidding! Deny it not, thou murderer, under the
curse of God and the wrathful detestation of all mankind!
From thy fiendish back let the cloak of hypocrisy be torn,
and thy detestable deformity be exposed.

Every aspiring effort of the soul to free itself from the fetters of superstition and rise to the throne of God, by his demonstrable laws of science, has been closely watched and bitterly denounced as heretical and contrary to the canons of the church. The power of the magnet and the discovery of the compass and navigation were supposed to be the work of evil spirits. The invention of gunpowder, by Roger Bacon, was condemned as an unquestionable work of the Devil—the presence of sulphur being too odorous for denial—and the author was thrown into prison, where he died. Printing was certainly of Satan, and the author sought to be put to death by the *learned clergy*. His house in which he printed, in Paris, with his paper and type, were all burnt, and a guard set to keep the devil from escaping. This is history. Again; Harvey's discovery of the circulation of the blood was reviled by the *learned clergy* as false and highly dangerous to the vitals of religion. For, said they, " If the bounding spirit (pulse) so plainly seen and felt struggling to escape from its tenement of clay, be nothing but the circulation of a fluid, it will render all those glorious doctrines of the immateriality of the soul doubtful, and render God's Holy Scriptures null and void." " If," said these same *learned clergy*, who burnt the first book on astronomy, "it should be shown that the sun and stars are not little lamps that turn round this world to give it light, it will destroy the Bible faith, which says that Joshua commanded the sun to stand still for a given time, and it obeyed." I now ask the honest reader whether these *learned decisions*, or the word and mighty works of God are true? Theologians strove to put down the science of geology, as wholly incompatible with the Mosaic account of creation; but their babblings against the age of the earth, as well as its movements, are now laughed at by boys. The writings of Puffendorf and

Grotius were, in like manner, denounced as unsafe, because their maxims and morals were taken from the laws of nature, as grounded in our constitutions by our Maker, and not from their interpretations of the Bible— a book not to be degraded by political parties or subordinated to the cupidity of church officials. The discovery of inoculation, by Dr. Jenner, was pronounced wicked and brutal—ingrafting the brute into the human—and should be put down by law. Proof was had before the courts, after the death of infants (it mattered not from what cause), if inoculated, that horns had been seen growing out of their heads, and sermons and harangues of violent denunciation against inoculation are yet extant.

If said all this was not from superstition but fanaticism, I would answer that superstition is the father of fanaticism, and though done in the sacred name of God and of his revealed will, it certainly was the work of Satan. Call it religious zeal, or what you please, I can not but pronounce it a Satanic and infernal malignity which fanned the flames of persecution, and prompted preacher to drag preacher to the stake and broil him alive, when devils in their hellish spite could do no more.

Had Franklin, who sacrilegiously drew lightning from heaven, lived in those days, he would have suffered as did Prometheus, for stealing fire from heaven ; and Morse, who wilfully harnessed this fiery element and set it to carrying the mail. would certainly have been put to the stake.

In regard to the cruelties of past ages there has been but little difference between Catholicism and Protestantism, and I would feel just as safe under the hierarchy of Olympus or pontificate of Rome, as under Protestant dogmatism with its adverse doctrines and warring creeds. It may be said that the divine influence of reason and the progress of science have extinguished those awful cruelties of man to man; but this is not so, for every reader who has any knowledge of the selfish and party-passions of man must see that but for the conservative power of skepticism and church divisions, the horrid and heart-sickening scenes of Smithfield and Bartholomew would be enacted over and over again. Yes, the fiendish fires of human sacrifices would be kindled, and the bloody sword, clotted with human gore, would again be unsheathed. And though there can not now be a sufficient concentration of power in any one of the warring sects to carry on those vengeful acts of inhumanity, there rankles in the heart a secret enmity that lacks but numbers to make itself known.

To show the taint and tendency of the human mind, and its deplorable credulity in matters of superstition, we have but to recollect what all the papers of the United States published a few years ago, in our own day and time, and that at our own doors. Matthias, the favorite apostle of Christ, appeared in person in the city of New York, where the wealthy recognized him, and dressed him in the most gorgeous robes; and woe to his devotee who had a pretty wife, for he soon disappeared. Yet still his worshipers kneeled before him till the number of strange deaths induced skeptics and infidels to raise the alarm, whereupon the great apostle vanished from earth, but soon after turned up alive again, in an adjoining city, as the classic god Adonis, and of course was again worshiped and adored, particularly by ladies of taste—for the virtuous and refined Lucretia worshipped Venus, the prostitute goddess, and Adonis, with all the other notorious debauchee gods, the rankest rakes of the land, and why not modern ladies do the same! And now, I say to you, my reader, there is no creed too absurd, no proposition too monstrous for the human mind.

WHAT IS A FACULTY?

FACULTY is a word coined and used by the manufacturers
of shoddy text-books on psychology, mental philosophy, or
metaphysics—all meaning the same thing; which books
are taught in our modern colleges, where old folks go to
listen to the wonderful answers of their sons and daughters
to questions they themselves know knothing about, and
(between you and I) of which the writers and teachers
know as little, yet by which they live and command the
admiration of the old folks, who wonder, and whose wonder grows at the mystic wonders of these *deep learned*
teachers, to whom they would not pay a dime to graduate
their daughters in a useful or culinary school. It is, then,
no longer wonderful that mystery should still be sustained
both by preachers and teachers, when there is so much
eclat and money in it. This same trait in the human
mind of reverence for things unrevealed and artfully made
difficult of comprehension, is the father of all the wild
ravings and religious fanaticism of the world.

If there are *faculties* anywhere, they are not in the
mind, but in the objects that awaken the mind, and
impress their nature upon the mind, which, being a mere
passive recipient, can not resist the ideas thus forced upon
it. And hence it would seem that sugar has the *faculty* of
sweetness, vinegar has a sour *faculty*, and fire has two
faculties, that of producing both pleasure and pain. Man
begets the idea or *faculty* of two legs, and a horse that of
four legs; which moots a question of much metaphysical
and abstract learning, whether a man or a horse has the
most *faculties*. The mind, I *repeat* it, is a mere passive
recipient, without power either to create or resist the

nature of those objects which beget ideas within it. For instance, suppose yourself in a dark room; your mind, with all its powers and *faculties*, falsely given it, can not create or see the sun, or even a candle; but light a candle, and it can not resist seeing it. Blow it out, and what? It can no longer see. This being the case with all our other senses, and the law and order of receiving all our knowledge of every possible description, why so falsely teach the nature of mind? All after-thoughts or ideas thus received are brought back to the mind by association.

Faculty is a word conveying a false meaning, gotten up by art and enforced by arbitrary authority. Yes, I repeat it, a word from which millions of money has been coined by writers and teachers; and by which as many brains have been addled and dwarfed by efforts to understand it. This word multiplied by each author's own number, then spiritualized, refined, classified, divided, sub-divided, and again multiplied by no defined number, for every writer has his own number of *faculties* to constitute what they call mind, which, being filled with a vast number of these *faculties*, and the innumerable elements belonging to each *faculty*, becomes a mystic marvel and an inexplicable enigma to writers, readers, and teachers! Now all this parade and apparent learning I detest and condemn, as not only false, but perplexing and unprofitable to the pupil, who never has, nor ever can be made to understand it; and could he comprehend it, it would be as a grievous and toiling error. Mind I hold to be a unit, an indivisible being, of which we know nothing beyond its will and acts, and whose laws are few, simple and easy of comprehension, by all who will think for themselves, and notice the operation of their own minds. It will be observed that the mind turns with as much certainty to the object that assails it, as does the needle to the magnet

that attracts it; nor are our ideas or thoughts either exclusively the mind itself or the object itself, which stamps
the mind with the nature and quality of itself. Authors
foolishly and assumptively take the one extreme or the
other, of subjectivity or objectivity; when, in reality, it is
neither, but simply the union of the two, as the union of
the father and the mother, in the production of a child.
Haven, when treating of this subject, speaks thus: "Is
beauty and sublimity subjective, an emotion of our minds,
or is it a quality of objects?" A true answer to which is,
it is neither the one nor the other, but a union of both.
It might, with equal propriety, be asked, is muriatic acid
table salt, or is soda table salt; when any man of science
will answer to this ignorant question, neither of them are
table salt; in other words, muriate of soda is a new creation
by the union of the two. Haven again asks: "Is taste
intellectual or emotional?" as though sensations and emotions were not simply modes of mind or intellect itself.
He further asks: "Whether the enjoyment of a beautiful
sunset is in the painted cloud or in the mind itself?" to
which true mental science answers, the cause (as in motive
and will) is in the cloud, and the effect or enjoyment in
the mind; which takes us back to my oft-repeated doctrine, and only productive principle of universal nature,
dualism; as, but for the cloud, there would be no cause for
such enjoyment of beauty, and but for the mind, there
could be no such feeling or idea of beauty; in proof of
which, a blind man might live forever without an idea or
enjoyment of a sunset, nor could the sunset enjoy itself,
or pronounce itself beautiful—the cause is in the cloud,
and the feeling or idea in the mind. In short, he might,
with as much philosophic propriety, have asked, is the
cause an effect, or is the effect a cause? He says: "Beauty is
a distinct and intuitive *faculty,* and not dependent upon our
feelings, sensations, or emotions." O, how ludicrous, when

feeling is the mind itself which enjoys the beautiful! He again asks: "Is taste a matter of feeling, or is it an intellectual discernment? evidently we can not depend upon authority for the decision of this question, since authors differ; evidently we must refer the ideas in question, of taste, to the intellectual, since it does not belong to the sensitive part of our nature." Surprising it is, that even a tyro should ask such a question, for the intellect itself is feeling; but admit them, *falsely*, to be separate beings, as Haven does, how is the intellect to discern without feeling? Where can that part of our nature be which is not sensitive and without feeling? By it we live, move, and have our being—by it we feel, think, will, and act, and without it we are dead. As, however, he makes the feeling and discernment of beauty and sublimity a separate and independent *faculty*, without feeling, we must infer its independence of the mind itself! and, consequently, without the pale of mental philosophy and the science of the feeling or sensitive soul; and thus it would appear that Haven has taught, as did Professor Alexander, that the soul is not responsible for acts of the will, nor any other of those independent *faculties!* In treating of conscience, or a knowledge of right and wrong, under the above treatise, he again asks: "Does the cognition of right belong to the rational or to the sensitive part of our nature; to the domain of intellect, or of feeling; a judgment, or an emotion?" What a jumbled folly! Is not cognition a necessary part of our nature? Is not the domain of intellect a sensitive part of our nature? Is not feeling a sensitive part of our nature? and is not judgment and emotion a sensitive part of our nature?

To relieve the reader from the farther pursuit of such absurdities, I will say to him, that taste is the mind tasting, and not confined, as Haven would have it, to painting and statuary, nor is it, as he says, a separate and independent *faculty*, but simply a mode of the same mind, in every possible case; whether of nature or of art, of bacon and cabbage, or of roast turkey; for I ask what it is that tastes but the mind? Call the tastes of our appetites low, vulgar, brutal, or what you please, it is all mind, intellect, soul; for without mind we could not relish or enjoy anything, nor make choice of that which suits us best; so that a choice and act of will, declares a mind which makes the choice and wills to act. And now, in fine, I will say, that the mind is not governed, in this or any other case, by those exotic things called *faculties*, but is led to its choice, wills and acts, by the objects of its choice. Suppose you cast your eye upon a gorgeous sunset, as Haven says, and enjoy it, where the necessity of a *faculty*, aside from the simple perception of the mind itself, through the sense of sight, any more than for every other sense and enjoyment of the mind? You see a pleasing object, and the mind enjoys it; you smell a pleasing odor, and the same mind enjoys it; you hear sweet music, and the same mind enjoys it; you shiver with cold, and the same mind suffers; enter a room of soothing warmth, and the same mind enjoys it. Yes, and well-flavored wine you may take with a gusto, and the *very same identical mind* enjoys it. How ridiculous, then, to assert different minds and bewildering *faculties* for the different senses, which all point alike, to the one indivisible and observing mind! To dwell no longer upon the gross and vexatious errors of authors, I refer the reader to Haven's text-book, as a fair specimen of all others; where he will see a hundred *faculties*, and a thousand elements of faculties, in his analyses, that are doggedly drudged and drilled into the student's mind, already crammed with other follies; but still he is bound, like the parrot, to senselessly answer!

And thus it will be seen that the preaching and teaching

of artificial minds, for more than two thousand years, have only served to darken the subject and make man the greatest enemy of man,—all the church divisions, persecutions, and bloody wars being derived from the union of theology and a false psychology. Haven says, "Evidently we can not depend upon authority for the nature of mind, since authors differ so much in their doctrines upon this subject." And Hamilton says, "If preachers and teachers had not, by their *learned ignorance and conceited arrogance*, transcended what God saw proper to reveal, preaching and teaching would have been simple and true, and the morals of mankind and peace of society improved." And yet, it is strange to see that both Haven and Hamilton are servile copyists of the old stereotyped errors, founded on superstition and a religious fanaticism, called a divine *conscience*—a selfish, bigoted creature, the degrader and destroyer both of religion and science. Yes, and when such men fill every pulpit and literary institution in the world, it is no longer a wonder that falsehood should be forced by authority, as it was upon wiser heads than ours during the days of Greece and Rome; and I feel well assured, from my knowledge of the human mind, that the same authority which now gives faith to the varied and endless creeds of the world, could re-establish the heathen mythology, and pin it down upon the duped and craven credulity of mankind! O, how sad, how degrading and low is the taint and tendency of human idolatry!

CONSCIENCE.

CONSCIENCE, as taught in our modern schools, is a *faculty* or divinity within us which, in all cases, tells us what is right and what is wrong, and should be implicitly obeyed as an infallible monitor. This doctrine, though maintained by the best of men, and for the best of purposes, is in reality the doctrine of Satan, who has caused those advocates of the doctrine to fight each other with fire and sword, and, as the divine Doctor Scott says, "*spit hellfire at each other.*" This sacred monitor not only tells us that we are right, but points out the errors of others against whom we are *conscientiously* bound to use our best exertions, and even to punish and put to death all who will not obey our dictations, creeds, and commands. Every man on earth is said to possess this unerring divinity, and yet, what is truly marvelous, every one is commanded, on the pain of death, to yield his divinity as false to that of others. This paradoxical and wonderful thing, *conscience*, that tells us what is right and what is wrong, what is just and what is unjust, becomes the cruel persecutor of the Christian Church, under which Michael Servetus, John Rogers, and thousands, yes, millions of the most pious men on earth have bled and died. Leaving the Christian world for the great arena of common life, we find this divine *conscience* deceiving men, and engaged in the most malicious and cruel strifes. The man of observation has but to look at the little transactions around him, and see the disputes, suits, and hard thoughts among the best and most *conscientious* of his neighbors. We have seen this unerring divinity in the prompting of men's deeds under the terrors

of the inquisition, and I will spend but a few sentences in
showing the reader that the desertion of reason for a
mystic theology, founded upon this vacillating and deceptive thing, *conscience*, has produced all the wild ravings
and confusion in the science of psychology and the profession of religion.

It appears that psychology (the science of the soul, or
metaphysics) and theology have been inseparably connected from the earliest dawn of this science, so much so
that the churches, from age to age have been convulsed
and split asunder by the books that have, from time to
time, been issued upon this subject, as though God's holy
and inspired Word was to be in subordination to the wild
and fanatical sallies of uninspired men. This is undeniably so, and so much so that my whole aim in this investigation is to show the misconceived duty and consummate folly of the clergy in leaving the plain and practical
precepts of the Bible, and entering the fields of distracting and interminable disputation.

Having no room for quotations, and preferring historical facts and sound reasoning to all authority, I will give
but a few sentences from Morell's History of Moral Philosophy, to show the vacillation and confusion of mental
science.

" What, then, is the next stage to which the human mind
advanced after sensationalism, idealism, and skepticism
had exhausted their resources, and left all in doubt?"
The resource, we answer, in which the mind, the last of
all, takes refuge, is mysticism. Reason and reflection
have apparently set forth all their power and ended in
uncertainty. The mystic thereupon rises to view, and
says to the rest of the philosophers around him : Ye have
all alike mistaken the road; ye have sought for truth
from a totally incorrect source, and entirely overlooked
the one divine element within you (conscience) from

which alone it can be derived. Reason is imperfect. It
halts and stumbles at every step when it would penetrate
into the deeper recesses of pure and absolute truth. But
look within you. Is there not a spiritual nature there
that allies you with the spiritual world? Is there not an
enthusiasm which arises in all its energies when reason
grows calm and silent? Is there not a light that envel-
opes all the faculties if you will only give yourself up to
your better feelings, and listen to the voice of God (conscience) that speaks and stirs within you."

Thus, as I have said, we are taught to listen to and
obey the "god that speaks and stirs within us." Yes,
this vagabond and lying god, which has produced all the
persecutions, church divisions, and wars of the world;
the father of Buddhism, Mahometanism, Catholicism,
Protestantism, and the innumerable brood of isms, cisms,
and dogmatisms of adverse and warring creeds of men;
the god who crucified Christ of old, and has caused his
ministers to crucify him anew; the God of mythology,
of soothsaying, and of astrology; yes, and who stirs up
ghosts and sight-seeing; who heads mobs, causes wars,
stampedes amongst mules and horses, and great revivals
amongst men. A lying god, who makes us *conscious* to-
day that it deceived us on yesterday.

Thus we see that the doctrine of an internal and unerring monitor, superior to reason, is but the offspring of
a chimerical and frenzied fanaticism, and as the ghosts and
phantoms of midnight vanish before the rising sun, must
these morbid musings vanish before the light of reason.
Where, I ask, in the name of the great and good God,
is this sacred and intuitive monitor when one Christian
drags the other to the stake? Are they not both prompted
by the same unerring divinity to the most unhallowed
and malignant deeds? This doctrine is opposed to reason,
and so is Satan; for well he knows that earthly thrones

have tumbled, and demon oppression, with all its Gorgon forms, has fled before the voice of reason; nor can the tricks of papal sorcery, or the wiles of the devil himself stand against the might and majesty of reason.

In closing this article, (*conscience*), let me say it is simply the mind being conscious of whatever we think or do To have a *conscience* is to be *conscious* of a thing, and to be *conscious* of a thing, is to know a thing, believe it, think it so, to be assured of it, to judge it so, to have reason to believe it so, to be confirmed, persuaded, or convinced of it; in fine, to feel that it is so, for *feeling* is the soul, and the soul is *feeling*, as we can not be *conscious* of a thing without feeling it, nor feel and know it without being *conscious* of it. Now all this, though undeniable, is attempted to be evaded by a name, such as a moral sense, an original and intuitive *faculty* of right and wrong; yes, and which gives us a knowledge of our personal identity, making it the only divine *faculty* of self-knowledge we possess. I will here say to such *faculty* writers who deny to the brute a soul, that if this intuitive *faculty*, as they call it, of self-knowledge and personal identity be divine, the brute has it in common with man; for when did a cat or dog, though belligerent by nature, ever fall aboard and maim themselves in mistake for another simply because they know themselves to be themselves and not another. It is this parade of names without meaning, and distinctions without a difference which has produced all the confusion, and obscurity, and perplexity in mental science, when the mind, in reality, is a simple unit without a single *faculty* or power belonging to it; all the *faculties*, so called, being nothing more than different modes of mind under the influence of objects that ingross it, which objects, and the ideas of those objects, it has no power to resist. For instance, if sugar be put into the mouth, the mind has no power to resist the impression and idea of sweetness, or sourness from vinegar; and just so with all objects that operate upon the mind. This creature, *conscience*, so much harped upon, is nothing but the division of the mind, which division is wholly the result of education, and the nature of objects that impress the mind. Were I, if educated as a savage, to burn my enemies, I should be impressed with a right; that is, I should have an approbating *conscience*; but if otherwise educated, I should have a guilty *conscience*. To call this creature of education an original *faculty*, an intuitive monitor, and to give it (as is done) priority and superiority over all the other *faculties*, is truly ludicrous; as being one of the many modes of mind, it can have no priority or superiority over the mind itself, or any of its other modes—*faculties*—as fiddling, dancing, laughing, and crying are equally old, and all but modes of the same mind.

WHAT AND WHENCE IS MIND?

SIR Isaac Newton, after tracing the laws of gravitation from its gentle hand upon the falling apple to its mighty grasp upon distant worlds that roll their hidden and eternal way through trackless space, when asked what was gravitation, answered, that he knew no more than the ploughman of the field. And with like humility we have to answer in regard to the mind—knowing nothing of its essence; yet, as in the case of gravitation, we can trace its laws from the gentle smile of the little babe to the fiendish scowl of those demon monsters of persecution. That mind is like the body (a forced state) no one will deny, and that it would soon die out from the world without support from the body, and, in like manner, would the body as quickly die out without food, as would a lamp without oil, or a fire without fuel. We can as certainly trace the origin of mind back to Adam as we can body—it being, as is the body, a seminal secretion; or, otherwise, when, and how, and by whom are minds made? and when, and how, and by whom are they put into the body? We see that mind comes into the world with the body; that it grows and strengthens with the body; suffers disease and infirmity with the body, and dies and disappears from this world with the body. We also see as many hereditary traits of mind as of body— showing its dependence upon its archetypes, on and on to Adam; and if this be not so, how can God hold the mind bound for Adam's sin? If new minds come fresh from God's own hands (say forty millions a year, for it seems that that many new bodies come into the world) it certainly can not be that so kind a Father, who creates these new children by the hour, will send them to hell for Adam's sin when they are in no way akin to him.

It must not be here understood that I believe mind to be perishable matter; for I feel assured that it will live beyond the grave, as it is pledged by Almighty Power to be immortal. The body, we know, is dissolved into its original elements, and goes into the laboratory of transmutation, to again be paraded out in new forms by the plastic and reviviscent hand of nature; which fact, no doubt, gave to Pythagoras and Zoroaster the idea of the transmigration of souls. Some of the most pious divines, however, have maintained that the mind was the result of the organization of matter; but concerning such speculations we have no occasion for uneasiness, as it is just as easy for God to make matter immortal as to resurrect and reanimate the body, as he has solemnly vouched to man he will do. Dr. Priestley and his school of divines contend for the materiality of mind, as more rational and consistent with the wisdom and power of God than the complicated and incongruous union of spirit (of which we know nothing) and matter.

This much, and this only, we know: that the mind is born into the world as blank as a sheet of paper—without the knowledge of anything; but soon, and by the sensibilities God has given it, it is impressed, through the senses, with everything around it, and by-and-by becomes intelligent. We have no self-creating power within the mind, and from the teachings of such false doctrines as mental omniscience, or self-creating powers, may be traced all the unfortunate difficulties in regard to religion, in moral science, yes, and in politics, which have rent society and perplexed the world for centuries past. If we will honestly grant the fact of our own limited destiny, of God's supremacy, and of his wise laws, and his steadfast government over mind, over body, over his vast and harmonious universe — yes, over all created things, to which he has given laws to keep them in their alloted spheres and make them what they are— we shall be better satisfied with ourselves, with our neighbors, and with the dispensations of Providence; for all will be by the will of God, who, in his wise and preconceived plans, saw what man can not—that these laws would work with undeviating certainty (fate) for the best.

As I have said, if we will grant, what we can not honestly deny, that God created all things, gave them laws and bounds — leaving nothing to a self-creating power, or to chance—the enigma of mind is at once solved; for we have nothing more to do than simply observe (as in the case of the begetting of children under God's laws of procreation) how our ideas are begotten by the laws of mentality. Against these established and sealed ordinances of the Almighty, however, men have rebelled, and given to themselves a self-creating power, by will—a power that the God of heaven can not himself possess; as for a thing to act and bring itself into existence before itself had an existence is wholly incompatible; and hence, it is held by all sound thinkers, that God is not self-created, but self-existent from all eternity; and these fundamental facts I shall often recur to in these essays.

Man, if he will but see himself aright, must know that he is but a fated link in the firm and eternal chain of causality—that all things originate and terminate in God, who gave the first impulse to life and motion, and who holds firm and fast the two ends of this vast and unbroken chain that binds his mighty universes in one harmonious whole, and in their bidden and eternal rounds. Thus it is, I hold, that the power and wisdom of God forbids the idea that he has created anything in vain, left anything to chance, or put it in the power of any being to disappoint him, frustrate his plans, or thwart his preconceived designs in the final issue of all things.

Authors speak largely of the powers of mind, which word figures powerfully throughout their powerful *big* books on mental philosophy. This term, power, as applied to mind, is as a solecism in language, and a gross absurdity in nature; and has always misled the pupil in the study of mental philosophy. Man has no power but that of yielding to his fate; he has the power of being born, the power of getting sick, and the power of dying; he has the power of digestion, a thing he knows nothing about; and the power of seeing and hearing, and smelling, etc., which he can not help any more than the contraction of his heart, and the renewing of his exhausted strength by the vital functions within. Yes, and he has the power of pleasure and pain, and of love and hatred, with the myriad of impressions that may be forced upon him. The mind has the power which a vessel has to receive, or the wax has, not to shape itself, but to be put in many shapes, and to receive endless impressions. The mirror has power, not to make, but to reflect impressions; and the blank-paper has power to receive impressions, and when those impressions are made, has the power of exhibiting a vast amount of intelligence. Gold has the power of being gold, and the cannon-ball has immense power with the common observer, yet it is a cold, lifeless lump of iron, with no intrinsic power to create itself or move itself by its own will, yet (by this false term, power,) has the power of being moved. A man has the power of being put in prison, and of doing all other things which he is forced to do; and in like manner has he the power (forced liberty) of being impressed by the surrounding objects and circumstances, amidst which he is placed, and by which he "lives, moves, and has his being." Thus it will be seen, by the most common observer, that there is nothing self-created or self-moved, either in mind or matter, but all is cause and effect, *dualistic* and *dynamic.* The cannon-ball, for instance did not create itself or move itself, but was sent by the explosion of powder, which powder did not create itself, nor could it explode itself. God made the materials, and man the powder by his will, which will was created and moved by an antecedent and motive cause.

These are great and vital facts but little understood, yet they lie at the foundation of all science, morality and religion—facts that the self-stultified pedant can not see, yet, upon which little children, not yet demented by art, base their thoughts. I have been asked by those not five years old, who made the toy-man? who made the horse? and when answered God, then, who made God? thus ascending in the inductive order from effect to cause. Yes, and right here, by-the-by, does the immortality of Lord Bacon rest; for his labors, in reality, were nothing more nor less than to bring philosophy, which had been lost by ignorant learning in word and art, back to nature, (its true foundation, laid by God himself) the child's order of induction.

I have in part, and will more fully show, that man is brought into this world without his knowledge or consent; that he is borne through the transit of life by the laws of necessity, and that his exit from time to eternity is determined and fixed by the indissoluble chain of causality. The life itself is a forced state, and would, as I have said, die out as quickly without the vital air and the food that develops and nourishes it, as would the flame without the fuel which sustains it. That thought, in like manner, has no independent, substantial existence apart from its causes. It is an effect, a result; it is relative, it is conditional, it is the product of subjective and objective unity. It is like life, has no intrinsic, or real, or prior existence; but is a begotten thing, a new creation, and, in turn, is possessed of creative powers. The powder, for instance, has an existence when made, and the spark, or fire, has a begotten existence, but explosion, in like manner, is a new creation, a result, the product by the union of both; but when thus begotten becomes a real, but momentary entity—a power and a cause of other results. In like manner, the child is not a real and independent entity—is an effect, a product, a result of the union of father and mother, or a subject and an object; but there was a germ from Adam in the father and the soil in the mother. This is the case in all organic existences. The grain of wheat that has been enveloped with the mummies of Egypt, for three thousand years, and from which whole fields of wheat have sprung, would have remained throughout all time without the stimulus of light, heat, moisture and soil to force it into existence and develop its intrinsic and inherent nature. Just so with mind, which would remain forever without ideas, unless it came in contact with the objects that develop their appropriate ideas. For instance, a horse begets the idea of a horse, and a cow that of a cow, the table, book, and ink-stand before me each beget their ideas of a table, book, and ink-stand. In positive proof of these facts we have but to know that a blind man has no idea of colors, and can not distinguish white from black ; but open his eyes and place these objects before him, and he can not, to save his life, help but see them and know them. Thus he has a knowledge of white and black, and, simple as it is, it is the great secret of how we receive all our ideas, or knowledge, of every possible kind, on which thousands of immense volumes have been written. Our senses are the only inlets to knowledge, and valid witnesses to the soul, which could never become intelligent, nor ever know anything but by their aid. The eye can not hear, nor the ear see, but each sense is wisely and beautifully fitted to its appropriate objects. Suppose one coming into the world deprived of all his senses but feeling (without which it could not live), he would be below an idiot, and on a level with the oyster. Think, then, what is mind, and how it is developed ; yes, and where those innate and divine ideas are that make us so intelligent without study, and give us all our knowledge of truth and falsehood, and of wright and wrong, as we are falsely taught by our text-books in our modern colleges.

We have many actual and undeniable facts in full proof of all I say, and one more particularly striking, of a deaf man in Paris, who was restored to hearing by the jar of his brain and nervous system from the sound of artillery. He soon acquired language, and told that he had no knowledge of a God, or that he should ever die, and when he saw funeral processions and herses pass, he could not think what they meant. Thus we see the amount of knowledge the loss of a single sense, in the beginning of life, deprives us.

The mind is a unit—it is one and indivisible, and yet do authors divide it into many parts, powers, faculties, and so on, making it so mystic and complicated by confused and unmeaning terms, as to render it incompatible with itself and wholly incomprehensible to the pupil. I have shown that the aggregate mind has no power but to receive and be subject to impressions, and if they can divide mind into many parts, giving to each external, internal, and all sorts of powers, they can make a part greater than the whole, a thing settled by science to be impossible. To the faculties they enumerate we might add the faculties of love, of hatred, of crying and laughing, of fiddling and dancing, and of ten thousand other emotions and passions of soul, all of which are mere modes of mind, produced by the nature of objects that excite them. These powers are lying sounds, without an archetype, they are words without meaning, pretending a difference where there is no distinction, and only calculated to confuse and mislead the reader. At every turn of the mind, like that of the kaleidoscope, there is a new form or mode that might have a new name for countless millions of times. The mind, like the wax, is a simple substratum that may be shaped to many forms, and stamped with endless impressions. Sensation alone constitutes that substratum upon which the whole superstructure of mind is founded.

Feeling, alone, gives us a knowledge of all impressions,

15

and of everything that we can, by any possibility, be made acquainted with. Now, from sensation arise pleasure and pain, and next follow desire and aversion, which beget a will to do or not to do. This, simple as it is, constitutes the whole foundation and sum total of the human mind. God has implanted in mankind, universally, a desire for happiness and an aversion to misery. This is steady, uniform and innate—it is in all persons and in all ages, and it is the first law of our nature, and assented to by all. God has so inseparably united virtue and happiness that it becomes our interest to sustain moral rule—our own property, life and liberty depending upon it. From this arises the moral sense, or knowledge of right and wrong, for feeling we do not wish others to inflict pain or suffering upon us, we are equally sure that others would not that we should wrong them. Thus sensation, or feeling, begets the golden rule to "do unto others as we would have them do unto us." Without sensation or feeling we could not be conscious of a single idea, or even of our own existence. Feeling or sensibility, in short, is the distinguishing characteristic and high boast of the soul, as rendering it susceptible of pleasure and pain, and, consequently, the subject of rewards and punishments. It must be granted by every close and unbiased observer that we can not be conscious of a thing without feeling it, nor feel and know a thing without being conscious of that thing. It must be, then, as Mill (author of Mill's Logic) says: "Feeling is the soul, and the substratum and sum total of mind." Again he says, page 13–34: "A feeling and a state of consciousness are equivalent expressions; everything is a feeling of which the mind is conscious; everything which it feels, or in other words, which forms a part of its own sentient existence." For this single sentiment of divine truth which Mill has dared to express in regard to mind he has been greatly censured by the clergy. Locke has suffered the same, and their pious old brother, William Paley, author of Moral Philosophy and Natural Religion, has been shamelessly slandered by them.

This doctrine they call sensationalism and utilitarianism, which they have thrown out of all the schools and substituted their own trashy books, made up of words without meaning and distinctions without a difference. It has ever been a marvel to me how men professing to be the ministers of God could so traitorously desert the plain truth of his laws of nature and substitute their own complicated and arbitrary inventions; nor could I credit it did I not know that they had taken the simple and plain truths of God's word out of his Bible, and appropriated them to their own selfish and party purposes. Pupils coming out of such schools are actually nothing more than parrots and learned pigs, demented by the memory, memory of learned and arbitrary nothings, for I have conversed with and pitied many such graduates, who could only answer my text-book so and so, just as a child will naturally answer: "Daddy says there are witches, and I believe it." Were students to throw away such manufactured trash, and apply their own minds, which they carry with them by day and by night, to nature, and objects and circumstances around them by which they are hourly impressed, they would soon learn how they gain their knowledge, and thus be better informed than any mechanical and routine book-teacher in the world.

Such teachers prefer art to nature, and pertinaciously holding to the allegorical and enigmatical mysticisms of the Bible, gain much pelf and power by deep learning, wonderfully and admirably incomprehensible to the duped and craven masses. This is certainly so (say the Protestant clergy) with the Catholic priesthood, and, I am sorry to say, there are but few exceptions amongst any of the profession. But to the argument. I have aimed to show that we have no innate ideas, but that all are gained through the senses — each idea being stamped by its specific object; vinegar, for instance, makes the impression of sour, and sugar of sweet. Nor is it in the power of the mind, with all its wonderful creative powers (falsely given) to alter the nature of God's decrees, of cause and effect—of *dualistic* and *dynamic* dependencies. Powder, as we have seen, can not explode itself, wood can not burn itself, an alkali has no power to act upon itself; but when an acid is applied an action takes place, and the result is a new creation of a thing that is neither one nor the other. Just so is an idea—a new creation, which is neither the mind which is operated upon, nor the object that operates upon the mind. An idea is begotten by the subjective and objective unity, just as a child is by the union of the father and mother. The mind operates upon nothing, but is operated upon by everything. It has simply, like the mother, a capacity or power (excuse the word) to receive and to conceive. The body does not operate upon medicine, but medicine, like all other things, operates upon the body — tartar pukes and calomel purges. The brain and nerves do not operate upon the rusty nail, but the nail operates upon them to lock the jaw in death. Our sensibilities do not operate upon fire, but fire operates powerfully upon them. In like manner do all things operate upon the sensitive mind, which has no liberty or choice but to feel and receive things as they are.

Sir William Hamilton, the great and admired philosopher of the day, after affirming that the labor of the last two thousand years, by philosophers and divines, had only served to darken and render doubtful the subject of

mind, and, consequently, condemning them all *en masse*,
as idle, arrogant and presumptuous speculators, professes
to take a "plain common sense" view of the subject; but
strange to tell, he is not philosopher enough to be consistent with himself, for he sets out by inventing almost a
new English language, and to make it plain, intersperses
it with all manner of languages, dead and living; and
has an index of an ordinary volume. But a big book
and a learned book it is, full of art, with little simplicity
or common sense. The only instance, I think, in which
he condescends to descend to common sense or common
opinion, is in regard to feeling, in which case he is
assuredly mistaken. He takes the position, that the
mind, the percipient or sentient being (all the same),
has no particular location in the body, but is diffused
throughout it; and that we really feel at our fingers'
ends as it seems we do. My reason for saying he errs in
this, is that we may take off arm by arm, and leg by leg,
and the mind will remain unimpaired. Besides, we have
many instances of surgical record, where, long after
having an extremity taken off with a painful ulcer or
broken bone, that pain was felt by the patient, and
complained of, showing the mind, which felt that pain,
not to have been in the limb severed and cast away.
This is a matter of common sense and of demonstration,
that spoils many a learned and beautiful speculation. I
here make known another reason why the mind can not
belong to every part of the system, as, in that case, each
part of the system would be a portion of the mind; and
as mind, like everything else, is made what it is by its
parts, taking any of those parts from it, as in severing a
limb, leaves it no longer what it was, with all its parts;
otherwise a part may be as great as the whole—a thing
held, by all the rules of science, to be impossible.
Another objection to the learned author's divisibility

of mind, is that all the senses point to the brain, and all the nerves, or telegraphic wires, originate in the brain, or its *medulla oblongata* and spinal cord. In short, the mind has its headquarters in the head, and the senses are its aids and sentinels that convey to it all its information; and those pickets, or messengers, may be cut off, one by one, the telegraphic wires may also be cut or destroyed, leaving the commander wholly without information, and yet that commander may live; for the mind, as I have aimed to show, has an existence independent of the objective world, yet it is dependent upon that world for all its information. The mind may be compared with a violinist, who can make sweet harmony when his instrument is sound and well strung, but when the strings become relaxed, or, one after another, break, the music is defective; but even the instrument itself may be broken, and the violinist live independent of it.

I had intended to hurry on with my own views of mind, and take no particular notice of Sir William's errors (or those of any other author), but as he is the conventional Hercules, and walking dictionary amongst artistic and ostentatious pedagogues; yes, and a living concordance with theologians, I am more inclined to show a few of his defects in science. In treating of perception, he confounds cause and effect, and makes them one and the same. He says, that in perception we receive the reality of objects just as they are—the idea, in other words, is the thing itself. That there is fragrance in a rose, sweetness in sugar, heat in fire, and so on. But little reflection will convince us that this is not so, and why: because the rose might exhale forever without the idea of fragrance, but for the feeling mind that perceives it; and in like manner might the mind remain without the idea of a rose, if no rose had ever existed. They are independent of each other, and have no resemblance to each other; but when the odorific particles exhaled from the rose come in contact with the olfactories of the mind, there is a new creation, an idea, which is neither the rose nor the mind. That there is fragrance in a rose, which can not smell itself, can not be true, nor can the rose go through the nerves to the mind, to be potentially or concretely there. In short, this perception of fragrance is simply an effect, and except cause and effect are one and the same, the idea is neither the rose, nor the exhalations from it. We see what we call a rose, which would have smelt as sweet by any other name, and we feel a certain impression from it, which we call fragrance; but what resemblance that impression bears to the sight of the rose we know not, but feel assured that the particles themselves bear no resemblance either to the rose or to the idea they produce: and farther, that a blind man can smell the odor without seeing or knowing anything of the appearance of a rose. All perceptions are mere sensations or feelings, and I hold that they bear no more resemblance to the objects that beget them, than the knife does to the pain it produces or the wound it inflicts. Prick the hand and there is at once a pain, and an idea of pain, which is not the pin, nor does it bear any resemblance to it; and so it is with all other perceptions. The nail which assails the nerve does not follow the nerve up to the brain, or the jaw which it locks (as I have said elsewhere) in death; nor does the effect or result resemble the nail. Light assails the eye, and sound the ear, as odors do the olfactories, but none of them go through the nerves of sense, or enter the mind in their formal and specific nature. We hear a drum and see it, but the idea can not be as big as the drum, nor can the sound resemble the drum. Fire has no heat in it, but has the quality of producing a sensation of pain, which we call heat, while it acts

upon a sensitive being; but the fire might exist alone
forever, and no such perception, pain, or idea take
place, without a sentient or percipient subject to be
acted upon. So it is seen that the sensation called
heat is not in the fire (except sensations are in the fire),
a thing that has no sensation or feeling of heat. If all
things which produce sensations in the mind, are themselves in the mind, according to Sir William, we must
have big ideas and little ideas, black and white, red
and blue, crooked and straight, round and angular, sour,
sweet, and bitter, soft and hard, etc. I have no thought
that the idea of a horse is larger than that of a man, for
if our ideas or perceptions bear any resemblance or proportion to things perceived, the idea of a state, a whole
continent, or the ocean, would fill the mind, to the exclusion of all other perceptions; and yet the mind can receive
the whole globe, languages, sciences, and millions of other
things. All sensations or perceptions are nothing more
nor less than the result of a subjective and objective
unity, and this result bears no resemblance either to the
subject or the object. In plainer language, our ideas are
neither the mind nor the objects that operate upon the
mind. For instance, muriatic acid is not table salt, nor
is soda table salt; but put them together, and table salt is
the result—a new creation which resembles neither; and
just so it is with our ideas—they are results, or new
creations, through the agencies of mind and the things
that operate upon the mind. In the language of philosophy, by subjectivity and objectivity, the mind being the
subject, and our ideas begotten in the mind are the effect
of objects. It is idle to dispute, as has been done, whether
mind or matter be prior, as we know we can not know
without a mind to know, and as knowledge is simply
what we know, the objects of knowledge must be prior

to knowledge. Mind, thought, and the object of thought, simple as it is, is the sum total of mind and its knowledge.

Another obvious mistake with Sir William in his order of perception, or mode of gaining knowledge, is this: he says, "Knowledge is the first step, feeling the second, desire the third, and will the fourth." Now it is evident to every observing mind that feeling is first, and is at the foundation of all knowledge; for we can not know or be conscious of a thing without feeling it. If knowledge comes first, as he teaches, it must come without knowledge, as we have no right to assert the presence of a thing without feeling or being conscious of it. Had he said the objects of knowledge are prior both to sensation and to knowledge, it would have been granted as the natural order of receiving knowledge by the mind, which must also have an antecedent existence to any and all knowledge. Another great and mischievous error is, that he makes *conscience* the divine dictator and ultimate standard and test of all truth, when we know that *conscience* is a lying witness and false guide, for *conscience* has often told us that *conscience* had deceived us. We are *conscious* we are right, and, by-and-by, we are *conscious* we were wrong. When men fight, each one's *conscience* says, lay on, you are right. The most pious and honest Christians fall out, and go to law, each one's *conscience* prompting him to action. The Catholic is *conscious* that the Protestant is in error, and the Protestant feels assured that the Catholic's *conscience* has deceived him; while the Mahometan knows they are both false to their great Prophet and to the God who sent him. The Hindoo, according to Sir William's standard, is certainly right, when he crushes himself under the wheels of a man-made god, by the irresistible promptings of a *divine conscience*. In short, conscience is a mere creature of education, and belongs to the country or neighborhood where it is raised. To assert absolute veracity, then, to a thing so

fortuitous and mendacious, is an absurdity. He gives
conscience, which he calls a *faculty*, priority and supremacy
over all the other *faculties*, in one place, and soon after
makes it co-ordinate with another batch of *faculties;* then
again the intuitional *faculty* rises far above and reigns
supreme over all the other *faculties.* He has high *faculties*,
low *faculties;* external and internal *faculties;* conservative
and elaborative *faculties;* primary and secondary *faculties;*
passive and active *faculties;* the *faculty* of knowledge and
a subsidiary *faculty*, with other complications too numerous
to enumerate. See his index. What he means by external
faculties bringing in knowledge, I can not tell (for he dis-
cards our brute senses), except it is that the mind sallies
out of itself in quest of knowledge, as many teach. He
also gives the mind a vast number of powers, such as
passive and active powers, etc. I have shown that the
mind has no power, except that of submission to be operated upon; just as lead has the power of being melted,
and wax of receiving impressions or being operated
upon. Passive power is no power, and is a contradiction
in language, calculated only to confuse and mislead the
reader; and should, as Reid says, be "discarded from our
language."

I have thus taken a brief notice of a few of Sir William
Hamilton's obvious errors, and had I space I could point
out many, many more—a waste of time which I should
not have spent had he not, by the dash of his pen, demol-
ished all other authors, human and divine, from the earliest
ages up to his time; leaving his book alone as the only
standard of truth. Yet he himself, in my opinion, is neither impeccable nor immaculate, but subject, like other
authors, to be misled by vanity as well as honest judgment.
In truth, he is entirely too learned ; but, with all his learning, he neglected to study well the inscription by Socrates
on the Delphic Temple—"Know thyself." Gregory the

Great says: "Religion should not be subject to grammar," nor should philosophy, in my opinion, be sacrificed upon the altar of pedantry, or subordinated to the forms of logic and the rules of rhetoric. No, nor should we victimize meaning to words, or modes and manner of expression, as the learned author has evidently done. "There is nothing (says he) too absurd for philosophy, or nothing so incomprehensible, but what has been asserted and believed." Yes, and this fact his own book shows.

And now, to be done with our author, and with his and with my idle speculations, from which no practical good can result, I will again, by repetition, impress a few leading facts upon the reader. I have said that there is nothing in God's universe that can create or operate upon itself, any more than the mirror can create the pictures it reflects, the wax its impressions, the photographic plate its objects, or the paper what is written upon it; and this is the secret which at once solves the whole enigma of mind, long sought for by philosophy, but now found. And why? They have sought for it in books and in the closet, where it dwelleth not, while I, ever regarding the voice of nature as the voice of God, have sought it where it was to be found: and though I now write where there are no paper and man-made books, the book of nature is ever open before me. Now think and think again, and don't forget God's order of *dualism, and of mutual and causal dependencies.* This I know to be original with myself, as here applied, for I have never consulted an author who had the same idea, or could tell why it is impossible for the mind to create its ideas and volitions, or look into itself and know itself. This simple fact, if heretofore known to authors and honestly regarded, would have saved the labor of thousands of volumes upon this mystic and perplexing subject.

Knowing as perfectly as I do the nature of mind, I feel

it my religious duty to say to the pupil, who may wish to
study the science of mind, that the trashy, stupid, stale,
stereotyped, and unprogressive books of the schools, will
be worth nothing to him, save to talk *big nonsense.*   I
have looked into more than one hundred of them, and
know them to be nothing more than copies of ten thousand previous copies of the original labyrinth of mystic
follies and falsehoods, and I do sincerely pity the student
who has to undergo the drilling and drudging of such
endless and perplexing errors.   As my article on volition
will give the whole science of mind, with its practical
results upon society, I shall close this article.

THEOLOGY OPPOSED BOTH TO RELIGION
AND TO SCIENCE.

It is not here to be understood, as it generally is, that
theology is religion, nor that religion is either opposed to
itself or to science, for God has not made two revelations
to conflict with each other.   Theology is not divine revelation, but the controversial hypothesis of vain, selfish, and
uninspired men, who theorize the Bible as though God,
the Lawgiver, could not or would not make his law to be
understood by his children, for whose benefit he made that
law.   He made his children, and made the law, and holds
them eternally bound to the obedience of that law, and,
consequently, would be a cruel tyrant instead of a kind
father if he involved it in mysteries beyond their capacity
to understand.   The tyrant of Rome, who wrote his laws
so fine and invisible, and hoisted them so high upon the

streets that his subjects could not read them, as an excuse to wantonly put them to death, might plead justification, as following the example of God himself.

What is the voice of theology in this great dilemma of God's blunders, as they think, in making a law not to be understood? Theology claims to be appointed of God to fill his defects, and make his law plainer than he himself could or would do; and that one half of his children might live upon the labor of the other! This is the true position of theology; and now what has it done? Theologists have fought with demon fury over the Bible, and have broiled each other alive. They have engendered malice, revenge, and distracted the whole world. Yes, they have thus sowed the seeds of skepticism and immorality, which are so rife in our midst that no man's horse or household is safe, while tyranny and brute force have had the mastery for years past, rendering life and property all unsafe. This is certainly not from what the Bible teaches, but from the desertion of its simple precepts, and the following of idols, uninspired, vain, and ambitious men. The apostle says to the Christian Ephesians, Acts xx, 29, 30: "I know that after my departure, shall grievous wolves enter in amongst you, not sparing the flock; also, of your own selves shall men arise, speaking perverse things to draw away disciples after them." This fact, with the bitter and deplorable dissensions produced in the church of Christ by theology, I shall abundantly show in the following essays. Next, hear what Origen says: "Most of the moral evils of the world arise from the liberty the clergy take in interpreting Scripture to suit their own views, and in adhering to the externals of religion, to the neglect of its practical teachings." Knowing, as I do, that not only the life of a Christian, but even his rapturous death, which wings his soul for eternal joys, is worth more than all the wealth and honor that earth can bestow, I can have no other object in view than that of maintaining the principles of true religion, which, I shall show, has greatly degenerated through the vanity and ambition of the world. That genuine religion, which heals the anguished heart, and bids the drooping soul look up with immortal hope, no longer exists; but church divisions give to every dying man his unhappy doubts and dreads. Christ says: " These things I have spoken unto you, that in me ye might have peace. In the world ye shall have tribulation; but be of good cheer, I have overcome the world." But sad it is to ask, how long did this victory, gained through the loving kindness, long suffering, and death of our blessed Saviour last? And where is the true religion amongst the ten thousand diverse and warring creeds now to be found? It is a most solemn and grievous fact beyond all quibble, that the selfish and vain-glorious ambition of leaders in the church of Christ, have extinguished almost every spark of vital religion, and substituted a puritanical and oppressive code of dogmas and artistic forms in its stead.

Practical religion is the most artless and unmistaken thing in the world. Simply this, a tie between the honest and pious heart and the God who made it that no power on earth or in hell can sever, and that no theological learning can better. And now, in proof of my position, I will make a few quotations to show what theologists say of each other; and first, from Sir William Hamilton, acknowledged to be the greatest writer of the age. In his condemnation of the clergy for their disputes and mystification of the Bible by their "learned ignorance," as he calls it, writes as follows: "Humility thus becomes the cardinal virtue, not only of revelation, but of reason. This scheme of reason proves, moreover, that no difficulty emerges in theology which had not previously emerged in philosophy; that, in fact, if the divine did not transcond what it has pleased the Deity to reveal, and wilfully identify the doctrine of God's Word with some arrogant extreme of human speculation, philosophy would be found the most useful auxiliary of religion. For a word of false, and pestilent, and presumptuous reasoning by which philosophy and religion are now equally discredited, would be at once abolished in the recognition of this rule of prudent nescience, nor could it longer be said of the code of consciousness (the Bible), this is the book where each his dogma seeks, and this the book where each his dogma finds !"

The distinguished Bishop Butler, author of analogy, in speaking of controversial theology, and of mystic and subtle refinings, says :

> " For they a rope of sand could twist,
> Firm as learned Sarbonist."

Having reference to the celebrated theological school at Paris. I quote next from Charron, who, in speaking of divines, in their opposition to reason, says: "Superstition, and most other errors and defects in religion, are owing chiefly to a want of becoming and right apprehension of God. They debase, and bring him down to themselves; they then compare and judge him by themselves; they clothe him with their own infirmities, and then proportion and fit their fancy accordingly. It is men's not being governed by the reason of things, which makes them divide about trifles, and lay the utmost stress on such things as wise men would be ashamed of. It is on the account of these that the different sects place the highest value on themselves, and think they are the peculiar favorites of heaven, while they condemn all others for opinions and practices not more senseless than those themselves look on as essentials ; and were it not in so serious a matter, it would be diverting to see how they

damn one another for placing religion in whimsical
notions, and fantastical rights and ceremonies, without
making the least reflection upon what they themselves
are doing." We will read next what the great Doctor
Scott has said: "While men behold the state of religion
thus miserably broken and divided, and the professors of
it crumbled into so many sects and parties, and each
party spitting fire and damnation at its adversary, so
that if all say true, or, indeed, any two of them in the
five hundred sects which there are in the world, and for
aught I know there may be five thousand, it is five hundred to one but that every one is damned, because every
one damns all but itself, and itself is damned by four
hundred and ninety-nine." Again, the pious Bishop
Taylor speaks thus: "We could not expect but that God
would, some way or other, punish Christians by reason of
their pertinacious disputing of things unnecessary, unde-
terminable, unprofitable; and for their hating and perse-
cuting their brethren, who should be as dear to them as
their own lives, for not consenting to one another's follies and senseless vanities!" The Rev. Isaac Watts, in
his work on the Improvement of the Mind, says: "A man
who dwells all his days amongst books, may have amassed
together a vast heap of notions; but he may be a mere
scholar, which is a contemptible sort of a character in
the world." This sentence speaks volumes in favor of
coming out from the dark and factitious closet of the
mystic recluse, to the glowing light of heaven, and the
unerring revelation and guidance of nature. We will
next hear Doctor Clark, who very justly says: "A teacher
of divinity may be a living concordance, and a walking
index to theological follies, and yet know nothing of religion!" Mosheim, the celebrated sacred historian, says:
"Let no one, for a moment, think that the bishops and
clergy of the present day compare with those of the days

of the fathers, when the gospel was preached in simplicity, and with Christian piety and love."

I have thus made a few quotations from good authority—a volume of which might be given to sustain my position, that speculative sectarian theology has drifted us far from the primitive principles of religion, and is not, therefore, religion itself, as some think. I will now give some unquestionable proofs that theology has been opposed to science. First I will give the trial and condemnation of Galileo:

"I, Galileo, aged seventy years, and on my knees before you, most reverenced Lords and Cardinals, and general Inquisition of the Universal Church, of heretical depravity, having my eyes upon the Holy Gospel, which I do touch with my lips, do swear that I believe, always have believed, and always will believe, every article which the Holy Catholic Apostolic Roman Church holds, and teaches, and preaches; and as I have written a book in which I have maintained that the sun is the center—which false doctrine is repugnant to the Holy Scriptures—I, with sincere heart, do abjure, curse, and detest the said error and heresy, and generally, every other error, and heresy, and sect, contrary to said Holy Scriptures."

Thus we see how a truly great and good man was treated by theology, simply because he regarded nature and nature's God as above all dogmatic theology and the machinations of man. The immutable and eternal laws of nature (established by God himself) discovered by the divine, but persecuted Galileo, have since been pursued by Newton and others, till we can now calculate the movements of the heavenly bodies, and predict eclipses to the second for thousands of years to come. Yes; we have seen the true minister of God on his knees before an ignorant and ungodly priesthood; a scene most horrid

in the sight of Heaven—not surpassed by the burning of
the pious Servetus and John Rogers. But so much, so
far, for theological learning, meriting only the curse of
God, and the eternal horror and wrathful detestation of
all mankind. It may be (as has been said) all such cruelty and murder of reason was under Catholic fanatcism
and priestly craft; but this the history of the reformation
proves to be false, and, knowing what I do, I should feel
just as safe under the hierarchy of Olympus or pontificate
of Rome as under that of Protestant dogmatism, with its
crushing despotisms, isms, scisms, and little antagonisms.

I will give a few historical facts, in farther proof of
the opposition of theology to science. Yes, for I shall
record nothing but facts—undeniable facts. When Harvey first discovered the circulation of the blood, by "poor
human reason," the learned clergy avoided him and vili-
fied him as an infidel, because of their very learned belief
that the pulse was the bounding spirit striving to make
its escape from its tenement of clay. Again, when Roger
Bacon discovered the mode of making gunpowder, the
learned clergy excommunicated him, as having dealings
with the devil, and threw him into prison, where he died.
Some say he was, after ten years of close confinement,
released; but this matters not, as all historians agree that
he was the greatest miracle of his age, particularly in the
science of chemistry, and in mathematical and mechanical knowledge; so much so that the learned clergy wisely
suspected him of magic, and persecuted him so as to make
him regret he had ever studied science—the laws of God.

Every intelligent reader knows that the first book
published on the true system of geology met with the
vehement indignation of theology, which feared it would
contradict the Mosaic account of creation, and thus run
counter to their learned calling. For the same reason
did they oppose astronomy; saying, if the sun did not

stand still three hours, while great stones were thrown down from heaven upon their betters, as Joshua commanded it, much doubt would arise in regard to Jewish history, and, consequently of the truth of the Bible itself. I say their betters, for they did not belie, betray, and murder Christ as did the Jews. All these learned and alarming predictions lacked prescience, for none have come to pass. Learning, in theology, professes to be dark, deep, and difficult of comprehension; for it has gone back, yes, far back through the dark and lengthened vista of time into past eternity, to find upon the tablets of the eternal Godhead, the records to suit its doctrine—that God, having the same power over his children that the potter has over his clay, makes nine hundred and ninety-nine in the thousand ill-shapen, and then damns them eternally because he *himself* has thus made them ill-shapen. This discovery, it is true, may induce many to say they believe in this learned theology, in order to be on the safe side; but for pelf and power it does not compare with the theology of the Pope, who received the keys of heaven, hell, and earth from Peter, of more recent date; and, by-the-by, his passports to heaven, at fair prices, make his members equally safe. The crest of theology has fallen much indeed since science has taught it that the sun, planets, and stars were not little lamps swinging around this only world in all God's creation—made, as it thought, for its special benefit. And more mortifying still to think, yes, to know, that those little lamps have turned out to be thirteen hundred and twenty-three millions of visible globes as large as this earth—but a speck of God's creation. O, theology, theology! vain theology! strive no longer to degrade God's glorious works or oppose his immutable and eternal decrees!

The discovery of the compass and the science of

navigation was pronounced by theology to be the work of evil spirits, and looked upon with inquisitorial vigilance. All readers will recollect the early history of printing; and that the first Bible ever printed was executed at Paris, where the inventor's house was surrounded by theology, to prevent the evil spirits from escaping, but the demon had, by timely hint, eloped. His printing-office, paper, and type were all consumed. This was by theological learning and high officials (of the Universal Church), who were worshiped by the people as gods. When Dr. Jenner made the god-like discovery of inoculation as a preventative to small-pox, he was traduced by theology as an infidel, and persecuted till he lost his standing, and had occasion, like Galileo and Bacon, to be sorry they had not obeyed the dogmas of men instead of the laws of their God. Proof was brought before the courts, by church-members, that horns had been seen growing out of the heads of those who had the brute matter of a cow inserted into them; and, oh, how cruel, that little children, made in the image of God, should be thus turned to brutes! There are sermons yet to be seen of that day, all in proof of this undeniable fact. Even Martin Luther, of whom better things should have been expected, was so blinded by fanaticism, bigotry, and selfish ambition of party, that he had no humility, humanity, nor Christian charity; for here is the expression of his feelings, which governed him alike in all other things. In speaking of witchcraft, which he vehemently denounced as a "diabolical sin," he says: "I would have no mercy on these witches, but I would burn them all." Yes, and history tells us that thousands of poor innocent creatures were annually burned throughout Europe. The last case of slander to God, and cruelty of man to man, from superstition, is on record in the English courts; where a poor, ignorant, and innocent old woman was had up before Lord Mansfield, and undoubted was the fact that she had been seen riding on a broom-stick through the air; but Mansfield mercifully let her off (though the respectability of the witnesses proved the fact), for there was no law to prevent any of them from riding on a broom-stick through air. Learned theology, however, condemned his decision. Did we dare express our sentiments, we would say we hate the Devil for burning people, and yet we worship theology for doing the same. The virtuous Lucretia, and other good Romans, worshiped the base and corrupt Venus; and so in modern times do good, unthinking people aid in putting down the science as well as the true Word of God, and worship the many-headed, paradoxical and vacillating theology, as the true voice of God himself.

I think the reader must see by this, how it is and why it is that two thousand years of teaching in mental science, and eighteen hundred and sixty-nine years of gospel preaching, have only served to make those subjects more doubtful and distracting than ever; for, as Sir William Hamilton justly says : " The past history of mental philosophy and of theology, have, in a great measure, been only of variations and errors." The perpetual oscillations of human opinion, with the palpable contradictions and astounding falsehoods propagated by the various leaders of their distracted parties, are all in proof of a grevious error in the education of man. We need not go back to the Brahminical sages, nor to Oriental pantheism, to Egyptian astrology, heathen mythology or the endless shades of paganism, to show that man has ever been chained to the greatest and most degrading errors; and led as an ox by the despotic opinions of others. There is an individual now in Italy, who, by his dictum, wields the minds of a large portion of the Christian world, with as much ease as a boy whirls his top. Joe Smith, the Mormon imposter, is a lamentable instance of the credulity and stupidity of mankind, in letting go what preachers may call the vulgar realities of life, and getting out of the sphere where God has placed them, and grasping after the mystic and magic power of theology. His craft and wily tricks have already grasped the four quarters of the globe, and creatures of all nations and languages are crossing stormy seas and traversing forests wide and wild to worship at his shrine. Thousands of smaller leaders are rising up, from time to time, to lead captive the craven and credulous in the various isms and dogmatisms of the day; while juggling demagogues and metaphysical fanatics have entered the vortex of mental distraction, and swelled the scene of unhallowed bickerings and revelings without charity. No brotherhood is found on earth; no bonds of union nor ties of friendship to be felt. No one God, one people, one church, is granted—all is left in darkness and in doubt, and each party impiously arrogating to themselves the special gift of heaven. All have agreed to disagree in all things, save only that reason, the great enemy of mystery and of faith in things unseen, is to be condemned by all, as heretical, and dangerous to falsehood and oppression. And well may everything ungodly fear divine reason, which has made tyrants tremble upon their thrones, and human oppression, in all its Gorgon forms, to fly before its voice; nor can the wiles of papal sorcery, or the tricks of the Devil himself, stand before the might and majesty of reason.

After the expenditure of myriads of money and the labor of millions of teachers in the training of mind, the world is not improved, but rendered more ungodly and open in its acts of fraud and cruelty. The bloody sword is still unsheathed, and crime is rife in the land; nation wars against nation, and man with man; the midnight dagger and the burglar's hands are bold in their daring deeds; while frauds, perjuries, and seductions have become the order of the day, from the precincts of divinity to the high functionaries of government; brother cheats brother, and neighbor overreaches neighbor, and openly boasts of his smartness. The greatest murderer of our late civil war has been made the admired hero; while high officials, without number, by the blackest crime of ingratitude known to the records of Heaven, have perjured themselves, robbed their government, and become leaders of society.

The first murder ever committed on earth arose from a quarrel about religion; and I, from long reflection and investigation of the history of man, am satisfied that all the murders and wars of the world, from that day to this, have arisen from false views of religion: and by this opinion did I for years prophesy our late bloody struggle. I saw preachers of theology, North and South, amidst the embroiled elements of human strife, and like "dogs of war," urging to havoc, blood, and devastation; and soon did they find such demons as Butler prone to do their bidding—a beast whom the Devil took into his service to steal spoons and do his kitchen drudgery, after which he sent him to Congress to sow the seeds of further strife from which to reap another rich harvest.

> " Why sleeps the thunder in the skies,
> While wicked men to fortune rise;
> Or why should innocence bewail
> Distress in bleak misfortune's vale?
> Just are the dark decrees of Heaven,
> Since short the date to either given;
> Vice earns but dread and constant shame,
> While endless joys are virtue's claim."

The Northern people being taught a conscience, by

theology that slavery was a crime, and the Southern people, being conscious of an intermeddling with their rights, their divine consciences brought them into deadly conflict. O, theology, why not, when it was so fully in your power, prevent such awful disaster, by the exercise of your profession, of meekness, mildness, and brotherly kindness?

Nor has theology been satisfied with "spitting hell-fire and damnation at its brethren," at the sad sobs of the widow and the piteous cries of the orphan at their hand; but they have since split the church of Christ, and cruci-fied him anew.

It might seem a condescension in an author to notice such creatures as Butler, who glory in infamy, and desire to be thus recorded, like the lepered wretch who openly and exultingly burnt the Temple of Diana in order to immortalize his name in history, having no other talent by which to make himself conspicuous. Could Butler now burn the capital at Washington, he would gain more immortality than all his petty pillagings and brutal oppressions can give him in Satan's black book of damning crimes.

All this will not be denied, when both secular and sacred prints make it known, and when it is daily heralded from the pulpit that crime is alarmingly on the increase.

And now, as Christian brothers, let us, in Scriptural language, reason together, and ascertain how and why is this most grievous state of things. Many years of obser-vation, among the various conditions and nations of man-kind, have proven to me that man is a creature of education, and that his education has actually been vicious instead of virtuous; for what but education prompted the slaugh-ter of seventy thousand men, women, and children, in France, all between the hours of midnight and the dawn, and the bloody and fiery scenes of Smithfield, and that in the sacred name of God? Nor is this one drop to the blood which has been shed in the cruelty of man to man, from the errors of education. And now I say, in brotherly counsel, what I positively know, that all the persecutions and cruelties of man to man, as well as every other crime and offense, both to God and man, arise from superstition, fanaticism, bigotry, and ambition. There is one thing here I wish to impress upon the reader's mind, which he may never have thought of, and that is, that the interpreter has, a hundred to one, more influence upon society than the writer of the book himself has; hence, it follows that the interpreters of the Bible have ever had more influence than God, the Author; for every party subscribes to the creed written by his pastor for him, and blindly follows his leaders; and particularly if they can, by the force of dogmatic theology, battle down all around them. And here I am reminded of the controversies between Campbell and Rice, and Bishop Purcell, and Owen, at Cincinnati, in modern times and at our own doors, where, all the time, Pluto was the busiest old fellow in the crowd, stirring up, not brotherly love, but fiendish enmities, and but for the balance of conservative power, now-a-days, in the hands of skepticism, the scenes of Bartholomew and Smithfield might have been enacted over and over again, for human passion and party prejudice are the same now they ever were.

I moralized upon this scene, and could not see where it was to have any better effect upon society than the meeting of Sayers and Heenan, in their pugilistic combat, so much condemned as a bad example to society. True, one sacrilegiously entered the scratch in the name of God; but we all know that the foulest cloaks have been worn, and the blackest and most damning deeds of earth have been committed, in the sacred name of God; not saying

17

this was an instance, but I name it, as many think everything done in the name of God is religious. Pirates have
acknowledged that they murder and rob in the name of
God, giving to him and his vicegerents a part; and when
a vessel appears in sight, they devoutly go through all the
commands prescribed by theology, as making the cross,
etc., and when successful they return thanks to the Lord
for giving them such rich booty; and now marvel not,
my reader, for this becomes the legitimate result of all
formal religions of the world, as well as that of the
Christian faith. Nothing more clearly shows the deplorable credulity of the human mind, and the power of
theology over it, than does the sale of indulgences; a few
of which items I will give as lessons to show the reader
what his mind is and would have been under the same
theological training:

The price of procuring abortion............ 7 shillings.
For simony.....................................10   Do.
For sacrilege.................................10   Do.
For taking a false oath........ 9   Do.
For robbing...................................12   Do.
For burning a house...........................12   Do.
For defiling a virgin 9   Do.
For lying with a mother or sister.................. 7   Do.
For murdering a layman.................... 7   Do.
For murdering a priest....................The whole fortune.
For keeping a concubine...................10 shillings.
For laying violent hands on a clergyman...........10   Do.

Thus has theology justified the most abhorrent of crimes
for the sake of the Lord. Countless millions have also
been filched from the pockets of the poor, for funeral
services, as well as for passports to heaven and security
against hell; and ungrateful did theology pronounce the
son who would not sell the coat off his back to pay
theology to have his father prayed out of the torments of
purgatory or hell; yes, and thus have we seen theology .
winking at sin and rioting in luxury, while its devotees

famished for bread. O, theology, theology, learned theology, easier would it be for a camel, etc. Part of these vast sums was given to the Lord in erecting gorgeous edifices, and in sustaining an ostentatious church paraphernalia; for it has ever been the idea of theology that God is very vain and fond of appearing before men, while the pride of party and pomp of power demanded a portion of this hellish booty. It ever has been, and yet is the idea, that God will sanction even the blackest of crimes for money to be used in his name. Cast your eyes all over the world, and back, throughout all nations, and you will find that sacrifices have been and are still demanded by, and given to, the gods that are worshiped. Every day of your life you will see thousands of innocent babes writhing in the agonies of death upon the altars of those theological gods, that must be appeased either by blood, or by the smell of cookery. It is sad, yet certain, that no nation on earth has yet ever worshiped the true God, the Great Jehovah of the universe; and had the first sons on earth have known the true God, who wants neither mutton or cabbage, one would not have murdered the other. Theologians have brought divinity down to a low standing, and given to God all their own human passions. When I say theology has done all this, I speak correctly, for everybody knows that every religion has its clergy or leaders, who write the creed and direct modes and manner of worship. Even the savages of North America have their prophets and medicine men, who direct all religious duties. At the close of the Black Hawk war, in the spring of 1833, I took the great prophet of that nation, Black Hawk himself, his two sons, Keokuk, the great Indian orator, and the whole royal family, on board my steamboat, when passing Rock Island, and landed them at the mouth of the Des Moines river, not then a white man in the now great State of Iowa. In conversation with this celebrated chieftain, I found that, though the oracle of his prophet had led him to war with the pledge of turning the balls of their enemy into mud, he had not lost confidence in him. Such is the wonderful devotion of all nations to theology! Each sect gets up its party theological schools to train young men in their particular dogmas, and they deserve just as much credit for their religion and their learning as the railroad cars do in tracking closely after their conductor.

If the theologian, when turned out, is able to meet his antagonist—not the Devil (take notice), but his brother in Christ—and can overcome him by his pugilistic training in the rules of logic and the artful tricks of subtilty and quibble, he at once has calls, not for his Christian demeanor in humility, meekness, brotherly love, and friendship, but for his worldly powers in pleasing party pride and passion. This is as true as that there is a God in heaven, and no honest man will deny it. It matters not how sincere, honest, and pious a preacher may be now-a-days, without the artistic paraphernalia of modern theology, he is at once an old fogy, and won't do; and if his piety places him beyond their power of impeachment, they will starve him out: for the novelty, the pride, and ambition of modern times could not tolerate the preaching and humble appearance of Christ and his apostles themselves. What sort of a figure would a modern preacher cut coming into a fashionable city riding upon an ass, or coming in from the wilderness, as John did, with his loins girded up with camel's hair. Sackcloth and ashes are no longer tolerated; but fine linen and broadcloth best suits finely-cushioned pews, fashionable bonnets, and shoddy members. These are certainly bad examples for morals and society; but not less so than the liberty theologians take in theorizing and allegorizing the Bible, till they have torn it asunder and picked it to pieces, so that no one finds enough of the old thing itself as a guide, but runs after some one of the five hundred who has snatched a piece of it.

I have said that the interpreter of the Bible has a hundred to one more influence upon society than God, the Author, has; and this is undeniable, for everybody knows that the leader of a party interprets Scripture to suit his party doctrines. It works just in this way: An uninspired man, of blind prejudice and full of ambition for party leadership, assumes a dogma to suit his purpose, and the Scripture then must bend to suit his hypothesis. I can defend any kind of wickedness and find Scripture to defend it. Theft, for instance, and ingratitude. God, says the Scripture, told the Jews, secretly, to borrow all the jewels they could get of gold and silver, and pretend they were only going just across the Red sea to worship, and would soon return; but God, as recorded by these rebellious, ungrateful, and slanderous people themselves, led them on with all their plunder, never intending their return. And thus they make God their cat's-paw of falsehood and of fraud. And again: "I saw," says the prophet Micah, "the Lord sitting upon his throne, and all the host of heaven standing on his right hand and on his left, and the Lord said, Who shall entice Ahab, King of Israel, that he may go up and fall at Ramoth Gilead? And one spake, saying, after this manner; and another spake, saying, after that manner. Then there came out a spirit and stood before the Lord, and said, I will entice him. And the Lord said unto him, Wherewith? And he said, I will go out and be a lying spirit in the mouth of all his prophets. And the Lord said, Thou shalt entice him, and thou shalt prevail. Go out and do even so." This may have been some little god of a petty party, but I hold it as a gross slander upon the great God of the universe, who, by a wish (without fraud and corruption), could have annihilated Ahab and his nation.

Thus it will be seen, as I have said, the leader of a religious party, or a sinner, may take any position, or commit any act, and find Scripture to support. The followers of Cortez, Pizarro, and Almagro found Scripture to justify them in butchering the poor natives by thousands and feeding them to their dogs. They acted under the authority of the 149th Psalm of David, which commands God's favorite people (the Catholics, of course) to "go out with the high praises of God in their mouths, and a two-edged sword in their hands, to commit vengeance upon the heathen [any they may fancy to call so], and to bind their nobles in chains and in fetters of iron. This power hath all his saints. Praise ye the Lord." And now, Lord, forgive me in saying, it was wrong, yes, very wrong, in you to give this authority, to have your poor, innocent, and unoffending children most cruelly butchered up by highway robbers, pirates, and murderers. I quote from memory, having no book of reference of any kind by me, but I think it is word for word. I make these quotations to show what I shall, by-and-by, insist upon—that there are passages in the Bible never dictated by God, and wicked things done in his holy name which he never authorized. I quote next from the great and true philosopher, John Locke: "No mission can be looked upon as divine that delivers anything derogatory from the honor of the one only true, invisible God, or inconsistent with natural religion and the rules of morality; because God having discovered to man the unity and majesty of his eternal Godhead, and the truths of natural religion, by the light of reason, he can not be supposed to back the contrary by revelation; for that would be to destroy the evidence and use of reason, without which man can not be able to distinguish divine revelation from diabolical imposture." I think it is Dr. Scott who says: "That had not the Mahometan divines had the knack of allegorizing nonsense, fools and frantic persons would not have been held in such honor and reverence amongst the Mussulmen, only because their revelations and enthusiasm transported them out of the ordinary temper of humanity." Hence, I say, if mankind were governed by the light of reason and the laws of natural revelation, they would not be dupes to mystic mummeries and slaves to the gross impostors who now rule the world.

Why should Dr. South speak thus of the Bible: "It is a mysterious and extraordinary book, which perhaps the more it is studied the less it is understood; as generally finding a man cracked or making himself so." This is not so; for God never uttered a word essential to salvation not to be understood. He might have said with propriety, what he meant, that the more designing and ambitious men tamper with the Bible by false interpretations and misconstructions, the less it is understood. Archbishop Tillotson says, that "It will be hard to determine how many degrees of innocence and good nature, or of coldness and indifference in religion are necessary to overbalance the fury of the blind zeal, since several zealots had been excellent men if their religion had not hindered them; if the doctrines and principles of their church had not spoiled their disposition." A solemn satire this upon blind zeal and human idolatry. I next quote what the celebrated Chillingworth gave as a reason for turning papist: "Because the Protestant cause is now, and hath been from the beginning, maintained with falsifications and calumnies, whereof the prime controversy writers are notoriously and in a high degree guilty." And upon his return to the church, he says: "*Iliacos intra muros peccatur et extra;*" which is, in plain English,

Priests (preachers) of all denominations will lie alike. From this, again, I in part dissent, feeling that he hits his brothers unjustly *en masse;* for they will not all lie, but, being the same erring beings that make politicians, they, like those corruptors of society, too often dissemble for the sake of popularity and party. Dr. Scott says: "Moral goodness is the great stamp and impress that render men current in the esteem of God ; whereas, on the contrary, the common brand by which hypocrites and false pretenders to religion are stigmatized is their being zealous for the forms, and cold and indifferent to the morals of religion. And, in general, we find mere moral principles of such weight that, in our dealings with men, we are seldom satisfied by the fullest assurance given us of their zeal in religion until we hear something farther of their character. If we are told a man is religious, we still ask whether he is honest and of kind temper ; but if we hear at first that he has honest, moral principles, and is a man of moral justice and good temper, we seldom think of asking the other question—whether he is religious and devout." And again : "A man who has, or pretends to have, a blind zeal for those things which discriminate his sect, though he be ever so immoral, too often finds countenance and credit from them; and though thought a devil by others, passes for a saint with his own party, so that the superstitious lie under temptations to be vicious, and the vicious to act hypocritically."

Being wearied with quotations, a volume of which I could give, in proof of the distracted and uncertain condition of religion, we will next look into the cause of this unfortunate condition of the Christian world, and then prescribe a remedy. Did we but know what makes Mahometans honest, and Christian professors rogues, we should at once be able to prescribe a cure ; but in lack of this knowledge, we must resort to palliatives. In this

Christian land, it is your life or your money, while in Turkey life and property are both held sacred; so much so, that all history tells us so, and every traveler is struck with the fact. All goods are left exposed, and, except there are Christians about, their doors are not shut. I saw Capt. Partridge, a well known military teacher of the United States, directly from Turkey, and he told that all he had read of the Turks' honesty was true. This can not be that Mahomet set a better example to honesty than Christ, but that his preachers and teachers better understand the training of the human mind than those of Christ; for, as I shall show, we are creatures of education; and that whole nations may be led into paths of virtue or vice by their rulers or guides. Long and close observation has convinced me that the great fault in our system of training men to honesty, is the loss of confidence in the truth of Christianity, owing, in a great degree, to our controversial divinity (theology); for who can have full confidence in a thing so doubtful as to admit of disputes and divisions amongst those who set themselves up as judges of that thing? Thus the flock is divided, scattered, and bleating about—lost in confusion. Professors now will grant this to be unfortunately so, and yet affirm the Bible to be simple, and certainly true, and admitted by all—a paradox indeed— yes, a self-contradiction; for that which is certain and admitted by all, admits of no discussion, disputes, or doubts by any; as, for instance, the whole is greater than a part, and that two and two make four. Frankly and honestly speaking, we have all lost confidence, more or less, in the Bible, and consequently that humility, meekness, kindness, long-suffering, charity, etc., of the primitive brotherhood is no more; nor have we any martyrs, even to the loss of a dollar these days. Hatred to their brethren, pride of party, and church parapher

18

nalia, will draw a little from love of pride and self; and
he who may wish to be prayed out of purgatory or hell
will put up more freely. The sacrifice of gain in traffic
to truth and honesty is no longer known to a Christian
profession; but money is our god, and worldly pride
and power is the ruling passion of the day.

In addition to the false and contradicting constructions
put upon the simple words of God, by learned theology,
we certainly have many mistranslations, interpolations,
and wilful forgeries in our Bible, calculated to increase
our doubts, and consequent disregard for its commands.
Good old William Paley, author of Moral Philosophy,
says, in his defense of Christianity: "It would be very
unsafe to establish for the Jewish history, what never
was established for any other history—that every word
in it must be true, or every word false; as this would be
to sacrifice Christianity upon the altars of Judaism." He
shows many passages to be evidently false—contrary to
common sense, and derogatory to the character of God
himself. Sir Isaac Newton, in his letters to Bishop
Horsley, affirms the same; and I could fill a volume
with quotations from the most pious writers in the
world, all to the same effect. Let any man of honest
and feeling heart, with the high estimate every Christian
should have of his Creator, but read the Old Testament
for himself, and he will there find things falsely recorded
as by the will of God, that would make a decent man
blush. Yes, and such other things as no honest man
could be guilty of. The two cases herein named, of
lying and stealing jewels from the Egyptians, and of
perfidy and littleness far below the dignity and honor
of man, in sending an angel to betray Ahab and have
him murdered. In other parts it is said, that "Lying
lips are an abomination to the Lord." This every
Christian will recognize as of Divine authority. But

establish the two cases here named, with many others equally atrocious, and who is there but could lie, steal, and murder, and justify it, by Scripture record, as the will of God. Again: God is made to falsify, and was boldly told of it face to face, and made to retract. I will make a short quotation or two more, to set the reader to thinking: "And Jehovah spake with Moses face to face, as a man speaketh unto his friend." Exod. xxxiii: 1, 11. "And Moses returneth to the Lord, and said, Lord, wherefore hast thou so evil entreated this people? Why is it that thou hast sent me? For since I came to Pharaoh to speak in thy name, he hath done evil to this people; neither hast thou delivered thy people at all. And Jehovah said unto Moses: I have seen this people (I do wonder if God did not see it before he thus committed himself), and behold it is a stiff-necked people. Now, therefore let me alone, that my wrath may wax hot against them, that I may consume them. And Moses besought Jehovah his God, and said: Lord why doth thy wrath wax hot—turn from thy fiery wrath, and repent of this evil against thy people. And the Lord repented of the evil which he thought to do unto his people." It seems, however, he did not repent till Moses rebuked him face to face; and in another place, the Lord was reminded of the solemn oath he had taken to support the Jews, which oath he was accused of violating. Here is a passage, pronouncing the above record false: "The strength of Israel will not repent; for he is not a man that he should repent." Many, many passages might be given, where God is mad, mutable, and mean; and others, in contradiction, making him immutable, honorable, and just. But to be done with authority, I refer every worshiper of a true God to the book, that he may read for himself, and he will see where acts of fraud, of cruelty, and of cold-blooded butcheries have been perpetrated in the name of a just and feeling God.

Having given, in as short a space as possible, ample proof of the distracted state of the human family in regard to what constitutes our duty to each other and our serving our God, I next ask who is to be umpire or judge of all these matters, and whether it is not safer for every man to be his own judge, as " every tub must stand upon its own bottom?" But few readers may know the fact that one uninspired and prejudiced man has put it upon all men to believe as he did, or suffer the imputation of heresy. Three hundred and twenty-five years after Christ some two hundred and fifty bishops met at Nice, and there and then, for the first time, collected and assorted the various gospels and epistles, making a book called the New Testament; and the history of this council justifies me in the belief that there were many errors embodied in that book, for they had no more authority than you or I to judge of what was or was not inspiration. Alexander, Bishop of Alexandria, and Arius, who, at the head of their parties, disgracefully quarreled for near two months about what was divine and what spurious, and the result was to throw out about one half (since published under the title of Apocryphal New Testament,) and one volume bears the stamp of divinity as much as the other. They there disputed, however, as leaders of parties are prone to do, till Constantine, Emperor, threatened to disperse them if they did not conduct themselves more orderly. Read what Alexander said of Arius and party: " They were heretics, apostates, blasphemers, enemies of God, full of impudence and iniquity, forerunners of antichrist, imitators of Judas, and men whom it was not lawful to salute or bid God speed." Yes, and what might be expected in retalliation from men of selfish feeling and of vile party religion? The

same gross and disgraceful language was hurled back
with Satanic piety upon Alexander and his monop-
olizing party. Sabinus, Bishop of Heraclea, says of this
council : "They were, with the exception of Constantine
and Eusebius Pamphili, *a set of illiterate simple creatures
that understood nothing.*" And Passias, in his Synodican
to that council, makes known that "they promiscuously
put all the books that were referred to the council for
determination under the communion table, in a church ;
then besought the Lord to aid them in assorting them,
and that the inspired writings might get upon the table
while the spurious ones remained under the table ; and
it happened accordingly." But it is reasonable to suppose that Alexander, having the keys, did the work
himself. Here in this council did Alexander get up
the first creed, a bone of contention thrown in by Satan
himself, over which the clergy have fought with more
malignity than dogs would over a bone of flesh, having
roasted each other alive. These facts must convince
every reader that these men of the Nicene council, who
selected and handed down to us our religion, were men
and nothing but men, honest and well designing no
doubt, yet no better, no worse than ourselves, and no
more right to judge than ourselves.

In further proof of the position I hold, that the Bible has
been greatly corrupted, both by design and by ignorance,
I here give one of Sir Isaac Newton's letters, published
by Bishop Horsley : "If the ancient churches, in de-
bating and deciding the greatest mysteries of religion,
knew nothing of these two texts, I understand not why
we should be so fond of them, now the debates are over.
And while it is the character of an honest man to be
pleased, and of a man of interest to be troubled at the
detection of fraud, and of both to run most into those
passions when the detection is made plainest, I hope

this letter will, to one of your integrity, prove so much the more acceptable, as it makes a farther discovery of frauds with the Bible than you have hitherto met with in commentators." He goes on to speak of many gross and grievous interpolations and corruptions committed both by the Latins and the Greeks, as well as by more modern creed-makers. Mosheim, in his Church History, says of this Nicene council, whose uninspired, blind and prejudiced selections we are bid to hold as emaculate: "The divine maxims of Christ and the teachings of the New Testament were entirely disregarded by the Ecclesiastics who modelled the church under Constantine." And farther: "Let no one confound the bishops of the golden age of the first two centuries, with those who came after them, for piety, sincerity, brotherly love and friendship." He further says that the Hebrews corrupted the sacred records of the New Testament in order to make the teachings of Christ and his apostles as ridiculous and incredible as possible; and that it was the interest and feelings of the early Christians to do the same with their cruel persecutors, the Jews.

Thus I think I have amply proven, by historical facts, that the human mind is governed in all nations and in all ages by the circumstances under which it is placed, and, consequently, not an inborn, infallible and immumutable thing; but a thing of education, and may be made ignorant or wise, and vicious and virtuous, according to circumstances; and all this I have more fully shown under the article of volition. To know the power of education and the degrading influence one man may have over millions of his fellow-mortals is but to cast your eyes into China and the vast east, and there see more than half the human family now on this globe worshiping to the dictation of one theologian, Confucius, who lived five hundred and fifty-one years before the birth of Christ. Then turn your eyes to Persia and behold the millions who are sacrificing their infants and even their own lives to the Magian religion, founded by Zoroaster and Pythagoras, about the same date as above. Next look over into Arabia and behold the Mussulman, the bravest soldiers in the world, willing to rush to the cannon's mouth to defend the faith of their prophet, the great theologian of Persia. Then look at the power of the Pope, who held the whole Christian world under his thumb, and who could dethrone crowned heads and give whole continents away as he might fancy. Yes, and in farther fulfillment of the influence of one man over many, Martin Luther broke those adamantine chains that bound heaven, hell and earth to the triumphant car of the supreme ruler of the Christian world. True, millions had seen Christianity dwindle down as it again has done to a mere cold and formal profession, and were prepared for the reformation, wanting only a leader. The reader may say, true, sir; I have read enough in your little book to see that mankind have, from age to age, vacillated in error, and that they have ever been under the control of a few leaders; but can man, with that taint and tendency to superstition which you have shown him to have in his nature, and the craven credulity you have also given him to submit to imposition and falsehood, ever be brought to the standard of truth? and, in fact, where is that standard, if any there be, which can be acknowledged by all mankind? I answer to this question that the remedy for this evil is in one single sentence, and if preachers and teachers will but recognize and enforce it, the world may be cured of its evils. It is this: but to grant that the God of the universe, the God who made us and sustains us, is the only object worthy of worship; and as virtue, truth, honor and justice are his attributes, they are the best

standard of man's actions, and this is all. The honest
reader may say: very good; but we Christians have always
professed to worship a God, and yet we are dishonest
and vicious, though, I must grant, we have not worshiped a God of truth, of honesty, or of honor, and this
may be that so many follow the example of the god thus
worshiped, and consequently, be as corrupt as he.
And now we come to the great and solemn question of
the government of man, who is said by our teachers,
to have an incurable perversity in his nature (and if
in his nature, of course given by God) that nothing
can cure but the power of God who gave it; which
teachings I pronounce to be false, and hold them to be
slanderous to man and to God, and dangerous to society,
which has greatly suffered by them. If God has given
man power to do anything, it is certainly to be good,
otherwise he is not a good God, no, nor a wise one, for
it would take him all his time in undoing his own works;
as in every good act of man, it must be seen that God
would have to be present to change the man from the
nature he himself had given him. The greatest dullard
in mental science must at once see that this universal
preaching from our pulpits to wait till God shall give us
a clean heart and renew in us a right spirit, is a divine
license to evil; for if God has decreed man to vice, he
has a right to it. Under this conviction of our church
teachings, a horse thief, if met by God in the stable for
the purpose of changing him, might, as an honest man,
boldly face him and say: "You can not accuse me of
a wrong in acting in accordance with the nature you
gave me." Had I room to moralize upon our past teachings I could demonstrate their great evil and show that
we shall never have an honest community while it is
taught we have no power to do good. But I must close
with a few more remarks.

We should, by revision, at once get rid of all the slanders in the Bible against our God, for so long as we worship a false, vicious, and dishonest god, will we be false, vicious, and dishonest. I am bold to say, we should admit nothing derogatory to the character of the one true, and holy God; then, indeed, would we be one people, with one faith, one church, and one God. Some nations, (showing what the human mind can be brought to) have no devil, but two gods; one vicious and vengeful, the other kind and just; that is, a good and a bad god; the bad god receiving almost all the worship, sacrifices, and prayers of the nation, particularly evil doers, because they fear him; and just so with our God, who is represented in the Jewish records, and in modern preaching as a jealous, vengeful, passionate, fickle-minded, lying, stealing, murdering, and unfeeling sort of a god, who determines to destroy his people one day, and regrets his rashness next, as in the case where Moses told him, face to face, "as one man talketh to another," that he had falsified, and failed to come up to his promises; and then it was, and not till then, when afraid of consequences, he backed out, and said he "regretted of the evil he had intended to do unto his people!" Nor does this slander stand alone, for there are many others, only one more of which I will name. The knavish and luxurious priesthood persuaded the people that our Creator was as fond of barbecued meats as we are, and that to send up a "sweet savour to the Lord" would induce him to immediately alter his eternal and immutable decrees, not knowing that this world turned over, so that up one hour was down next; but thought it a flat, fixed speck of earth, and that God lived just a little above us, and would quickly smell the frying of meats. But so it was, the "Lord smelled a sweet savor, and the Lord said in his heart, 'I will not again curse the ground any more for man's sake.'" Thus

were the eternal purposes of Almighty God controlled
simply by the "sweet savor," while the priests got all the
rich flavor, and the well roasted meats. Just hear what
those priests say to the people: "But ye shall offer a
burnt offering, for a sweet savor unto the Lord. Ye shall
offer a burnt offering, a sacrfice made by fire of a sweet
savor unto the Lord; thirteen bullocks, two rams, and
fourteen lambs of the first year!" But now comes out a
rational and divine contradiction of all their culinary
trickery. "I will take no bullock out of thy house, nor
he goats out of thy folds; for every beast of the forest is
mine, and the cattle upon a thousand hills. If I were
hungry, I would not tell thee; for the world is mine, and
the fulness thereof. Will I eat the flesh of bulls, or drink
the blood of goats?" Farther, "Offer unto the Lord,
thanksgiving." Psalm 1: "Thou desirest not sacrifice,
else I would give it; thou delightest not in burnt offerings." "To what is the multitude of your sacrifices unto
me, saith the Lord. I am full of the burnt offerings of
rams, and the fat of fed beasts (such as the priests were
fond of); and I delight not in the blood of bullocks, or of
lambs, or of he-goats." Isaiah, i : 11; "Wherewith shall
I come before Jehovah, and bow myself before the high
God." "Shall I come before him with burnt offerings, with
calves (which are very good when well cooked) of a year
old? Will the Lord be pleased with thousands of rams,
(like the priests,) or with ten thousand rivers of oil?
Shall I give my first born for my transgressions, the fruit
of my body for the sin of my soul? He hath showed
thee, O man, what is good; and what doth Jehovah require
of thee but to do justice, love mercy, and to walk humbly
with thy God." Micah vi : 6-8.

The reader may see by this that we must get rid of the
inconsistencies, and the slanders upon Christ, and upon
the New Testament before we can have full faith in our

book of faith, or an honest community. Why theologists should hold so pertinaciously to the Jewish records I can not conceive, when they know that nation to have been the most rebellious, cold-blooded, cruel, and perfidious people on earth; so much so that they have been cursed of God and scattered abroad. They slandered God; persecuted, betrayed, and murdered Christ; and yet, as good old William Paley says, we by our leaders, are ordered to sacrifice (not only Christ,) but Christianity upon the altars of Judeaism. I say it again, and for the last time in this article, that man is governed by his education, and that the only way of bringing him to truth and honesty, is to give him confidence in a truthful and honest God, through his mighty and marvellous works. "The heavens declare the glory of God, and the firmament showeth forth his handy work; day unto day uttereth speech, and night unto night showeth knowledge!" "Thine, O Lord, is the greatness, and the glory, and the majesty, for all that is in heaven, and in earth is thine." "Lift up your eyes on high, and behold who hath created these things, who bringeth forth the host by numbers; I, the Lord, who made all things." And, again, "We know God (says the apostle) by the things that are made." Thus it is that the Scriptures themselves gives us a knowledge of God, through his works. Doctor Chandler, the great advocate for the Christian religion, says: "Natural religion is the only foundation upon which revelation can be supported, and which must be understood before any man is capable of judging, either of the nature or evidences of Christianity; and I am persuaded it is to the want of a due knowledge of the first principles of all religion, those mistakes about the Christian religion are owing, that have obscured the simplicity of it, and prejudiced many good people from entertaining and believing in it."

These are exactly my sentiments, and from the exalted

opinions I have of the God of nature, I never could have had faith in the Bible doctrines, with its Jewish false-hoods, but for the simple, the beautiful, the kind, and the lovely character of Jesus, whose whole life being without a spot or a blemish, I have been forced, in despite of my doubts, to believe in his divinity, and to love him dearly. And yet, when I read the Old Testament, and there see the detestable cruelties, frauds, and impositions practiced by the Jews, and that most impiously, in the name, and by the authority of a great, kind, and holy God, I at once have an unavoidable doubt of the whole fabric of our faith, and this is why I wish to purge the book of its disgusting filth, and of the gross slanders against the God I worship. The clergy, who have acquired a low estimate of the petty and fickle god of the Jews, as represented by them, must exalt their views of God, by the study (as the pious Doctor Chandler has said,) of his natural reve-lation, before they can ever make an honest community, or a worthy Christian; for God, in disgust, has deserted our country as he did the Jewish nation, and left it in full and unstaid possession of Satan, who is nightly tempting debaucheries, forgeries, perjuries, robberies, and murders, which fill the columns of our daily papers. Yes, as I have before said, and will repeat, God's illustrated book of nature, speaking in the unmistaken language of God himself, is ever open before us with its classifications simple and its nomenclature perfect. As the light of heaven is adapted with kindness to every eye, so is the language of nature to every tongue and capacity on earth. The outer eye requires no arbitrary learning, nor does the inner eye of the mind; it is but to open either and see for ourselves. From the grand and colossal exhibi-tions of nature, we infer boundless power, and infinite wisdom, and from the exquisite designs—adaptation of means to ends, we infer a Designer. Through immensity,

we launch into eternity, and in endless variety we find
perfect unity. Transcendent beauty, order, and harmony
fill all the departments of God's vast domains, while
vitality and thrift spring from every pore in nature.
Search from the depths of old ocean's oozy bed to the
concave heavens which span the whirling globe, and from
the hidden coverts of earth to the starlit skies, and all
is filled with life and activity. The glowing heavens are
replete with light, and the laws that rule the celestial
orbs, while the waters beneath team with organic being.
Plenitude and power is seen everywhere, and the unmistaken presence of the great Jehovah is made manifest to
the most common observer. God's own hand writing is
seen upon the face of nature, leaving no room for subtle
follies or verbal quibbling. Those glittering diadems
that stud the mighty dome of heaven are the crowning
glory of God, and the green earth, with its rolling rivers,
its waving forests, and blooming lawns, are all sweet expositors of their Maker's greatness and goodness. We see
worlds, ten thousand times ten thousand worlds, and on,
and on are worlds, and systems of worlds beyond worlds,
while this globe on which we stand is whirling with lightning speed upon its axis, and shooting forward with a
velocity two hundred times greater than a cannon ball,
on its hidden round through trackless space, spilling not
one drop of water, nor disturbing a tender twig. O God,
Almighty God, thine infinite greatness and tender goodness are unknown to the professed ministers. Poor
specks of creation, who, by aid of the rebellious and
wicked Jews, aim to slander thy greatness and thy goodness in bringing thee down to little, dirty, and dishonest
tricks, that would make the "angels weep to see." We
are fanned by the life-giving zephyrs, soft as angel whispers, freighted with the forest fragrance, more pleasing to
the olfactories of God, the Maker, than the smell of any

kind of cookery, saving that of rams, bulls, and billy-goats. O, poor, ignorant, and vain worms of the dust, and of a day, to suppose God has made all things for their special benefit, when thou knowest not of what he has made.

> " Behold, says man, all things made for my use.
> And man for mine, replied the pampered goose."

And now, having spoken with some severity against controversial theology, in theorizing and allegorizing the Bible, as it has done, to the distraction and almost destruction of religion, I feel it my duty to say that my heart and hand is with practical theology; in other words, with good and pious preachers, and my life fully shows this part. I have clothed and fed our missionaries amongst savages of the far West, which some yet living can testify; and I have contributed as largely as any man in Kentucky, to charity and church purposes. Moreover, I have never traveled with a clergyman that I did not ask the privilege, and take pleasure in paying his bills. As I have elsewhere said, that religion is the plainest and most unmistaken thing in the world. It is simply a tie between a sincere and pious heart, and the God who made it, that no power on earth or in hell can sever, and which no theological learning can better; and I am well assured, from actual observation, that our little, embrowned, poppinjay circuit riders (as pampered theology calls them,) of the far West, at whose hungry coming the chickens instinctively fly, have more true and saving religion than the learned and adored theologists of Europe, whose vast salaries, filched from the pockets of the people by law, enable them to hire their vicars to do the drudgery of preaching, while they stay at home and crack jokes over their inspiring wine; and this, in reality is the only inspiration that great and learned theology generally has.

I think now, in view of the facts in the foregoing essay, that the reader may thank me for opening his eyes to the present condition of the moral and religious world; and with kindly feelings do I here say to my brethren (the clergy,) that when I speak of some, I do not mean all, for well I know that many labor faithfully for the good of souls, while others counteract the success of their pious efforts.

WHAT IS INSTINCT?

INSTINCT I hold to be simply the nature of a thing—be that what it may. The instinct of gold is its inherent properties that make it what it is. The instinct of organic being is its laws of life that make it what it is. It is instinct in a bird to have feathers and fly in the air; while with a beast it is to have hair and to walk on the earth. Every gift of God is an instinct, and the why, the how, and the what, must be left with him—which will save a vast waste of paper, brains, and money.

If asked why it is that chickens and ducks hatched under the same hen will one run into the water and the other from it? I can only answer, It is because of their nature; and the question is with God, why he made them so. There is nothing more thoughtless and silly than these questions about instinct—which is nothing more nor less than the nature of a thing; which nature is the result of its laws, stamped upon it from first creation, that makes it what it is and nothing else, and thus is the question constantly returned upon Deity. There are no two men on earth, though of the same family and name, exactly alike, either in mind or body; nor is this variety by whim of free-will or by accident, but by a fixed and fatal cause—no effects (recollect) without a first cause. If (as free-willers and teachers of casualty affirm) we can do as we please, that pleasure to do, being something, must have been caused by something, and that again by something else; so that, it will be seen, we are led back along the fated chain of causality to Deity himself—the Great First Cause of all things. Thus having given a guide to the study of nature, we will go on to results.

The cruel and silly experiment made by the celebrated Dr. Boerhave to prove that brutes have instincts (a thing by nature self-evident) has figured through all the works on instinct from his day to this. Doubting whether the knowledge of brutes was by instruction from the parent, or from instinct, he opened a goat, and taking out the kid, put it in a room where he had placed milk, corn, hay, and oil; and the kid, after smelling around and refusing all else, at last came to the milk and sucked it. Now, the mother being dead before the birth of its young, could have given it no instruction; therefore congenital instinct is inevitable. A wonderful discovery indeed. Cæsar, who was taken from his dead mother's womb, I presume sucked milk, just as did the kid. It is no great discovery, or secret, that children suck more perfectly at birth than adults do.

All animals, I have observed, are led to their proper food by smell—having watched them for hours—particularly cattle feeding amidst a great variety of herbs, where poisonous and succulent plants grew side-by-side; passing over one and instantly grappling the other, as though instructed by immediate wisdom from above. Now, God himself, as is generally taught, was neither in the mouth nor the nose of the cow to direct its judgment; but he was the author of that law which he interwove into all organic matter. The male of all animals can tell, by their law of nature, when the female is in season to receive them, and dogs can tell, by this wonderful *faculty*, if a proud slut be within miles of them.

Thus we see that all animals are, like ourselves, governed by their nature, and, if we wish to be wise and safe, we must study that nature—God's fixed and fatal law of organism. In short (for this question is not worth a sheet of paper, beyond the detail of curious facts, showing that brutes have quick and sagacious intellects), brutes have their instincts and their nature, and men have their instincts and their nature; brutes can be instructed and so can men be instructed, and the only difference is in degree—men being susceptible of the larger amount of improvement. Crows are as quickly instructed in the danger of a gun as the human; and such is their acuteness of observation that, without a gun, you may approach within a few rods of them, while with a gun, you can not get within gun-shot of them. I once saw a drove of turkeys (in the Rocky Mountains) so fearless of men that we could have killed them with sticks, but, after shooting a few of them, they observed the danger, and took to their wings. Capt. Cook mentions a similar fact. In his voyage round the world, when on uninhabited islands, the foxes ran about their feet, and birds alighted upon their heads and shoulders. It is said of Alexander Selkirk, on the island of San Juan Fernandez:

> " The beasts that roam over the plain,
> My form with indifference see;
> They are so unacquainted with man,
> Their tameness is shocking to me."

Thus it is seen that beasts gain knowledge by observation and experience as do men.

The reader of natural history may recollect the acts

of an elephant, who, when being led down the streets
of Alexandria to water, put his snout through a window
to reach an apple on a bench, and, having been pricked
by a tailor's needle, the beast went on with vengeful
feelings, and, filling his trunk with muddy water, spurted
it all over the tailor when he returned, spoiling a royal
dress which was being made up for the ruling prince.
Educated elephants are instructed to go out and bring
in wild ones over a pit-fall prepared for the purpose of
entrapping them, and, if this educated creature be caught
out after such perfidy, those who may have escaped beat
him to death.   Dogs are trained in France to smuggle
goods across the line, and, seeing as well at night as in
the day, a dog will pass the guards with a thousand
dollars' worth of lace upon his back.   It is well known
by all sportsmen that when there is a gap in a close
hedge or fence, through which rabbits might escape,
part of the dogs will make chase, while others run to
the gap.   Deer, when wounded and hard pushed, always
make for a water-course, and, having sagacity to know
that if they go up stream the scent will float down to the
dogs, they invariably swim down ; but their enemies,
with equal sagacity, divide into two packs, one swim-
ming across the stream, then both packs run down on
either side, soon find whether the track has come out,
and, if they find no trail, they hunt back along the
stream, amongst the rocks and drift—for well they know
that deer will hide and even sink themselves all to the
nose, which they will protrude through the drift just sufficient to breathe ; all of which I have again and again
witnessed.   An old deer will try to elude the hounds by
returning occasionally upon its own track and then bounding off with a great spring at right-angles, thus perplexing
its pursuers till it gets ahead ; but the pack soon learns to
put the best trained dog upon the direct track, while the

others divide and run on either side, and thus unerringly
find the side track. It is known by all huntsmen that
no attention is paid by the pack to the cry of the young
ones; but let an old one open, and they all rally at once
to the spot. Young fawns are so much like young children that I can tell, miles off, when the pack is after them
or an old deer; for, knowing nothing beyond their place
of birth, the dear little creatures will run round and
round about their home, while an old buck, for instance,
will strike square out, and seek the most distant and
difficult passes. I once saw a fox come to a fallen tree,
and, leaping upon the roots, run the whole length to
elude the chase; but no sooner did the dogs miss the
ground track than they divided, running on either side,
and meeting at the top, pursued on.

There is a small wolf in Mexico that has the cunning
and caution of a human; and, when cautioned by my
guide to keep my meat better secured, as these wolves
would steal it even from under my head, I made the trial,
and, it being moonlight and they howling around, I kept
awake and watched the movements of one, who came
nearer and nearer, often standing upon his hind feet
above the high grass and looking around him. When
very close, I raised my arm; whereupon he laid himself
flat upon the ground, and kept motionless till he thought
me fast asleep. Silently then he crawled up and snatched
the meat with a juggler's skill. This incident, though it
occurred many years ago, has oft returned to mind and
caused me to moralize upon the actions of both brute and
human. Audubon was never a closer observer of birds
than I have been of all animals; so much so, indeed, that
I have learned the language of many of them. I can tell
by the voice of birds when they see a serpent as well as
if I were to see it myself. They, with distressing notes,
call all the birds within hearing, and flying round and

round in a circle, get nearer and nearer the snake, while he remains perfectly still, with mouth wide open and glaring eyes, so terrifying to the little birds that they become paralyzed, flutter, and fall into his coil. This I have often seen, and am satisfied that what is called a charm is simply a paralyzing terror.

I can recollect, when a child, of being belated in getting home, and seeing an old, black stump, which in the glimmering darkness grew into most frightful forms, when from it I had no power to run, but walked tremblingly up and put by hand upon it. Sublime and awful scenes of sight produce the same feeling upon the human, so much so, that persons have thrown themselves over destructive heights. Byron relates, that when in the Alps, and leaning with his breast over an awful height, it was with difficulty he could withdraw himself from destruction; and the same thing occurred with the celebrated Chateaubriand at the Falls of Niagara. Horses will, with open doors, stand in a burning stable and be consumed; while the human will do the same on burning boats, as well as in houses. 1 have seen persons at a fire so paralyzed and panic-struck as to be unfitted for thought or action.

From long observation, 1 am well assured there is no such thing as a destructive charm; but all is terror, horror, and affright, destroying all power of resistance.

In recurring to the nature of the mind in the brute, it is well known, from common observation, as well as from natural history, that the female brute has more kind and heavenly affection for her young than the human; and the gander, for instance, when mated (married) will set time about with his goose during incubation, and is never known to notice any goose but his own; while man will cheat his own wife, yes, and cheat the world, if he can. If any man could see as well at night as in the day, and had the exquisite sensibility that the dog has, and could trace the thief to his covert place, he would be looked upon as a God-gifted man ; and yet we degrade this gift of God as brutal. Nor is this all. The dove may be taken from its nest in England, shut up on board a vessel, and taken five thousand miles from home (as they have been), into the far northern seas, and let go, with the date and place of the vessel around their neck, and they will cross the whole continent of America, then three thousand miles over the ocean, to their home in England. And now, though man claims to have a divinity within him, he has nothing to compare with this, which transcends all the powers of science. Think you, then, the mind of the brute is matter, or that they have no mind ?

Helvetius felt quite certain that we only owe our superiority over the orang-outang to the length of life conceded to us, while the gifted Darwin felt equally sure that if the brutes had hands, instead of hoofs, they would be our equals. All idle surmises, and false to the truth. This we know, and it is all we know : The brute can feel, think, and act, in common with man ; and, consequently, if these qualities distinguish mind from matter, brutes have minds in common with man. Yes, and if *conscience* be divine, as is taught, they have a divinity within them ; for they, like children, are quickly taught a consciousness of guilt. Children, if physically able, will take each others toys, but by-and-by they are taught the private right of property. And just so with the brutes ; they may not be conscious of a wrong in their first depredation upon our corn-fields or gardens, but are taught a conscience and a cunning to depredate at night when all is asleep, and be off before day, just like roguish men.

Memory is considered a great *faculty* with *faculty* writers, and the horse is known to have this *faculty* in a higher degree than man ; for they never forget their

home; and if taken to a distance from it, they will unerringly return on a direct line to it, over mountains and
through woods, without compass or guide. And now,
though not poets, they have a prolific imagination; for
oft have I been jostled, and once left for dead, by their
conversion of an old stump or log into Gorgons and
phantasms of the most frightful forms. They also have
a will (*faculty*), and had they language they would
answer to the nature of it more correctly than do
free-will and *faculty* writers. The horse will wilfully
follow the corn to his trough; and when empty, and
green grass in sight, his will will lead him to it. And
now, if asked what caused him to go to the trough, he
would answer correctly, the corn was the cause; and
now why did he leave it for the grass? simply because
the motive for the green, rich grass was stronger that
that for the empty trough ; thus putting Haven, and all
free-will writers to shame.

Having long been a close observer of the conduct of
brutes, I could give many startling facts to show wherein,
for sagacity, they excel the lower grades of our own
race. But having already passed my intended limits, I
shall say but little more upon the subject, and that to
claim some sympathy for our poor, dumb creatures, who
are ever obedient to their Maker, as well as to ourselves;
while we, by our own acknowledgements, have ever been
rebellious against our Maker; and yet most arrogantly
and unblushingly do we claim all the gifts of heaven,
and a right to treat all God's other creatures with
injustice and cruelty.

The Rev. Sidney Smith, in his Moral Philosophy, says:
"There are observable in the brutes faint traces and rudi-
ments of the human faculties." This position, he goes on
to say, has been maintained by Dr. Adam Clarke, Reid,
Locke, Hartley, Stewart, and all others of the best writers

upon this subject, and begins his lecture on instinct thus: "I confess I treat on this subject with some degree of apprehension and reluctance, because I shall be very sorry to do injustice to the poor brutes, who have no professors to avenge their cause, by lecturing upon our faculties; and, at the same time, I know there is a very strong anthropical party, who view all eulogiums on the brute creation with a very considerable degree of suspicion, and look upon every compliment which is paid to the ape as high treason to the dignity of man."

Tupper, in his Proverbial Philosophy, says: "What hath the faithful dog less than reason, or the brute man more than instinct?"

Again, Tupper says:

"The dog may have a spirit as well as his brutal master,
A spirit to live in happiness, for why should he be robbed of his existence?
Hath he not a consciousness of evil, a glimmer of moral sense?
Love and hatred, courage and fear, and a visible shame and pride?
There may be a future rest for the patient victims of cruelty,
And a season allotted for their bliss, to compensate for unjust suffering."

Once more:

"What, man! are there not enough of hunger, and disease, and fatigue;
And yet must thy goad or thy thong add another sorrow to existence?
What! art thou not content—thy sin hath dragged down suffering and death
On the poor dumb servants of thy comfort, and yet must thou rack them
         with thy spite!"
"The verdict of all things is unanimous, finding their master cruel,
The dog, thy humble friend, thy trusting, honest friend,
And all things that minister alike to thy life, and thy comfort, and thy
         pride,
Testify with one sad voice that man is a cruel master.
The dog can not plead his own right, nor render a reason for exemption,
Nor give a soft answer unto wrath to turn aside the undeserved lash.
"The galled ox can not complain, nor supplicate a moment's respite.
The spent horse hideth his distress till he panteth out his spirit at the goal.
"Alas, in the winter of life, when worn by constant toil,
If ingratitude forget his services, he can not bring them to remembrance.
"Behold, he is faint with hunger—the big tear standeth in his eye.
"His skin is sore with stripes, and he tottereth beneath his burden.
"His limbs are stiff with age, his sinews have lost their vigor,

And pain is stamped upon his face, while he wrestleth unequally with his toil.

" Yet, once more—mutely and meekly endureth he the crushing blow.

" That struggle hath cracked his heart-strings, and the generous brute is dead.

" Liveth there no advocate for him, no judge to avenge his wrongs ?

" No voice that shall be heard in his defense, no sentence be passed on his oppressor ?

" Yea, the sad age of the tortured pleadeth piteously for him,

" Yea, all the justice in heaven is roused in indignation at his woes.

" Yea, all the pity upon earth shall call down a curse upon the cruel.

" The burning malice of the wicked is their own exceeding punishment.

" The angel of mercy stoppeth not to comfort, but passeth by on the other side,

" And hath no tear to shed when a cruel man is damned."

From one among the many celebrated poets who have borne witness to the dog's attachment to man, we quote the following bitter, but beautiful reflections:

" When some proud son of man returns to earth,
Unknown to glory, but upheld by birth,
The sculptor's art exhausts the pomp of woe,
And storied urns record who rests below :
When all is done, upon the tomb is seen,
Not what he was—but what he should have been.
But the poor dog, in life the firmest friend—
The first to welcome, foremost to defend—
Whose honest heart is all his master's own—
Who labors, fights, lives, breathes for him alone ;
Unhonored falls, unnoticed all his worth—
Denied in heaven the soul he held on earth.
While man, vain insect, hopes to be forgiven,
And claims himself a sole exclusive heaven.
O, man ! thou feeble tenant of an hour,
Debased by slavery or corrupt by power,
Who knows thee well must quit thee with disgust—
Degraded mass of animated dust.
Thy love is lust—thy friendship all a cheat—
Thy smiles hypocrisy—thy words deceit ;
By nature vile—ennobled but by name,
Each kindred brute might bid thee blush for shame.
Ye who perchance behold this simple urn,
Pass on—it honors none you wish to mourn—
To mark a 'friend's remains these stones arise—
I never knew but one, and here he lies !"

[BYRON's Epitaph on his Newfoundland Dog.

WHAT IS FATE?

This is a question that has exhausted human thought and ingenuity for ages past, and all is left in darkness and in doubt. Men, like Milton's fallen angels (as before related). have "reasoned high of providence, foreknowledge, will, and fate; fixed fate, free-will, foreknowledge absolute, and found no end, in wandering mazes lost." And why? Simply because they have attempted to reconcile free-will and fate—a thing impossible. Foreknowledge, decree, election, and fate, all mean the same thing, and are terms used to express the will of Deity. No one who professes to be of the elect, can deny the veracity of the doctrine of fate, for if, as he thinks, God has foreordained him to a particular end; he, the creature, *under the decree of his Creator*, can not evade that end. To assert freedom, then, in one who is elected (fated,) is too absurd for anything but derision, as the incompatibility is too gross and glaring for reconciliation. We should not evade God's truth and craven to vulgar prejudice as did Galileo in astronomy, and Edwards, Hamilton, Haven, and others, in mental science; but stand firm in his immutable and eternal laws. If God foresees what a thing will do, and makes that thing, he most assuredly made that thing to do what it is does do, or otherwise he makes things in vain. To say that his works operate differently from what he made them to do, is to declare him a short-sighted botch, and without power to remedy his own defects. Foreknowledge, then, and decree can not escape necessitation, and every effort to separate them will only involve us in absurdity, for God can not be

20

robbed of his supreme government over his own works, and in carrying out every wish he may have. God, himself, is under a law of necessity (as before shown,) and his wisdom and power certainly forbid the idea of his allowing anything to exist contrary to his wish. Our births and deaths are fated, and every step we take between birth and death is fated. And now, where I have spoken of the influence of education and training over the conduct of men, I have meant (whether there explained or not,) that the very law of education itself is a fated law. For instance, it is fatally certain that we can not even learn our mother tongue or the alphabet without instruction ; and when learned, it is fatally certain that we can not help but know them.

WHAT IS REASON?

Upham, in his "Philosophy of Mind" (page 190), under the head of Reason, says: "That without original suggestion we could not have any knowledge of our own existence, and without consciousness we should have no idea of our mental operations, and without judgment," which he says is also a distinct source of knowledge, "there would be no reasoning; and unassisted by reasoning we could have no knowledge of relations." "Reasoning, therefore," he says, "is to be regarded as a new and distinct fountain of thought, which, as compared with other sources of knowledge, just mentioned, opens itself still farther into the recesses of internal intellect ;" as though we had two intellects— one external and the other internal. "Reason," he says, "is a distinct source of knowledge, that enables the internal mind with a new and valuable form of ideas, and that it brings to light hidden truths, that no other faculty could do."

I have quoted Upham as a popular work, and one that pretty fairly embodies that chaotic mass of nonsense to be found in the text books that our schools generally teach. All, in common with Upham, assign to the mind a number of faculties and powers, which they say can create, call up, handle, and turn about, or set aside, ideas at pleasure. It is true, but hard, yes truly hard, that our youths, intended for future usefulness, should be compelled to memorize and answer, as the learned pig, to all this abominable and wholly unmeaning jargon of external and internal minds, and of intellectual faculties and powers, that have no archetypes in nature.

The pupil is perplexed and confounded by these external and internal intellects, and mental states of mind (as though they were not the same), external and internal knowledge, original, secondary, and subordinate faculties, active and complex powers, with the classifications, divisions, and sub-divisions, and abstractions, making, as the reader can see, by looking into those books, an ordinary volume of index, taking up, most unfortunately, as much space as the entire science of the human mind should occupy. These fountains of knowledge, and their almost innumerable departments, powers, and faculties within our little heads, are greatly more extensive than the "Mammoth Cave." Indeed, these fancied divisions of minds have been carried to such a ridiculous extent, that a great preacher and divine teacher, Dr. Alexander, Professor of Theology at Princeton, has affirmed, in his book of Moral Science, that "the corrupt principles of a man do not vitiate the essence of the soul," which must mean that each of those independent faculties or powers acts for itself, and contrary to the desire of the soul ; and again, "that the mind is not responsible for the acts of the will, which is an independent faculty." This doctrine of the great professor, though glaringly false and mischievous, is but the legitimate consequence of the numerous divisions of an indivisible thing, and the many independent faculties, not to be found in the mind, but taught in all the works on moral and metaphysical philosophy. When such mendacious doctrines, then, can be maintained by such minds, and enforced by their divine mission and official authority, what can we expect better from the tyro in science, or a community indoctrinated in such institutions.

As I have before affirmed, the mind is a unit, indivisible and unextended, occupying some portion of the solid brain, needing no great cavities or numerous spaces for the location of those many powers and faculties. The doctrine then taught of its many parts and distinct divisions, is at variance with facts and ridiculous in its tendencies. Those who believe in the spirituality and identity of the soul, can not consistently teach its material divisibility and inidentity. It is granted by all sound thinkers that no two objects or actions can occupy the same space at the same time; and how is it possible then for the mind, occupying but one space, to occupy or entertain within the same space all the faculties, powers, and distinct agencies so ludicrously allotted to it by metaphysical writers.

Reason, or reasoning, is simply one of our mental modes of exercise, and nothing separate from the mind or its other modes of action, except so far as the objects presented to the mind turns the mind to their own nature. For instance, if a black and a white object be presented to the mind, the mind at once sees and knows one to be black and the other to be white, and no comparison or exercise of mind is necessary. Again, the affirmation that the whole is greater than any of its parts, carries a conviction to the mind without puzzle or exertion. But suppose I announce that you must die, you may answer, I never have died, and why then say I shall die? A reason is now demanded, and a succession of facts to prove the future by the past becomes necessary to a judgment; all of which is simply an addition of facts to facts, and no separate faculty from the indivisible mind. And again, if the mind looks at the midday sun, no reasoning can make it more convincing than the unavoidable perception that the sun is shining; but when said it will cease to shine by night, an additional thought becomes involved. We want a metaphysical nomenclature, as well as a chemical, which would greatly abate the nuisance of endless quibbling about words. If we were to substitute experience for reason, the word would explain itself, as it is impossible to reason without past experience or instruction. A child can not reason, and would as soon take hold of a coal of fire as a rose; but if asked, after once taking hold, why not do it again, it could quickly give a reason; and now this, as short and simple as it is, is the law of mind in every case in life. We little think how we gain our knowledge, and the books upon this subject generally complicate and render everything doubtful.

In short, anything that supports or justifies a determination is a reason for that determination. The testimony of any case gives a reason to judges and juries for their decisions. The original meaning is simply an utterance or talk about something, it matters not what, that gives the ground or cause for an opinion, and consequent decision. It being a waste of time to prate about the etymology of the word reason, I here give the reader what the great metaphysician, Locke,

says in favor of its practical use, which everybody under-
stands: "No mission can be looked on to be divine, that
delivers anything derogatory from the honor of the one
only true and visible God, or inconsistent with natural
religion and the rules of morality; because God having
discovered to man the unity and majesty of his eternal
Godhead, and the truths of natural religion and morality
by the light of reason, he can not be supposed to back the
contrary by revelation, for that would be to destroy the
evidence and use of reason, without which men can not
be able to distinguish divine revelation from diabolical
imposture."

I next quote what the Rev. Sidney Smith says in
regard to the use of reason, under the head of Reason
and Judgment, in his book on Moral Philosophy: "We
connect together two ideas in early life, which we find it
impossible to separate in advanced age; we reason from
them as from intuitive truths, and upon such topics
are utterly impregnable to every attempt at conviction.
These are the principal obstacles to the progress of the
reasoning faculty; and they are disorders of the mind
so common and so detrimental, that I shall speak of them
more at large in my next and concluding lecture. When
they happen not to exist, or when they have been guarded
against by a good understanding or a superior education,
the conclusions we draw upon most subjects are sound
and just; for if a subject be discussed coolly, if the
parties have no other interest in its termination but
that of truth, if they thoroughly understand the terms
they employ, if they are well informed upon the related
facts, and if they are, both, in the habit of guarding
against accidental associations, the conclusions in which
they terminate will probably be the same. There is
hardly any difference of opinion not resolvable into one
or the other of these causes. Here, then, we have an

outline of that manly and high-prized reason, which,
under the blessing and direction of God, arranges the
affairs of this world; which cools passion, unravels
sophisms, enlightens ignorance, and detects mistake;
which wit can not disconcert, nor eloquence bear down;
which appeals always to realities, and ever follows truth
without insolence and without fear. For it is disgraceful
to the immortal understanding of man to be governed by
sounds and to be the slave of that speech which was
given to him for service. It is beneath the loftiness of
his faculties to take his notions of truth from the little
hamlet in which he was bred, or from the fashions of
thought which prevail in his hour of life; for truth
dwells not on the Danube, or the Seine, or the Thames;
she is not this thing to-day, and to-morrow another; but
she is of all places and all times the same, in every
change and in every chance—as firm as the pillars of
the earth, and as beautiful as its fabric. Add to the
power of discovering truth the desire of using it for the
promotion of human happiness, and you have the great
end and object of our existence. This is the immaculate
model of excellence that every human being should fix
in the chambers of his heart; which he should place
before his mind's eye from the rising to the setting of
the sun, to strengthen his understanding that he may
direct his benevolence, and to exhibit to the world the
most beautiful spectacle the world can behold, of consummate virtue guided by consummate talents. 'For some
men,' says Lord Bacon, 'think that the gratification of
curiosity is the end of knowledge; some, the love of
fame; some, the pleasure of dispute; some, the necessity
of supporting themselves by their knowledge; but the
real use of all knowledge is this, that we should dedicate
that reason which was given us by God to the use and
advantage of man.'" Divine truth, and eloquently said.

The first lesson given a child should be to discriminate between things natural and necessary in nature, and the fortuitous dogmas of man. They should study well the laws of nature which controls the succession of events, both in the physical and moral worlds, that we may anticipate the future from the past, and thus be able to meet the emergencies of life. Medical doctors are like divine doctors—ever prone to magnify inessentials in medicine from mere casual results, that the after experience of impartial observers explode. Strange, that this kind of association should have so far blinded the great M. Boyle, who has given the following grave prescription for dysentery. I copy it verbatim from his works: " Take the thigh-bone of an hanged man, calcine it to a whiteness, and having prepared the patient with an antimonial medicine, give him one dram of this white powder for one dose, in some good cordial, whether conserve or liquor." Some one doubtless took this prescription and got well; and from this accidental recovery of the patient was inferred a necessary and efficient connection. This case reminds me of what is recorded of a doctor with slender science, who commenced the practice of medicine with a single nostrum. His first patient was a Dutchman, who got well, and his second patient a Frenchman, who died; from which casual results he recorded, in his book of experience, the following facts: " Be careful to recollect that what will cure a Dutchman will kill a Frenchman." The dying of the privet, the flight of crows, signs in the heaven, and many other coincidences with war, have been taken as causes of war simply because of their association. In this casual connection, augury, astrology, and all the forms of prognostication and superstition have had their rise. Advantage has been taken by the designing of this trait in the human character, and they have, by grafting these superstitious ideas upon weak minds, reaped a bountiful harvest, and given to the capricious masses a fanatical devotion to the most absurd and corrupt institutions in religion. And right here is the danger from our versatile and erratic nature of total scepticism; for, seeing the deception and depravity of religious supremacy, minds equally weak are prone to revolt from all authority, human and divine. If we were instructed from early life in the immutable and eternal laws of nature, upon which alone human harmony and happiness depend, instead of riddles, enigmas, and inexplicable mysteries of controversial theology, we would not be found at this late period of the world degraded by a vasalage in superstition and human authority.

Just as rational are the devotees of the legend of the Talmud and Alkoran—yes, and to the more recent tricks of Brigham Young, as our deluded devotees to the distracted dogmas of our day. Such craven credulity is beneath the dignity of an immortal soul, and nothing can redeem us from the venal and debasing grasp of human authority, but the sublime truths taught in the book of nature, which elevates the soul and kindly unites the heart of man to man and to the Author of his being. Let us then return to her simple and easy lessons in the laws of mind; guided by the reason our Maker has so kindly given to seek him.

Our metaphysical books, as I often repeat, are full of technicalities that in reality have no meaning, and, consequently, only encumber the subject and distract the pupil, who is always looking for their application, and not finding it despairs of understanding the subject which, without such language, would be perfectly simple and easy. But thus it is that those petty pedagogues, by the dexterous use of senseless sounds, and harmonious nothings, get the name of wise-acres, and fatten upon the credulity of their demented and enslaved fellow-mortals. Yet these books being established in our schools from long authority, have unfortunately mislead the pupil by inducing him to believe that such divisions in terms, as powers, faculties, etc., must mean and represent some real difference and division of the mind itself. There is proof ample of all that can be asked for mind without resorting to such impotent and unmanly subterfuge.

A man's belief is nothing aside from his thoughts, for, as before stated, we believe, we think, we imagine, we presume, feel, and are conscious, and know, that it is mid-day and not midnight. These are mere solecisms or repetitions of sounds, to express a simple feeling of soul. The light, flashing upon the mind, at once makes its un-avoidable impression, as the seal upon the wax, the picture upon the daguerreotype plate, the writing upon paper, or the object thrown by light upon the face of the mirror. There is a oneness of mind, and a oneness of action, and the multiplicity of words are but contraventions of the fact. Reasoning is said to be very complicated and complex, the drawing conclusions from the comparison of two or more ideas, as though many ideas or actions of the mind could exist in the same space at the same time; when the "*sensorium commune*" can act but one act at a time, how can we, with the existing state of mind, compare two other states of mind that do not exist? This would be the same as a thing acting when it is not and where it is not. Comparing must be an act of that which thinks or compares, so that to compare two or more ideas would be to admit that an action of compar-ing, and two or more ideas compared must occupy the same space at the same time, a thing known by philo-sophic writers to be impossible, having lain it down as an axiom that no two things can occupy the same space at one time. It is impossible that the same mind can be in two or more different states at the same time. Comparing is thinking; so if we compare two other thoughts, three thoughts must exist in the same mind at the same time. There is no such thing, therefore, as complex thoughts so elaborately treated of by authors, each thought being perfectly simple, but succeeding each other in such rapid succession as that they all seem to be present at the same time. If we whirl a fire-brand rapidly around in the dark, it bears the appearance of one continuous, unbroken and luminous ring, when in reality the fire-brand is not in but one place at a time, one impression not dying till another is presented, thus forming a continuous unbroken chain, though each link of that chain is different in time, in space, and in nature, when moving. Nor is there such a thing as simultaneity in the chain of causality, but all is succession. We may imagine an endless chain so united and dependent, that when the first link is moved, every link is in motion, yet it will readily be seen, that though the whole chain moves through space, no two links occupy the same space at the same time. It is common to speak of "synchronical," actions in physiological phenomena, but there is no such thing in the same organ. There are "peristaltic" or "vermicular" motions in rapid succession, and there is the intimate connection or tie of cause and effect, yet the cause must precede the effect in nature, as well as in time and space. It is common also to speak of simultaneous and synchronous actions of the mind, but there is certainly no such thing. All are successive modes of action, in quick succession, like the turning of the kaleidoscope. Nor is there any more mystery in this than that one body, as a ball in motion, should put a large number in successive motion. One idea will often stir up a whole concatenation of ideas. How this is done seems to be an ultimate fact, for which I have no satisfactory explanation.

This I know, however, that these associations are not stored away in cells, nor shut up in caves like the winds by Æolus, to be let out at pleasure, as some authors have taught, who speak of large stores of ideas, and shelves upon which select ideas can be placed for ready purposes, as merchants store away their goods. Speak one word, and it often happens, that ruminating thoughts crowd upon us for hours, simply by suggestion or association, pretty much in the order and connection in which they have been received.

> " Lulled in the countless chambers of the brain
> Our thoughts are linked by many a hidden chain ;
> Awake but one, and lo, what myriads rise,
> Each stamps its image as the other flies."

It is just as difficult to account for how it is that intermittent fevers and other diseases lie dormant in the system, and are stirred up by trifling causes, of which we are not conscious, or how small-pox or vaccination should remain unknown and unfelt for life, to the exclusion of certain other diseases. There is another fact in the animal economy but little noticed, and which bears a close analogy to the phenomena of mind, that no systemic or generic diseases can exist in the same system at the same time, one counteracting the other, which will lie dormant till the first subsides, and then rise up and run its course. To the just opprobrium of medical science, and to the neglect of mental alienation and suffering humanity, the dependent relation of mind and body has been almost wholly neglected. A close attention to our nervous influences would mitigate many a sorrow and prolong the period of life. It is often asked, if the mind is not entirely separate from and independent of the body, how do we remember for many years, when the body has undergone so many changes? to which I am sorry to reply, that small-pox, as I have just said, vaccination, and many other influences remain for life in the body, every particle of which, we suppose, has been lost in the constant renewal of the body.

I have said there are no such things as complex ideas, every idea being in itself plain and distinct. Color and extension, as I before observed, have no necessary connection, and may be separated, yet we invariably receive them as one simple idea. Each part of every letter in the alphabet, when we first begin to learn, is closely scrutinized. The single letter A having many parts which are examined by the young beginner to distinguish it from B; but, by-and-by, A with all its parts, first separate and distinct, now coalesce and become one simple idea. Time brings not only entire letters but whole words and sentences as equally simple as a single side of A. The word man, for instance, is perfectly simple and expressive, without going back and, by analysis, making a whole volume of metaphysical learning in giving every part of every letter in M–A–N, and then that he is a biped with many thousand peculiarities and relations of mind and body in the great scale of organisms. If we look at a table with two legs, it is simple, and one with four legs, though more complicated, is equally so, as an idea being neither black, blue, red, nor green, nor are they solid, extended, rough, smooth, angular, or circular, but a mere simple feeling.

The doctrine of an internal and unerring monitor superior to reason, is the mere offspring of a chimerical and frenzied fanaticism, and as the ghosts and phantoms of midnight vanish before the rising sun, must these morbid musings vanish before the light of reason. Those supposed intuitional promptings are but vain and hopeless delusions, which, if indulged in, would plunge us into the vortex of wild distraction and bitter contentions, from which would again arise the old scenes of horrid inhumanity. Where, I ask, in the name of *sacred reason*, is this divine and intuitive monitor when one Christian drags the other to the stake? Are they not both prompted by the same unerring guide to the most unhallowed and malignant deeds? How wide from the truth, then, must be such doctrines, when God himself is a unit and made of love; and were his professed followers possessed of the same spirit they would most assuredly be united in the bonds of divine unity and brotherly friendship. This doctrine I strongly suspect as being from Satan, as it is this, and this alone, that has produced all the church divisions and fiendish feuds that we see prevailing every-where, and that has destroyed millions of the best men on earth. Satan, on this account, has ever been opposed to reason, for well he knows that earthly thrones have trem-bled, and that demon oppression, with all its Gorgon forms, has fled before the voice of reason; nor can the tricks of papal sorcery or the wiles of the Devil himself stand against the *might and majesty* of reason. Reason, in short, is the voice of God, and the best boon of Heaven to man. Shall we, then, discard reason as the mystic divines have done, and rest the salvation of souls and the happiness of man upon a mere creature of education? This adored conscience is as beguiling to the indolent mind as the *ignis fatuus* or the glaring meteor that thwarts the vault of heaven and dies upon the welkin's bound—fair to be looked at, but false to follow; an evanescent, ephemeral creature, governed by time and place, and resting wholly upon the veering conventionalities of man.

Thus we see the danger of being carried away by such allurements—those mere feelings and emotions of soul. They are dangerously attractive to the superstitious and fanatical, and are the exclusive generators of witches, wizards, and all the fearful monsters that alarm children and fools. We must not forget that God has endowed us with reason as well as imagination, and that these lofty emotions, though pleasing to the aspiring soul, will not bear us out in the vicissitudes and struggles of life. A mystic lethargy among mental philosophers, who found it easy to fall in the wake of the superstitious masses, and a sordid pusillanimity among the priesthood, who catered to the same feeling, led both religion and philosophy wildly astray for many ages.

After more than two thousand years of bewildered struggle in mental science, a great and leading light appeared in the person of Francis Bacon, who dragged those scholastic mystics from the dark closets and exposed them to the light of day. He showed by unanswerable arguments that reason was given by God as our only guide to truth, and that whenever we deserted poor *human reason* for a supposed *divine* monitor within, science would sink to insignificance, and our guide would prove a delusion and a mockery of all our hopes. Under Bacon's rule of Rationalism there arose a Locke, who rid the world of innate ideas and of *divine monitors*, and subjected all things to the test of reason. And, secondly, a Newton came forward, who, by the aid of reason, not only looked through the departments of this world, but ascended high amidst the celestial spheres, among other worlds and systems of worlds. But soon, however, philosophy fell back into the dark realms of superstition, and gave way to the mere feelings and delusive suggestions of soul. Amidst this distracted state of things, there appeared a Bishop Berkeley, who was so transcendental in his impulses that he boldly denied the existence of a material and external world. He contended that everything was ideal, that wo had nothing in the mind but ideas, and as these ideas were not matter, we had no proof of the existence of matter; and thus was established Berkeley's system of IDEALISM.

Next upon the stage came David Hume, who, with the greatest mind of the age, saw that the mystic and idealistic doctrine involved a gross absurdity, and that it struck at the foundations of all human knowledge. So he at once exposed it to ridicule and contempt, by plainly showing to the world that Berkeley, by his own principles, had destroyed both mind and matter, leaving us without either soul or body. From this scene of doubt and confusion arose Hume's system of scepticism, and next came Pantheism and a renewed mysticism, and, lastly of all, we have the school of Eclecticism (at the head of which is Cousin, of France), which in reality is nothing more nor less than a system made up of errors, but the least of errors of all the other schools.

I might emblazon my pages with the most glowing lights that ever shone upon earth, and yet could truthfully say, that after all those mighty minds have been exhausted in the cause of human improvement and knowledge, that the world is left in darkness and in doubt. The schools of the present age, particularly in Germany, are psychologized. They are asleep and subject to all the vagaries of their morbid imaginations. They yield to the fervid impulses and to the longings of their hearts, and hence the hallowed charm that encircles the soul, and buoys it up in its fond and ecstatic delusions and its Elysian reveries.

To convince the reader that I have not misrepresented the distracted condition of Mental Philosophy, I will here introduce a quotation from "Appleton's Cyclopædia of Biography: American edition; by Rev. Francis Hawks, D.D., L.L.D., of New York." From the notice of Hume which occurs in that work, I make the following extract:

"The place and functions of the metaphysical speculations of this great thinker (Hume), are not only peculiar, but unique in the history of Modern Philosophy. At the

period in question, Mental Science had fallen into the
lowest possible state, not only in Britain, but over Europe
—that, viz: of a conscious inconsistency; principles were
accepted and conclusions evaded; beliefs timidly relied
on, betwixt which and all grounds of certainty then
acknowledged, lay an impassible hiatus. The sensational
philosophy, always agreeable to the practical tendencies
of the English mind, had just reached its culmination
under the guidance of the genius and earnestness of John
Locke, and we were undergoing its consequences in the
dwarfing of systematic morals and the gradual impover-
ishment of religion; saving ourselves as to the mere form
of faith by refuge in tradition, or, what is worst of all,
willing subjection to gross paralogisms. When science
exists only through paltering with reason, when it accepts
as its function, not the office of discovering Truth, but of
finding excuses for Belief, it is science no longer, but a
corruption and hypocrisy; and however it may come, its
destruction is a blessing. Hume appeared as the destroyer.
Gifted with an intellect clear and fearless, he carried principles remorselessly to their consequences; and proved
beyond question, that on the grounds of the existing philosophy all belief must disappear.

" If he reached the Uuniversal Scepticism, it may be
said that he yet had a faith sounder than any in the
philosophy he had destroyed ; he trusted in the only
ground of human certainty, viz : in our *human reason*,
and had the rare courage to follow where it seemed to
lead. It is not easy to conceive the degree of consterna-
tion spread through every region of existing speculation
by the ' Essay on the Idea of Necessary Connexion,' the
' Enquiry concerning the Principles of Morals,' the
' Natural History of Religion,' and their other compan-
ions. Hume had divested himself by this time of the
scholastic rudeness of the author of the ' Treatise on

21

Human Nature,' and become one of the most pleasing and accomplished writers of any period. His blows resounded accordingly through all cultivated society. It was heard everywhere with amazement, that by a logic apparently invincible, the basis of all certainty concerning man, nature and God, had been destroyed ; and that doubt irremediable was the sole inheritance of our race ; It is needless to say that the resting place of humanity was saved ; but not by invalidating the *reasoning* of the trenchant Scotchman. Hume's triumph was complete, only it was the *existing philosophy* that he laid in ruins."

Thus we have seen the practical result of this unerring intution (conscience) upon which a grave philosophy, and one that governs the world, is based.

Discarding those thingless and distracting names as powers and faculties, with their innumerable progeny of of subordinate and hidden agencies, we will turn our thoughts in upon our sensitive soul, thus cleared of its rubbish, and see what is there to be found. Let us ask ourselves, what is a thought or idea if not an impression made upon our feeling mind? We can not think without feeling nor feel without thinking. They being identically one and the same but in sound. Twice two make four, and four ones or three and one will be the same, though very different in sound. We can not think without reasoning, and we certainly can not reason without thinking. We can not judge without reasoning, nor reason without judging ; reasoning being nothing more in fact than a connected train of thoughts. Apply a coal of fire to the surface, and we think we feel it, and infer the cause ; we believe we feel it, we judge we feel it, and reason tells us we feel it, we are conscious we feel it, we imagine we feel it, we suppose we feel, we presume we feel, we perceive that we feel, we conceive that we feel, and in fine we know that we feel. These, now, I will say to the pupil, are nothing but arbitrary associations and lying sounds, and not even as much as different modes of sensation or thinking, showing the fact, as I have said in many parts of this work, how deceptive, bewildering, and vague the language used by metaphysical writers is. Such books are not entities in nature, nor are the words they contain the representatives of real things. But such is the supremacy of habit over the human mind, and such, also, the indissoluble tie of association of things that have no real or necessary connection in nature, that it is hard to convince the credulous and ordinary thinker but that every word must have its separate and appropriate meaning, and, therefore, that feeling, reasoning, thinking, etc., as they differ in words, must be different in nature.

The despotic power of fashion is sustained, in like manner, not from any merit in the object itself, nor from any real existence in nature, but from our accessary and associated ideas. A fashion may be formless and even offensive and forbidding at first, but soon it becomes tolerable, and by a farther association with the idea of the great and fashionable, it becomes beautiful and irresistible over the taste of the aping and fashionable world. A borrowed and factitious beauty is engrafted upon the human mind, the fruit of which there is no archetype or stable existence in nature. Things obtain a common rusticity or nobility, according to their intimate associations. A costume habitually worn by persons of high rank acquires an air of elegance and beauty, when the same form, if associated with the idea of low life, would be repugnant to our erratic and fastidious taste. Hence the studied and constantly guarded effort of snobs to an air of elegance and of exclusive importance. Dugald Stewart very justly remarks. that the only reason why the Scotch language is esteemed as rough, disagreeable, and vulgar, is that Edinburgh is a provincial town, and

London the seat of court! All who are thus warped and swayed by artistic taste and human conventionalities, I call weak-minded and vulgar, for upon such impotent minds have ever been entailed the vices of their adored and corrupt models. Thus, by artful authority, based upon the same credulity, has our moral judgment been perverted, and the better feelings of the human heart been overwhelmed with a flood of petty and party prejudices. Thus, too, upon the same principles of association, has the priesthood, by coupling the most unhallowed things with the sacred and overawing name of divine vicegerency been able to pin down the galling yoke of vassalage upon the masses. Frauds and seductions innumerable have been perpetrated under the foul cloak of hypocrisy by the soft whisperings of divinity and the tender ties of sisterhood, and the books of heaven are blackened by the records of filchings from the poor and oppressed. As may be seen elsewhere, many mistakes in the name of the Lord are bound up in the Bible, but such is their genuine and sacred associations that we do not dare to grant our own judgments, and are afraid to separate them, though we may not believe in their canonical and inspirational infallibility. And thus has time, with its divine associations, hallowed some of the grossest and most libellous personalities against the great Jehovah himself.

In farther illustration of the deception of association, we often couple the cause and effect as one inseparable idea. For instance, we receive the words color, smell, solidity, etc., as the objects themselves, when, in reality, they are only arbitrary sounds to express the cause of our inner feelings or ideas, which can not, in the nature of things, be red, fragrant, solid, or like sound. These are mere feelings and exist in the soul alone, and bear no exact resemblance to the external thing, to which we arbitrarily give a name for convenience' sake. The rusty nail bears no resemblance to the lock-jaw which it produces; the knife does not look like the pain we feel from the wound it inflicts, nor does the miasma bear any resemblance to the fever it occasions. The matter of the rose might exhale forever, and no such idea or word as fragrance could ever exist, but for the existence of the sentient being, upon which the thought is impressed by such specific particles of matter; in like manner might the soul have a separate and eternal existence without such sensation, but for the actual existence which impresses it. Vinegar does not look sour, nor does sugar smell sweet.

APPENDIX.

As stated in my preface, not having a book of any kind before me, what I have written has been from memory, a few notes taken during my reading days, but mainly from the long experience and observation of my own mind in its adventurous and meditative journey of life. Since finishing this essay, however, I have procured Haven's Mental Philosophy, a very popular and artistic work, which is now used as a text-book in all the colleges throughout the United States. Having no space for a review, or for strict criticism in pointing out all the palpable errors of the author's dictum, and his astounding contradictions in his frenzied and bewildered attempts to sustain his dogmas, I will make but a few quotations, from which the reader may judge for himself.

Page 557. Haven says: "A volition may be certain to take place, and it may be motive that makes it take place, or certain," and yet attempts to escape by the quibble of saying: "It is not the motive, but the mind, which acts, and therefore, though motives and choice may be the unavoidable antecedents and precursors of will and action, they are only the occasion or reason why we act thus and so, and not otherwise." And by way of illustration he says: "There is a *cause* why the apple falls—it is gravitation. There is a *reason* why the mind acts and wills as it does—it is motive." Here he attempts, as the reader will see, to make a distinction

between the *reason* why we act and the *cause* why we
act, where there can be no difference, except in sound,
for if motives produce action, as he admits, are not
motives the *cause* of action—call them the occasion, the
reason, or what you please, when motives, by his own
admission, are the authors, yes, the *cause* of their effects?
Whatever produces action I call the cause of action.
Again he says: "I have all along admitted that there is
such a connexion between volitions and motives that the
former never occurs without the latter, that they stand
related as antecedent and consequent, and that motives,
while not the producing *cause* of volitions, are still the
reason and *occasion* why the volitions are as they are, and
not otherwise."· Now admitting, as the author does, that
such is the connection between motives and volitions
that volitions can never occur without motives, and that
they stand related as antecedent and consequent, the
reader will naturally ask, how the author can possibly
deny the *causal* influence of motives in the production of
will and action? If he will read a little back, he will
see the evasion to be this: That as motives can not act,
the mind must be the ultimate agent and author of its
own acts; that is, the mind is the proximate *cause* of
mental acts. Now this, while true in words, is false to
the spirit and truth of the subject matter. Yes, false
to inevitable results and to the decreed laws of casuality.

> " Mighty fuss, what can the difference be ?
> 'Twixt tweedle dum and tweedle dee.''

Haven blindly looks *only* at the last link of the moving
chain of causal events. He might, with equal propriety,
affirm that the miasma, which caused the fever, did not
kill, but the fever was the *cause* of death, and that the
miasma which *caused* the fever should be called the *reason*
or *occasion* of death. The man who stabs another might

say: "I did not kill, it was the knife which did the mischief." Our author, when a man is found dead by a shot, could, by his crafty and subtle shifts, contend before the court that the ball did the killing, and that his client only pulled the trigger, and, consequently, was not the cause, but nothing more than the *reason* or *occasion* of the fatal event. If Haven's logic be legitimate, the mother in great distress might be told that the loss of her child was not the *cause* of her distress, but that it was her own mind, which was independent of circumstances and the author of its own acts. He makes a distinction between remote and proximate *causes*, calling one a *cause* and the other the *occasion*, or *reason* of an act, when in reality they are both *causes*, the remote being the first mover and main *cause* of all events. When one laughs at an anecdote our author would say, it was not the anecdote that laughed, but the mind, it being the author and *cause* of its own acts; while I affirm the anecdote to have been the cause, and the whole cause and efficient agent, the mind being the subject upon which it acted, and the laughter the effect or product of the two. And now this takes us back to my *dualistic* doctrine, and to my favorite illustration of the chloride of sodium (common table salt) wherein neither muriatic acid nor soda constitute table salt, which is an effect, a result of the union of the two, wherein neither alone could possibly be a cause. In like manner it is impossible for the mind, which is simply the subject to be operated upon, to be the sole agent or author of any act, all acts being results, or the effects of something that awaken the mind and causes it to act; "otherwise," as Hamilton says, "motiveless acts, were it possible for them to exist, would be perfectly worthless, as having no object in view, good or bad." The mind, I again and again most positively assert, can do nothing of itself; otherwise blind and deaf persons, who have minds, but without means of being operated upon, could see, hear and know the objects of sight and sound.

In speaking of the causes of will, he says: "What are the essential phenomena of an act of the will? Let us arrest ourselves in the process of putting forth an act of this kind, and observe exactly what it is we do, and what are the essential data in the case. I am sitting at my table. I reach forth my hand to take a book. I observe in this case under consideration a motive impelling or inducing to that end (true fatality), a reason why I willed the act. It was curiosity, perhaps, to see what the book was, or it may have been some other principle of my nature (fatality), which induced me to put forth the volition. Previous to my putting forth the volition to move my arm, there was a choice or decision to do so. In view of the end to be accomplished and influenced by the motive (fatality), I made up my mind, to use a common but not inapt expression, to perform the act. Reasons to the contrary of an intended act may suggest themselves (fatality); counter-influences and motives (yes, motives), in view of which we hesitate, deliberate, decide; and that decision, in view of all the circumstances, is our preference, or choice."—Page 525. Again: "Different motives may act in different directions; they frequently do so. Desire impels me one way (true fatality), duty another. Conflict then arises. Which shall prevail, desire or duty, to act at all, is a desire to act whether of duty or otherwise (miserable tautology), depends on circumstances (yes, circumstances), on my character already formed (fatality), my habits of thought and feeling, my degree of self-control, my conscientiousness, the strength of my native propensities (fatality), the clearness with which, at the time, I apprehend the different courses of conduct proposed, their character and their consequences."

In speaking of how the will is influenced he again

says, page 527: "Now as regards the actual operation of
things, our choices are, in fact, always influenced by circumstances (fatality), and these circumstances are various
and innumerable; a thousand seen and unseen influences
are at work upon us to affect (fatally) our decisions.
Were it possible to estimate aright all these influences,
to calculate with precision their exact weight and effect,
then our choice under any given circumstances might be
predicted with unerring (fatal) certainty." Here, mark it,
he has fully granted the imperious influences of motives
and circumstances on the mind in the production of will,
"impelling the mind," as he says, "this way, that way,
and the other to an ultimate decision;" an argument
wholly inconsistent with a self-created, free, and motiveless will. Further comment here would be a waste of
time, as the reader can without effort see that the author,
though a professed free-willer, is forced to grant the
paramount motivity of will that inevitably confirm the
doctrine of fatality. I further quote a sentence to show
the vexatious error and folly in complicating, confusing,
and rendering a thing incomprehensible which in itself
is so simple and comprehensible. But here it is: "It is
a matter of some importance to ascertain the relation
which the will sustains to the other mental powers.
There can be no doubt that the activity of the will is
preceded, in all cases, by that of the intellect."

The most common observer must have learned from my
previous views, that will is nothing but the simple, indivisible mind willing; that is, it is nothing more nor less
than one of the millions of modes of mind, under the influences of causes producing all the sensations, pleasures,
pains, desires, and aversions of mind; so it will be seen
that will bears no relation to anything but the specific
object which creates it, or rather induces the mind to put
forth such will. Power is a powerful and multifarious

word with loose writers; but if the reader will read back, he will see that the mind has no power other than that of the wax to be impressed with endless impressions, each and every object creating in the mind an idea of its own inherent and specific nature. The mind has no power to create ideas within itself any more than the daguerreotype to create its pictures aside from its objects of will or desire. Our author says that the activity of the will is in all cases preceded by the activity of the intellect. This is a loose and blundering tautology, devoid of meaning; for the willing mind is the will, and the will is the mind willing. It is the same as to say, the activity of mind is preceded by the activity of the mind, for what is intellect but the mind, and what is willing but a mode of the mind.

I again quote, speaking of an object of volition, he says: "I must first perceive some object presented to my understanding before I can will its attainment." Here is a positive affirmation of the author that the mind has no power to will but by the promptings of its objects; but to proceed: "In the case already supposed the book lying on my table is an object within the cognizance of sense, and to perceive it is an act of intellect. Until perceived, the will puts not forth any volition (miserable tautology, will and volition being the same,) respecting it; in a word, whatever comes in as a motive, (yes, motive,) to influence the mind in favor of or against a given course, must in the first instance address itself to the understanding, and be comprehended by that power before it can influence mental decision (fatality). A motive which I can not comprehend is no motive; a reason which I do not perceive or understand, is to me no reason." You observe here that no fatalist could be more fatal than our author. "A motive (he says) which I can not comprehend, is no motive to will or act:" page 532. Now it must be plainly perceived that if the mind was free to create its own objects within itself, it would not be dependent upon outward objects which it must first comprehend before it can will or act. Once more: "It is not until some feeling is aroused, my curiosity or desire in some form awakened, that my will acts. The object must not only be perceived, but perceived as agreeable, and the wish to possess it be entertained (fatality,) before the volition is put forth." Much more might be quoted, but all to the same effect of *positive fatality*.

I give the following sentence to show additional errors: "I have already shown in presenting the psychological facts respecting the will, that our motives of action are from two grand and diverse sources, *desire and duty.*" Here, again, there is an obvious misrepresentation of the very nature of mind, its laws, and its course of action. Mind is simply a being endowed with sensation, or in more correct language, a susceptibility of sensation, when acted upon by objects that produce sensations. If sensations and ideas (all the same) were concrete things, and permanent in the mind, we should have millions of ideas and sensations present all at the same time, when in reality we have but one at a time. They are momentary results or effects of a subjective and objective unity; a product of the *dualistic* law which I have maintained throughout

He says: "Our motives of action are from two grand and diverse sources, desire and duty." In the first place, there is no diversity in a willing act; it is a unit, a simple desire to act. If we act from a sense of duty, it is no less a desire to act. In short, desire must precede every voluntary act of life, and where then the necessity of making complicated divisions, as he goes on to do, of a unit and a thing indivisible. There may be, and are many remote causes of will, but they all resolve themselves into one—a simple desire to act before we do act.

In speaking of God's foreknowledge and full control

over the thoughts and actions of man, he says: "Nothing must take place without his foreknowledge and permission. But how are these things to be reconciled—man's entire freedom and God's entire control and government over him. They appear inconsistent, and many do not hesitate to pronounce them so. Some, who accept them both as true, regard them still inexplicable and incomprehensible. The fatalist secures the supreme government of God only at the expense of human freedom. Others again (free-willers), in their horror of fatalism, preserve the freedom and accountability of man at the expense of the Divine government and purposes, thus virtually placing man beyond the power and control of Deity."

Now we will see how the author attempts to reconcile man's independence and freedom with the Divine government: "We choose thus and thus, because we are, on the whole, so disposed or inclined; and this inclination or disposition, depends on a great variety of circumstances (*yes, circumstances*), on the nature and strength of the motive (*yes, motive, I say*) presented, our *physical and mental constitution* and habits, (*who gave us our physical and mental constitution?*) our power of self-control, the strength of our desires, as compared with our sense of duty, the presence or absence of exciting objects; in fine, on a great variety of predisposed causes and circumstances (*yes, circumstances*), all of which are to be taken into account, when the question is, why do we choose thus and not otherwise?"—(*true fatality*). "Now, these circumstances, which go to determine our inclinations, and so our choices and volitions, are, in a great measure, beyond our direct control—(*strong fatality*). Our *physical and mental constitution*, our external condition, our state of mind and circumstances (*circumstances*) at any given moment whatever in the shape of motive (*yes, motive*) or inducement may be present with moving power (*yes, power of circumstances*) to the mind, inclining us this way or that; *all this lies much more under Divine control than under our own—(double fatality)*. Here, then, to speak reverently, lies the avenue of approach, through which Deity may come in and take possession of the human mind, and influence and shape its action without infringing in the least on its perfect freedom—(*nonsense*). He has only to present such motives as shall seem to the mind weighty and sufficient (*shame! what, Deity thus tampering personally with man!*), has only to touch the main-spring of human inclination, lying back of actual choice, (*yes, just as I constantly say, motive lying back of choice, will, and action*), has only to secure within us a disposition or liking to any given course, and our choice follows with certainty (*yes, Deity can force us with certainty*) and our volition and our action; and that action and volition are free in the highest sense, because our choice was free—(*astounding nonsense*). We acted just as we were inclined. Now this is just what we, in a limited way, and to a small extent, are constantly doing with respect to our fellow-men. We present motives and inducements to a given course, we work upon their inclinations, we appeal to their sensibilities, their natural desires, their sense of duty; and, in proportion as we gain access to their hearts, we are successful in shaping and controlling their conduct.

"The great and difficult art of governing men lies in this: We have only to suppose a like power, but complete and perfect, to be exercised by the Supreme Disposer and Controller of events (yes, so says fatality), so shaping and ordering (ordering) circumstances as to determine (to determine) the inclination of men, gaining access, not in an uncertain and indirect manner, but by an immediate approach to the human heart, all whose springs lie under his (yes, under) control, so that he can touch and command (command them) as he wills: we have only to conceive this, and we have, as it seems to me, a full and sufficient explanation of the fact that man acts freely and just as he is inclined, while yet he is perfectly under the Divine control (what but Deity inclines him—and yet free? Monstrous nonsense!) And this, if I mistake not, is precisely the sort of control and power over man which the Scriptures always ascribe to God, viz: power over the inclinations, affections, dispositions, from which proceed all our voluntary actions. In his hands are the hearts of men, and he can turn them as the rivers of water are turned."

I now ask the reader to pause and meditate seriously upon what he has just read. He will see here admitted by the strongest and ablest free-will writer of the world, that man must and always does yield to the irrevocable mandates of his original and unavoidable nature, state of health, education, and the motives presented to the mind for action. Yes, and God himself presents motives. Read and read again, think and think again solemnly upon every sentence, and you will see, unwillingly, but unavoidably, a clear admission that man is fated to his nature and the circumstances attending his condition in life, as well as his helplessness under the divine government. I quote again for further reflection: "But suppose I have really no inclination, no disposition to do right. My affections and desires are all wrong, inclining me to evil, and my sense of duty or moral obligation is not strong enough to prevail against these natural desires and evil inclinations; suppose this, which, alas! is too often true, and what then becomes of my power to do right? Does it any longer exist? Have I any power to change these affections and inclinations; or, their remaining as they are, have I any power to go contrary to them? A question, this, at once profoundly philosophica and intensely practical. To the question, then—can a man whose inclinations are evil, whose heart is wrong, do right? a true psychology answers, yes. He can do what he is not inclined to do (absurd); nor is that evil inclination a fixed quantity; he can be, he may be otherwise inclined. It must be admitted, however, that so long as the heart is wrong, so long as the evil disposition, so long the man will continue to do evil—(that is certain), notwithstanding all his power to the contrary—(no power of himself). Left to himself, there is very little probability of his effecting any material change in himself for the better. In order to do this, there is needed an influence from without and from above; an influence that shall (yes, shall) incline him to obedience, that shall make him willing (make him willing) to obey. This is precisely the want of his nature which Divine grace meets. It creates in him a clean heart, and renews within him a right spirit. This is the sublime mystery of regeneration. The soul that is thus born of God is made willing to do right· The inclinations are no longer to evil, but to good, and the man still doing as he pleases does the will of God (what! made by God to do his will, and still free?) The change is in the disposition; it is a change of the affections, of the heart; thus the Scriptures always represent it. This was what was wanted to secure obedience, and this Divine grace supplies."

It is here admitted by our author that God created our nature and holds our hearts and wills in his hands, and though bound by these destinies and the motives and incidents of life, which imperiously lead us this way, that, and the other, we can do as we please; that our hearts are continually evil, and that of ourselves we can do nothing, requiring the grace of God to give us a clean heart and renew within us a right spirit, and yet we can do as we please! So long as the heart is wrong, so long will we continue to do evil, notwithstanding all our power

to the contrary; yet we can do as we please. Man left
to himself can make no change in himself for the better,
which requires a power from above, yet he can do as he
pleases; that we have no power to go contrary to our
nature, but yet we can do as we please; that our Maker
has full possession and control of the main-springs of our
hearts, of our affections and dispositions, and yet we can
go contrary to the will of our Maker, and do as we please.
I admit (and so ought every fatalist to admit) that we can
do as we please, but deny that we can avoid doing as we
please, having no power over the causes which make us
pleased any more than we have over the causes of pleasure and pain, of sickness and death. As I have before
said, and fully explained, this great question of will is
not whether we can do as we please, for that is inevitable;
but whether our unavoidable nature, and the motives
presented to the mind for a choice, is not the course of
that choice, and, consequently, of the pleasure to do or not
to do, according to circumstances. The pleasure to do or
not to do, I affirm to be as compulsive as the pleasures
and pains that constantly come upon us; but there are
effects, take notice, of sufficient causes, which causes are
without and beyond our control.

Now, as simple and easily understood as this word
pleased ought to be, and would be if changed to force,
the whole quibble and wily subterfuge of authors has
hinged upon it, and I regret to see that Haven, who must
have known better, has made (I hope unwittingly,) a false
application of it to deceive his readers, and that in a case
so momentous in its bearings as the human will by which
the world is governed. Read back a little and you will
find another great error and inconsistency in this author.
After affirming all along that we do what we are inclined
or pleased to do, he says: "We can voluntarily do what
we are not inclined or pleased to do." Such ludicrous

inconsistencies convince not, but provoke derision. He
says when God enters the heart, takes possession, and
makes us pleased to do a thing, then we can do as he
makes us pleased to do. Who can deny but that God can
make us do as he pleases—vexatious folly and waste of
paper. His assumptions and conclusions constantly run
counter. In a single sentence the affirmation is that we
are induced by circumstances and temptations which give
motives to action, and in conclusion, we act free and independent of all circumstances, temptations, motives, and
desires. We can do not only what we are forced to do,
but that we can do what we are not pleased to do, and
can not do. In short, that a thing is, and is not at the
same time; that white is black, and black is white. His
blundering shifts to escape the truth, has nutralized his
whole work, and proven the title false, as no philosophy.
In this, however, he is not alone; for his book is nothing
more than a copy of ten thousand stereotyped copies of
the old drivelling, stayed and stale errors of two thousand years standing. I say Haven is not alone in his
quibbles and subterfuge to escape the truth, for what is
the language of Hamilton, Upham, and, indeed, all other
free-will writers. It would be tedious to give all of Hamilton's argument (though a free-willer) against free-will,
so I shall quote only a concluding sentence or two, thus :
Page 586. "How the will can possibly be free, must
remain to us, under the present limitation of our faculties, wholly incomprehensible. We are unable to conceive an absolute commencement; we can not, therefore,
conceive of a free volition. A determination by motives
can not, to our understanding, escape from necessitation.
(O how strong!) Nay, were we even to admit as true
what we can not think as possible, a free will, still the
doctrine of a motiveless volition, would be only casualism,
and the free acts of an indifferent will are morally and

rationally as worthless as the preordered passions by a determined will—(divinely true). How, therefore, I repeat, moral liberty is possible in man or God we are utterly unable, speculatively, to understand." All his reasoning in favor of necessity or fatality are equally as strong and clear as those here quoted. And now, for the views of Upham, Mental Philosophy, page 265: "In volition we are at first pleased or displeased, or have some other emotion in view of the thing, whatever it is, which has come under the cognizance of the intellect. And emotions, in the ordinary process of mental action are followed by desires. As we can not be pleased or displeased without some antecedent perception or knowledge of the thing which we are pleased or displeased with, so we can not desire to possess or avoid anything without having laid the foundation of such desire in the existence of some antecedent emotion; and this is not only the matter of fact which, as the mind is actually constituted, is presented to our choice; but we can not well perceive how it could be otherwise. To desire a thing which utterly fails to excite within us the least emotion of pleasure, seems to be a sort of solecism or absurdity in nature; in other words, it seems to be impossible, from the nature of things, under any conceivable circumstances. At any rate it is not possible, as the mind is actually constructed whatever might have been the fact if the mind had have been constructed differently."

Farther comment would be a waste of paper, as the laggard in science and dullard in perception must at once see that Upham grants the paramount power of motives over the mind, and consequently the doctrine of necessity.

He says: "Before we can will or act we must be pleased or displeased with some object in view." Now as the mind can not create those objects of desire or

necessaries of life, and as we can not will or act without
them, what is the sequence? "That motives control the
mind as it is now constructed is a matter of fact, and we
can not perceive how it could be otherwise. At any
rate (*free-will*) is not possible (*he repeats it*), as the mind
is actually constructed, whatever might have been the
fact, if the mind had have been differently constructed."

After all this, however, Upham, like Hamilton and
others, craven to vulgar prejudice, and disprove their
own testimony and granted fact by an inconstant and perfidious witness, conscience, a thing that has caused all
the wars, intollerance, persecution, and bloodshed of the
world. That has made Mormonism, Shakerism, Catholicism, Protestantism, Spiritualism, Mytholicism, Moham-
medanism, with ten thousand adverse and warring creeds.
Yes, and dragged thousands of the best men on earth to
the stake. But I must close these reflections, having
already passed far beyond my intended limits.

As the reader may wish to know something of the
different systems of philosophy, I will say there are two
great divisions—the conditioned and relative, or finite.
and the unconditioned, or infinite and absolute. In plain,
common-sense terms, the conditioned means that the
mind is limited and can not transcend certain bounds,
and is dependent upon our senses and the external world
for its knowledge. For instance, the finite mind can not
look into the infinite designs of Deity. Space and time
are good examples of our conditioned or limited thought,
both of which advance as we approach, and even in
thought we find no end. Of this branch of conditioned
philosophy, Hamilton may be named as the master
spirit, sustained by the Scotch philosophers generally;
whereas, amongst the advocates of the unconditioned
and absolute philosophy, Bishop Berkeley was the most
transcendental and rhapsodic. The eagle, though soar-

ing high in the heaven's unfathomable blue, has to
return to earth for food and rest; but this philosopher,
skylarking it all the time, and librating between heaven
and earth, disclaimed all connection with matter, when,
if he had had the common-sense of the *buzzard*, that
glides on easy wing, he would have known he had to
live on matter in common with all other animals.
Swedenborg, and almost all of the German philosophers,
belong to this school, which teaches that the human soul
is a spark of divinity itself, and that it is possessed of
innate and eternal ideas, independent of our gross senses
and the external world. Now as all things are made up
of its parts, any part taken from it leaves it less than it
was with all its parts; from which it follows that forty
millions of parts, sparks or emanations taken from God
annually to endow human souls, would by-and-by leave
him without a soul of his own; and this is not the only
danger or hardship, for it is distressing to think that
countless millions of the little souls or sparks of Deity
should be in hell, and enveloped in the flames of Satan;
for those very philosophers teach that souls, with the
sparks of Deity, go to hell. Moreover, if human souls
are of God, he certainly can not punish them for Adam's
sin; nor is it probable he will do it, because they are a
part of himself. This they declare to be a refined,
spiritual, and elevating philosophy, compared with the
common-sense philosophy which condescends to teach the
vulgar realities of life, and confines man to his fated and
legitimate sphere. True, this philosophy lifts man, with
his Elysian reveries and tipsy joys, to the third heavens,
but it is both degrading and destructive to Deity. In
short, it is founded upon a phrenzied fanaticism, which
acknowledges no bounds to human thought, and subordi-
nates reason to the vagaries of imagination—the clinging
curse of science and the blight of religion. The efforts

of those writers have been fervid and sincere, but their reasoning is rhapsodic, ludicrous, and adverse to every principle of science. If the clergy and fanatical writers had not transcended what God saw proper to reveal to man, the preaching and teaching of eighteen hundred and sixty-eight years would not now find the Christian world more divided and distracted, and mankind more wicked and dishonest than at any previous age of the world. To allegorize the Bible, take the words out of God's own mouth and appropriate them to their own sectarian purposes, has produced a doubt with all, and destroyed the unity of faith in Christ. And now, with profound humility, do I ask of the ineffable Jehovah a pardon in anything I may have said amiss in my honest efforts to do good.

Thinking the reader may also wish to know something of the age and extent of the various opinions of the world upon the subject of human liberty, I will say it has existed for thousands of years, and been observed in all parts of the world where philosophy and theology have been sustained. A difference of opinion prevails in all the systems of theology in India, and throughout the East. The Christian missionary meets with it in the remotest regions, and amongst nations of but litttle cultivation. Also amongst the Greeks conflicting opinions prevailed. The school of Lucretius taught the doctrine of necessity, as also did Epictetus of the Stoics. There were two rival sects amongst the Jews—the Sadducees, holding to the doctrine of freedom, while the Pharisees taught that of necessity. The Arabian schools of theology have been hotly divided, but the Koran, teaching the doctrine of necessity, the Kaarite sect, teaching the freedom of will, has had to give way. Amongst the modern reformers, Luther and Melanchthon were advocates for freedom, while Calvin and Bucer maintained the doctrine of necessity. Amongst the writers of the last and present centuries, we find Hobbes, Locke, Liebnitz, Collins, Edwards, Priestley, Diderot, Belsham, Lord Kames, Hartley, and Mill, author of logic, open advocates for necessity; while on the other hand, Cousin, Jouffroy, Stewart, Ried, Brown, Hamilton, Descartes, Kant, Upham, Tappan, Haven, and Bledsoe are advocates for freedom, but these are only a few on either side of the question.

The discussion amongst these authors has been in regard to the power to do as we will, when it should be, as I often repeat it, whence the power over the determinations of the will.

In closing this essay I will once more call attention to the main question—what it is that causes us to do as we please? Is it nothing, or is it something? If something, what? Is it a spontaneity rising from nothing within the mind, or is it an object to be gained without the mind? For instance, we desire a wife; is it the desire which creates the woman, or does the woman create the desire? We want money; is it the want that creates the money, or is it the money which creates the pleasure and the act to take it? Once more; in all our acts of obligation to God and man, is it the pleasure that creates the obligation, or is it a knowledge of the obligation which begets the desire or pleasure to fulfill that obligation? And now for the essence of truth. If the object to be obtained creates that pleasure, so much harped on, to do as we please, the whole question is at an end, for it can not be that the pleasure is prior to and creates the object before it has any knowledge of the object.

If asked why a question so plain and easy of solution should have distracted the world so long, I would answer in part by asking why the rulers of the world should

deceive the people for the sake of power and pelf; and in
whole, the clergy being at the head of all the institutions
of learning in the world, give a tone and turn to thought,
and in addition to the temptation of our temporary
rulers, for the clergy, or human, do honestly, sincerely
and piously aim at doing good, and act under a belief
that the truth would weaken our Christian faith and
give strength and encouragement to the deeds of the
wicked.   Astronomy, geology, and almost all great discoveries were in like manner to destroy religion, but
they did not, nor can any of the works of God destroy
his book revelation, for he has not made two revelations,
natural and supernatural, one to destroy the other; so if
truth be of God, grant it, and leave the consequences
with him.   This is my aim and end, and feeling that
I have the approbation of my Maker, have strove in a
hurried and desultory manner to impress the the truth
upon others.

And now, in fine, I will say to the reader, that, having
written afar off, amidst the voiceless wilds and slumberous
solitudes of the gray old forest, where, in God's own
sacred fanes, the thoughts here recorded were inspired;
he must look at the object, the matter and the argument,
for which I ask nothing, and from which I fear nothing,
but having not a book by me, and lacking the skill of
the drivelling and mechanical book-maker, he must excuse any artistic defect he may see.

www.ingramcontent.com/pod-product-compliance
Lightning Source LLC
Chambersburg PA
CBHW020816270326
41928CB00006B/568